SEXUALITY, STRUGGLE AND SAINTLINESS

In memory of Dick (CR) and Pauline Hensman
and Vijayatara

SEXUALITY, STRUGGLE AND SAINTLINESS

SAME-SEX LOVE AND THE CHURCH

SAVITRI HENSMAN

Ekklesia

First published in 2015

Ekklesia
235 Shaftesbury Avenue
London
WC2H 8EP
www.ekklesia.co.uk

Production: Bob Carling (www.carling.org.uk)
Photography: Michael Marten (www.marten.org.uk)
Cover model: Tyne Roberts
Editors: Jill Segger (uk.linkedin.com/In/jillsegger), Simon Barrow
Business: Virginia Moffatt, Henrietta Cullinan

ISBN: 978-0-9932942-0-4

A Catalogue record for this book is available from the British Library.

Contents

Series Preface

Ekklesia is delighted to launch its new publishing imprint with Savitri Hensman's groundbreaking collection of essays on *Sexuality, Struggle and Saintliness*. As a think tank concerned to link reflection and theory with practical action and advocacy for change, we are honoured to be able to work with a range of associates who exemplify those characteristics in the way they work – and one of the aims of our imprint is to bring such work to a wider audience. This will include both collections of material adapted from Ekklesia's website, and original titles that help reshape major concerns in church and society.

The volume you have in your hand exemplifies something important about the way Ekklesia seeks to think and act as a Christian think tank. First, it is written in an inviting way, which we hope will be open to people of all faiths and none. Second, it nevertheless seeks to develop its argument from the deep, subtle and rich resources of the Christian and biblical tradition – instead of casting these aside, or, just as unhelpfully, solidifying them into a rigid ideology.

In her writing Savitri Hensman invites the churches towards a change of heart and mind on matters to do with human sexuality and same-sex love. But she does so on strong theological grounds (rather than as a matter of compromising with fashion), and in continuity with the central tenets of the Christian gospel. Like much of Ekklesia's work, this book therefore eschews simplistic 'liberal versus conservative' dichotomising, and challenges us all to costly and imaginative transformation.

None of our endeavours would be possible without the support of the Andrews Charitable Trust, Bloomsbury Central Baptist Church, and many others who help sustain the work of Ekklesia in myriad ways. For this volume we would especially like to thank those who contributed to underwriting part of the production costs through crowdfunding. They are listed at the back of the book.

Future plans for Ekklesia Publishing include a significant contribution to the debate about housing, and other titles related to our priority areas: living economy, equality, peacemaking, and people and power. We also plan to be looking at the intersection of politics with beliefs and values, which is a central, distinctive concern in our work.

Simon Barrow
Co-director, Ekklesia

Acknowledgements

I would like to express my appreciation of the work of Jill Segger, who played a major role in editing this book. Thanks are also due to Simon Barrow, Virginia Moffat, Henrietta Cullinan and all at Ekklesia, as well as to Bob Carling and Michael Marten for assistance in production and cover image respectively. As an independent, not-for-profit organisation, Ekklesia promotes discussion on the role of beliefs and values in public life and transformative approaches to challenges facing society (for further details see the note at the end of this book, and also www.ekklesia.co.uk). My book draws heavily on pieces which I previously wrote for Ekklesia's website, many adapted for this publication. However there is also new material and, inevitably, it has been necessary to be selective.

Over the years, certain organisations and networks, especially the Lesbian and Gay Christian Movement (LGCM) and Inclusive Church (in addition to other groups that Ekklesia engages positively with, such as Accepting Evangelicals), have helped me to develop my thinking on Christianity and inclusion. I am also grateful to those whose views on the theology of sexuality are different from mine but who have expressed these with courtesy and clarity, prompting me to think more deeply. The focus of this work is heavily directed towards Anglican and Catholic conversations, which I know best. But I hope that friends in Methodist, Baptist, Reformed, Lutheran, Anabaptist, Orthodox and other traditions will find the overall approach helpful and respectful of their own contributions.

On a wider level various friends, particularly Kenneth Leech (recently deceased), and family members, including my sister Rohini Hensman, have nurtured me in reflecting and writing on faith and society. Others have helped me through good times and bad and, without them, this book would not have been written.

I owe a particular debt of gratitude to my parents, Dick (CR) and Pauline Hensman, gifted teachers and communicators with a profound faith and keen interest in theology, and my partner

Vijayatara (Sharon Smith), a sociologist of religion whose research touched on the ways in which faith communities deal with diversity. All three died in recent years but their love, humour, compassion and encouragement continue to enrich my life and the lives of many others.

Savitri Hensman
Winter 2015

Foreword

Perhaps the defining practices of the Christian faith are 'remembrance' and 'reconciliation'. Indeed, the Eucharist – the meal which institutes the Christian faith – is an act of remembrance that gestures towards reconciliation. It rehearses the profound and disturbing truth at the heart of Christianity: that God gives her very being, her body and blood, to reconcile the world. The Eucharist embodies the claim that 'remembrance' – at its centre – is no sentimental backwards-looking act, but a work of formation and reformation.

Reconciliation and remembrance are at the heart of Savitri Hensman's new book. *Sexuality, Struggle and Saintliness* gathers together wisdom on matters of sexuality and church polity collected over an extensive career. At a time when debate over the Christian faith's position on LGBT people and our relationships has profound charge and is extraordinarily divisive, Hensman's approach is welcome.

The author helpfully remembers the stories of how Christianity – in its various guises and formations – has travelled towards its current crises over sexuality. This very act of remembrance is a 're-membering' – an act of putting back together in a creative way. It offers an opportunity for the attentive reader to see the established narratives and positions on sexuality in fresh, unexpected ways.

Yet *Sexuality, Struggle and Saintliness* is also a work seeking reconciliation. Rather than accepting the awkward peace of those forced, by exhaustion, to a truce, it gestures towards a peace based on God's hunger for justice. The work of justice Savi Hensman is interested in will not allow fake victims. Nor will it allow questionable readings of biblical texts, notably Paul, to justify readings of God's love that diminish the status of queer people. Savi invites us to remember the richness of God's invitation to sanctification: that is, if we are to be the 'saints of God' this is not based on a narrow reading of 'purity' as a privatized morality, but on our being formed into a community shaped by

God's radical love.

Savitri Hensman's meditations on sexuality, then, are not about 'point scoring' against those who would treat the varieties of sexuality as a question of personal morality. They are timely and valuable precisely because they place them in a political context: what is at stake in the Christian faith's wrestling over sexuality is what it means to be the community of love in a fractious world. Her passion to remake Christian Community in God's Image makes this book truly valuable reading.

Rachel Mann

Chapter One

Introduction

Arguments among Christians about sexual morality are often in the headlines. This is partly because conflict, especially over sex, may seem more newsworthy than more common activities such as prayer, repairing leaky church roofs and giving food to the hungry. After all, rows and romance are often central to popular songs and soap operas.

However it is indeed the case that, in recent decades, Roman Catholics, Baptists, Anglicans, Presbyterians, Methodists, Lutherans, Anabaptists and other Christians across the world have been grappling with various questions linked with sexuality, in particular whether same-sex partnerships can be right.

Sometimes disagreements have led to threats of (or actual) splits if churches become more accepting. Elsewhere people have dropped out because they feel that they, or their loved ones, who are lesbian, gay, bisexual or transgender (LGBT) have been treated in an unjust and hurtful manner. In some cases, congregations and wider networks have been finding ways to live with difference, allowing freedom to others to act in line with their consciences while continuing to study and debate the topic.

It may seem strange to outsiders that churches are so concerned about who has sex with whom in a world where environmental destruction, mass poverty and war threaten human survival. Certainly it is important to keep a sense of proportion, which does not always happen.

Nevertheless sexual desire and relationships can be a cause of deep joy or sorrow, give rise to damaging selfishness or sacrificial love. In Christian tradition, matters affecting human wellbeing are not only social or psychological, but also spiritual issues. So even churches which champion the right of adults to make choices about sex, provided these involve informed consent, may take an interest in what kinds of relationships should be supported or discouraged.

Legal changes are opening up marriage to same-sex couples in some countries while, elsewhere, LGBT people and those defending their human rights have been targeted by repressive laws. Churches have often become involved, sometimes on different sides.

It is sometimes claimed that churches in favour of celebrating committed loving relationships are simply following the lead of secular culture, whether this is regarded as sensible or deplorable. Yet Christian thinkers have sometimes taken a far more positive view of same-sex love than that common in their day.

Part 1 of this book, 'Towards acceptance: the theologians' journey', begins with Chapter 2. This looks at how the Bible, tradition, reason and experience play a part in the work of theology, which might be described as the study of God and God's relationship with the universe, including humankind. Chapters 3–6 outline how, over the past century or so, numerous Christian theologians have come to believe that churches should not only welcome LGBT members but also take a more positive view of same-sex partnerships.

Part 2, 'Conflict and change: snapshots from the churches', covers chapters 7–25. This seeks to give a flavour of the upheaval which has been taking place in Christian circles around sexuality, while also delving beneath the surface to make sense of the conflicting positions and connected concerns, such as unity. This touches not only on the actions of church leaders and official bodies, but also on the responses of Christians in various walks of life, including instances when legislators have shared their views on faith and sexuality in the midst of debates on equal marriage.

Part 3, made up of chapters 26–32, focuses on 'Looking afresh at the Bible and tradition' and relating these to the challenges of today's world. I believe that the Bible's handling of sexuality is far more complex than is sometimes recognised and that on balance, it points towards acceptance of faithful, self-giving partnerships. At the same time, those on both sides of the sexuality debate sometimes make questionable assumptions that downplay the radical nature of Jesus' witness.

Finally, in Part 4, chapters 33–34, the challenge of 'Living with disagreement' is examined. This includes the suggestion that churches which have been open to discussing sexuality in a thoughtful and mutually respectful manner are moving towards a middle ground where those with different views can coexist until a broad consensus is reached. If Christians can get better at remaining in fellowship without pretending that deep disagreements on this and other issues do not exist, while handling conflict in a constructive way, they may have something to offer to a wider community.

At the end there is a brief autobiographical note and more information about Ekklesia.

Part 1: Towards acceptance: the theologians' journey

Since the early twentieth century, numerous Christian theologians have come to believe that sexual relationships between same-sex partners are sometimes morally acceptable. Among Christians in general too, views have become more accepting, though some remain firmly opposed.

Chapter 2 looks in general at how Christian thinking draws on the Bible, tradition, reason and experience. Chapters 3–6 focus on the shift towards greater acceptance while throwing light, more broadly, on how Christians approach social issues and questions of right and wrong. Debates on same-sex partnerships have also focused attention on why love, desire and human relationships in general matter. Such concerns deeply touch most people's lives, whatever their views on sexual ethics and whether they identify as lesbian, gay, bisexual, transgender (LGBT), heterosexual or none of these.

Many people today are aware of only a handful of the thinkers who have questioned the views held by most churches at the end of the nineteenth century, and have come up with profound and thought-provoking ideas, whether or not one agrees in full with their conclusions. Some (on both sides of the debate), seem to think that the Bible and tradition offer a clear-cut perspective which has been called into question by changes in culture and society, but the reality is far more complicated. Theology has also had an impact on wider social attitudes and practices.

Space is limited so some of the boldest pioneers or most profound thinkers of the past century receive only a brief mention (if they appear at all). However, there are many references in case any reader would like to find out more about the journey of which I have tried to provide a sketch-map.

Chapter Two

Thinking theologically: Bible, tradition, reason and experience

Sometimes Christians get caught up over the relative importance of the Bible, tradition, reason and experience in the way they interpret themselves, the world and their understanding of God. Some define themselves as 'Bible-believing' Christians, or use terms like sola scriptura (Latin for 'by Scripture alone'), while others regard themselves as 'traditionalists', or 'liberals' who put more store by reason and experience, respectively, discarding what seems irrational and outdated.

The media is often keen to pigeon-hole with these labels too, leading to some misleading or caricatured descriptions of what is at stake when Christians disagree –when, like any interpretative community, they frequently do.

However it is questionable whether it is possible, let alone desirable, to separate the effects of the Bible, tradition, reason and experience when grappling with theological questions and ethical issues.

It may be suspected that many who regard themselves as staunch Protestants or evangelicals, for whom Scripture is the sole authority, are more influenced by tradition and reason than they realise, and many who claim that tradition is their main guide – including a number who call themselves 'Catholic' (whether recognised by the Vatican or not) – are guided largely by the Bible and reason as well as by experience.

Meanwhile, those who believe that in their lives the Bible and tradition are far less central than the fruits of reason and experience, may in practice, be more 'Bible-believing' and 'traditionalist' than they think. But failure to recognise the subtle ways in which these factors overlap makes it harder to find common ground.

Let us imagine some different scenarios to illustrate how this might work.

Acting rationally and heeding experience

Do you see yourself as a modern Christian, not too heavily weighed down by the baggage of the past, making rational and unprejudiced decisions, or as someone for whom experience is central? Then imagine that the vehicle in which you are travelling breaks down, and you are offered a lift by a passing driver in a large, comfortable, 'gas-guzzling' car. It turns out that he is a senior manager in an oil company with a dubious environmental record.

You do not want to be rude, but he himself raises the issue of the environment. He cheerfully tells you that widespread alarm about oil spills and global warming is exaggerated: apparently his firm has commissioned a report by some scientists which shows this. He also explains that there are few experiences he finds as wonderful as driving at high speeds in his car with the window open, the breeze on his face. Noticing that you are looking slightly alarmed, he reassures you that he is a very good driver and has never had a crash.

Life is good and sometimes, he tells you, he thanks God that he has been born into an age of such progress and prosperity, and in which he can enjoy innocent pleasures like driving his fine car.

Now, to someone more objective than he is (whether or not complete objectivity is possible to achieve), it may well be apparent that the warnings from many sources about the impact of pollution and excessive fuel use deserve to be taken seriously. But how likely is he to admit this even to himself, given the twin forces of self-interest and peer reinforcement of questionable beliefs?

Likewise, even if the regular practice of walking through an unpolluted countryside, attentive to the singing birds and fluttering butterflies, might turn out to be even more enjoyable than driving fast in an energy-inefficient car, how likely do you think he is to try?

Reason and experience are indeed important. But humans are often less rational than we think, and the ways in which we approach and interpret experience are likewise shaded by a variety of factors of which we may sometimes be barely (if at all) aware.

Even if we are conscious of the influences on us, helpful as this is, it may not be enough for us to be confident that our judgement is right. For instance, if someone you liked very much were to be accused of a serious crime, could you be wholly objective about the evidence?

Faithfully obeying Scripture

Do you see yourself as a 'Bible-believing' Christian, mistrustful of any influences other than Scripture? The Bible is indeed hugely important – otherwise how would we even know of Christ, or have language in which to thank the Creator and seek the Holy Spirit's guidance? Yet faithfulness to Scripture is rather more complicated than it might at first seem.

Imagine that you find yourself on a plane and the passenger next to you looks familiar. You realise with a shock that you have seen him on the news: a notorious warlord known for kidnapping children and sending them into battle, and seizing girls to serve as sex-slaves to his troops.

He notices your reactions with some amusement, and starts to talk to you. He explains that he is a devout Christian, and was inspired to recruit child-soldiers after reading the story of David and Goliath (1 Samuel 17.1–54). Similarly, his massacres in the villages he conquered were prompted by the punishment of the Amalekites (1 Samuel 15.1) and the inhabitants of Jericho (Joshua 6.21) in what Christians call the Old Testament.

According to him, girls are taken from their homes to service his soldiers because, in Deuteronomy 22.28, it states that if a virgin not pledged in marriage is raped, her rapist is required to marry her and never send her back to her family, though of course he can have sex with other women too, in accordance with God's law. Those leading worship in his army, however, must have no more than one wife (1 Timothy 3.2, 12, Titus 1.6).

Though you challenge his interpretation, he is supremely confident that he is doing God's will, in accord with the 'plain meaning' of the Bible, which indeed he frequently quotes. Though some think him harsh, he sees himself as a 'soldier of Christ' (2 Timothy 2.3) in a time of turmoil, sent to rule with a rod of iron, as when earthen pots are broken in pieces (Revelation 2.27). How likely are you to be able to persuade him to rethink his views if this would mean re-examining his life, giving up the power he wields and coming to terms with the harm he has caused?

Such a version of Christianity would of course be strikingly at odds with the Gospel call to love one's neighbour, even one's 'enemy', and be a peacemaker. But, through the centuries, the Bible has often been quoted to justify various kinds of cruelty and violence. For example, a sizeable number of people believed that to oppose apartheid was to rebel against God's will revealed in Scripture. Even today, those claiming to follow Scripture obediently, indeed literally, often disagree with one another, each convinced that their own interpretation is the God-given truth.

This illustrates, incidentally, that interpretation is unavoidable. It is not a 'liberal' invention, just as the text it reflects on is not a 'conservative' one. There is no unmediated way between text and context, and much in the Bible that is plainly not 'literal' (another much-abused term).

Being faithful to Scripture in a meaningful sense is very different to the use of texts for self-justification or offence, and not always straightforward. It is all too easy to read the Bible through the filter of self-interest or one's preconceived ideas, or those of one's community or peer group, to misinterpret, or give priority to what is less important.

This is not a new concept: indeed it is found in the Bible. The prophet Isaiah writes of God's frustration with those who obey the detailed instructions of Scripture about religious observance (e.g. Numbers 28–29) yet fail to do justice and show mercy (Isaiah 1.11–17). Satan ('the Deceiver') quotes Scripture at Jesus in an attempt to undermine his mission (e.g. Matthew 4.1–11), and he faces hostility from religious leaders who believe he is undermining scriptural observance (Matthew 12.1–14). Paul's epistles emphasise that Christianity is not a legalistic faith: instead, love is the fulfilment of the law (Romans 13.8–10; Galatians 5.1–14).

Many learned volumes and academic papers have been written about how to approach the Bible in a way that increases the chances of discerning God's will. But there are also works on this subject that are scholarly yet accessible to the general reader.

Examples include *Struggling with Scripture*, a short book by Walter Brueggemann, William C Placher and Brian K Blount, published by Westminster/John Knox Press in 2002, and an even shorter booklet by Brenda Watson, *Towards Sound Interpretation of Scripture*, published by Aureus in 2003. As Watson puts it, "Can any of us – Catholic, Orthodox or Protestant, traditionalist or radical, liberal or evangelical, or by whatever label we wish to be known – claim to have a God-like understanding which rules out the possibility for further correction or enlightenment?"

Following tradition

Tradition is very important: almost every Christian learns about their faith through the witness of others in present and past generations, part of a church in which beliefs and practices are shared. Yet this too is not straightforward.

Do you see yourself as a 'traditionalist'? Then imagine you hear that a state governor in another country will be taking part in an online debate about a controversial policy he wants to introduce, with the encouragement of the denomination to which he belongs. This church has held fast to the view that religion should play a prominent role in the civic sphere. He is trying to prohibit those who are not 'proper' Christians from being awarded degrees by, or teaching at, any university in his state.

He argues that, since the earliest times, Christians have sought to penalise those they regard as heretics, to protect the faithful from wrong beliefs and encourage those in error to return to the truth. According to him, this is an important part of church tradition and it is only in the modern era, supposedly in response to secularist ideas which play down the importance of religious belief, that many churches have abandoned their heritage.

The penalties he is proposing are quite mild, he points out, considering that numerous people in history were imprisoned or even killed for heresy. As recently as 1871, all academics and students at Oxford and Cambridge universities had to be Anglicans and even since then, many have held on to the belief that virtue and learning should not be separated.

You are concerned about the effects if this policy is adopted, not only on the students affected but also on the image of Christianity and relationships between Christians and their neighbours. But if you were to email or phone in a comment to the governor, will he respond? However persuasive you were, do you think it likely that he would reconsider?

There is much that is precious in church tradition. Indeed the words of a 'Church father' or mediaeval nun may cast more light on some of today's headlines than the spin-doctoring surrounding many politicians and corporations. But there are other aspects which are less admirable. Mistreatment of non-Christians and fellow-Christians with the 'wrong' beliefs has been all too common in church history. Treatment of women as inferior, or even dangerous, is another example.

Thankfully, however, tradition continues to develop: the relationship between the church and God is a living one, and openness to change as well as appreciation of the past plays a part. Practices such as religious tolerance and carol concerts, which at one time might have seemed like extraordinary innovations, have become common. Similarly, churches sometimes modify, or even abandon, doctrines on which they formerly insisted, or adopt beliefs which later become 'traditional'.

What is more, tradition is often diverse, though official church histories do not always recognise this. For instance, in Britain and beyond during pre-modern times, many Christians may have married by having their hands tied together or jumping over a broom with no clergy present; but this is probably rather different from most people's notion of a 'traditional Christian wedding'!

Hence 'tradition', by itself, cannot be a completely reliable guide to what is right. Nor is it the sole basis for doctrine (the codification of core Christian beliefs), which as Cardinal Newman set out, requires development and reception.

The interplay of Scripture, tradition, reason and experience

In reality, people do not rely entirely on Scripture, tradition, reason or experience alone to form their picture of God, the world, the church and themselves.

Even the most ardent 'Bible-believing' Christian is generally guided not only by the words on the page, but also by the powers of reason required to understand these and the tradition which helps to shape his or her assumptions. For instance, it is rare, perhaps unknown, for modern Christian men to seek to become, literally, eunuchs for the sake of the kingdom of heaven (Matthew 19.12). Instead, this is usually interpreted as a figure of speech, even by biblical literalists, though modern medicine would make such a procedure less risky than in ancient times!

Certainly, many who condemn others for not being faithful enough to Scripture bypass Jesus' memorable saying that "it is easier for a camel to go through the eye of a needle than for a rich person to enter the kingdom of God" (Matthew 19.24, Mark 10.25, Luke 18.25). It is far easier to condemn groups with lower social status or which are unlikely to make things uncomfortable for the church if they feel hurt or angry. Ironically, if more 'Bible-believers' were aware of the degree to which they (like others) interpreted the words they read, they might be more aware of the risk of failing to engage with challenging biblical truths.

Likewise, someone who puts more emphasis on 'tradition' or 'reason', while being a frequent churchgoer, may end up absorbing numerous biblical stories and other passages which then enter their imagination and influence their reasoning, sometimes subconsciously. As well as Bible readings and psalms, some of the hymns they sing, the images on stained-glass windows, murals and altar-cloths and so forth may evoke biblical events or images. Indeed someone who goes to morning prayer or Mass practically every day on her way to work, as well as worshipping on Sundays, may end up familiar with more of the 'good book' than those unfortunate enough to go to churches where the preachers constantly refer to the Bible but almost always quote the same handful of texts!

In any case, tradition is often based heavily on the Bible, filtered through the lens of reason. And what seems reasonable may be affected by the experience of Christians past and present, whether written in the pages of the Bible, passed on in other ways or encountered in the attempt to be open to Christ in prayer, worship and everyday life.

Wider recognition of the diverse ways in which divine grace and wisdom may be nurtured would support faith and fellowship, helping to break down some of the barriers in the church. A biblical passage which jolts a reader into looking at an issue in a new way, an encounter which brings fresh insights, unexpected findings by scientists, an old hymn or prayer in a new context – in these and other ways, deeper understanding and spiritual growth can occur.

In this, Christians have much to learn from one another and indeed, from other people of goodwill, and sometimes even from our fellow-creatures. The sometimes surprising way in which a child looks at the world, an elderly person's rich store of memories, the fruits of a scholar's patient work, thoughts which occur in the midst of everyday routines, insights from different settings which reflect different backgrounds and gifts – sharing such things can offer wonderful opportunities and a chance to adjust what is unbalanced and correct what is wrong.

Scripture, tradition, reason and experience cannot always be separated, and none in itself offers a fail-safe guide to the truth regarding controversial matters. This may be worrying to those who like certainty or fear getting things wrong. Yet if more people who might classify themselves in different ways – 'evangelical' or 'liberal', 'Catholic', 'Orthodox', 'Anabaptist' or 'Protestant' – could share with and learn from one another, there would be a greater chance of discovering what God has done and is doing, and how we can better respond.

God is not, as some have believed, a kind of celestial sadistic schoolteacher, giving snippets of sometimes ambiguous information and then punishing pupils if they fail to give perfect answers. Far from it: God is wonderfully loving and patient, though also awe-inspiring and challenging, and the universe is full of pointers to the divine, which can appeal to, and be grasped by, people of every background and educational preference. We inevitably make mistakes, but with God's help and hopefully with the support of other Christians and people of goodwill, we can fix these and move forward.

For Christians, in particular, 'the Word' that we seek in challenging times is not fixed in texts and thought alone, but shown to us in the flesh: in the incarnation of divine love and freedom in the life, person, work, death and resurrection of Jesus Christ.

Chapter Three

Relationships reconsidered: the early-mid twentieth century

Sexuality and the work of theology

Faith cannot always be put into words. Nevertheless, language is essential if people wish to communicate their experiences and beliefs about the Divine, however imperfectly, and together reflect on how they might respond.

Theology might be described as the study of God and God's relationship with the universe, including humankind, and theologians as people who undertake this in a focused way, discussing their findings with one another and the wider community. There are Jewish and Muslim as well as Christian theologians. However, Christian theology is a particularly widespread field of study, including in universities, and theologians can help churches to think more deeply about important questions.

Over the past century or so, numerous Christian theologians have turned their attention to the issue of same-sex love, desire and relationships. Many have come to believe that under certain circumstances, lesbian and gay partnerships are acceptable, though not all are convinced. The debates over this issue reflect some of the developments in theology during this time.

Non-Christians sometimes think that the church (the community of Christians past and present, that is, rather than the leadership of institutional churches) reaches its view on particular ethical issues on the basis of unchallengeable commands set out in the Bible or doctrinal statements. This is largely the fault of Christians, who have often failed to explain the kind of reasoning that goes on within the church, and the rather authoritarian way in which some congregations and networks function. God is sometimes portrayed rather like a distant general whose orders (passed on by lower-ranking officers) must be obeyed even if they make no obvious sense and many foot-soldiers are destroyed.

However, in the Gospels, Christ invites his followers to be not as slaves, unthinkingly doing what they are told, but friends growing towards maturity in relationship with him as they treat others lovingly (John 15.1–17), apprentices and heirs of a generous God whose ways are filled with wisdom (Luke 6.17–49).

There are certain core beliefs – about the nature of the Divine, including the Trinity whose love embraces humankind – which have remained more-or-less constant for many centuries, though theologians continue to reflect on the implications and strive to express these in terms to which people in a particular time and place can relate.

However, on particular matters of right and wrong, from slavery to the role of women, there has been much debate and what were initially minority views have sometimes gradually won wider support. [1] Questions have also been raised by economic, social, scientific and technological changes. Archaeological finds, historical research and fresh translations have also prompted scholars and communities to look at the past in new ways, and sometimes to rediscover what had been forgotten.

Some theologians (sometimes labelled 'conservative') tend to be reluctant in rethinking long-held beliefs. Others, (sometimes labelled 'liberal' or 'radical') give more weight to new developments when grappling with particular ethical questions. In addition, theology may be especially inspired by, or grounded in, particular aspects of Christian experience (e.g. being a Baptist, farmer, hospital chaplain or specialist in the Synoptic gospels or mediaeval Russian spirituality).

However, in general, whatever their 'label', theologians tend to explore – drawing on the insights of the Bible and church tradition – how human flourishing is, and can best be, promoted in the context of the relationship with God and neighbour. They are influenced – in good and not-so-good ways – by the wider church which is filled with people who have their own ways of talking about God but who would usually not regard themselves as theologians, and by society.

Theologians may also draw on insights from a related discipline, such as the study of religion, and the social sciences in general, to illuminate the historical context, how certain beliefs and practices have come to be regarded as acceptable or otherwise, and how they are understood by practitioners.

Even in church circles, some commentators talk as if there were a set of clear-cut beliefs on sexuality which earlier generations of Christians all accepted but which have largely been set aside today simply because of developments in modern society and thinking. Whether this is regarded as a good or bad thing, it is a distorted view of a far more complex reality.

To begin with, thoughtful and spiritually insightful thinkers in ancient as well as modern times have often pointed to the need to go beyond superficial piety, and look more deeply into what God might be doing and inviting people to receive or do, even if the conclusions were unsettling. The Bible itself is a collection of books written at different times and sometimes reflecting different perspectives – even the New Testament contains diverse views – and the beliefs and practices of Christians in past centuries have varied greatly.

The pace of change in the modern world is however, probably greater than at almost any time in the past and there has been intense study and debate during recent decades on a range of issues from economic justice and ecology to gender and sexuality. This has sometimes prompted Christians to read the Bible and writings of earlier Christians afresh.

For instance, while at one time the first few chapters of Genesis were taken as an invitation for humankind to exploit the earth and other animals ruthlessly, it is now widely believed that the kind of leadership which humans are required to exercise is more about care and responsible stewardship. Again, now that the world is indeed full of people, the call for humans to "multiply and fill the earth" (Genesis 1.28) may not apply in the way it once did.

This and the following chapters are by no means a comprehensive account of changes in the theology of sexuality, which have led many (though by no means all) Christians to believe that same-sex partnerships may be morally justified. A number of theologians who have played a part in that journey have not even been mentioned, and others have had their work only briefly described. What is more, while I have tried to reflect something of the diversity of views even among those who support greater acceptance, there are some whose writings have been particularly important to me at some point in my life: I am not wholly objective.

The focus is on relationships where both partners identify as male or as female. Issues specific to trans or intersex people are not generally addressed, though the theological changes outlined here have had some influence on their experience as well as that of lesbian, gay and bisexual people.

I also say relatively little about the work of those theologians who continue to argue that same-sex relationships are always wrong. But some of their arguments will probably be familiar to anyone who grew up when such beliefs were dominant, attends certain churches or follows media coverage of what prominent church leaders say on homosexuality. [2]

Changes in opinion on human sexuality in many churches throws light more generally on the way in which Christians grapple with ethical issues. And the extensive work which has taken place on the theology of sexuality, how the Bible is read and on church tradition deserves to be properly acknowledged.

A time of questioning

Faith-influenced reflection on same-sex love and relationships is not new, including the affirmation that these could be positive. Yet up to the early twentieth century, this happened more often in the context of spiritual reflection, pastoral care or creative writing than through formal theology.

In the ancient and mediaeval world, disease could speedily wipe out huge swathes of the population, so unsurprisingly, procreation was seen as vital for survival. Moreover marriage bonds between men and women could play a role in increasing social stability, which was especially valued as the church overall became less critical of the existing order. Marriage could connect extended families and provide new generations to whom knowledge and norms could be handed down, and who could inherit land (if any was owned) and care for parents in old age.

This is not to say that people's most important emotional relationships, or the direction of their imagination, were necessarily directed to the opposite sex. For instance, intense bonds could develop between pairs of monks or nuns, though these might not have always been physically expressed. [3]

In addition, the language of human love and desire has long been used to describe the human encounter with the Divine, including homoerotic or gender-crossing expressions by men yearning for a Christ pictured as male. [4]

Over the past hundred-odd years, however, many theologians have studied and written on human sexuality, including desire, intimacy and partnership between women and between men, and there has been much discussion in church circles.

The twentieth century was an era when changes within the church and society led to a re-examination of a range of issues. At the beginning, leaders of different Christian denominations generally held that contraception was always wrong, even for married couples. Differences remained over whether priests and bishops could marry, and whether celibacy or marriage was a higher state. But churchgoers and Christians thinkers were increasingly questioning whether the only proper place for sexual intimacy was between husband and wife with openness to conceiving children if at all possible. [5]

A few decades earlier, across Europe and its current or former colonies, there were rigidly-held views in society and the church about the roles of men and woman and the importance of upholding men's mastery in domestic as well as public settings. Similarly, people of certain classes and ethnicities were usually assumed to be divinely chosen to lead. While many in the early church had taken a more egalitarian view, by the Middle Ages those Christians who held on to this were marginalised and often persecuted, though this did not entirely silence dissenting voices.

Likewise, marriage was sometimes seen as a tool to assist better-off families to hold on to and accumulate more wealth and prestige – a notion starkly at odds with New Testament values, but which had come to be regarded as 'Christian'. In some denominations, monks and nuns were also part of strongly hierarchical 'families' with great wealth and power. Elsewhere, the monastic tradition, with the opportunities it still sometimes offered for alternative lifestyles and value-systems, had been undermined or had fallen into disarray.

In practice, churches often accepted that companionship might also be valuable and did not take a hard line on sex between married couples who could not have children because of the age or infertility of one or both partners. And not all men and women in church circles fitted gender stereotypes. What is more, marriage did not always involve much emotional closeness, and could co-exist with other kinds of intimate relationship. But entering into an openly acknowledged same-sex union instead of marrying a member of the opposite sex was not usually an option for respectable, religious folk.

Yet in recent centuries – amidst social upheaval, greater cross-cultural communication and an increase in literacy and availability of books, including the Bible in various translations – some of what had been held certain by most in mediaeval times was called into question. There was also a surge of interest in gender, sexuality and difference in the nineteenth century, when some thinkers argued for rigid hierarchies on the grounds of nature as supposedly revealed by science, while others questioned this and took a different view of 'normality'.

Changes in women's status, family patterns, healthcare and environmental awareness increasingly led people to question the desirability of having numerous children: responsible use of resources and protecting the earth and its inhabitants were seen as equally, if not more important.

Self-giving love, past and present
Some of those seeking a freer, more affirming environment for people attracted to the same sex looked backwards to an idealised version of the Graeco-Roman pagan past (despite the deep class and age-based inequalities of that era). Others were rooted

in Christian tradition.

"Loving, we love by God and in God," wrote Russian Orthodox theologian Pavel Florensky, a mathematician, scientist, priest and mystic, in The Pillar and Ground of the Truth, published in 1914, [6] mentioning 1 John 4.7–8: "Let us love one another, for love is of God (*hoti hē agapē ek tou*). And every one that loveth is born of God, and knoweth God. He that loveth not knoweth not God, for God is love." Discussing the different terms for love in New Testament Greek, he suggested that love for everyone could not substitute for a close personal relationship; indeed "in order to treat everyone as oneself it is necessary to see oneself in at least one other person, to feel oneself in him; it is necessary to perceive in this one person an already achieved – even if only partial – victory over selfhood."

He quoted St Jerome among others: "Two by two are called and two by two are sent the disciples of Christ, for love does not abide with one." Citing the Bible and writings by influential figures in the early church, he argued that self-giving friendship between same-sex pairs, in which "one grows intertwined with a friend," had been critically important to the church from the outset. His approach drew on the Orthodox notion of partnered love as essentially ascetic, not in the sense of avoiding pleasure but rather involving the discipline of self-emptying. While Florensky did not specifically address the question of sexual intimacy, he suggested that, "in communal life even the bodies become one, as it were." He drew attention to an ancient service for the "pledging of brotherhood" with certain similarities to marriage. He would later be sent to Siberia and martyred in the Stalinist purges. Many decades later, historian John Boswell and theologian Eugene F Rogers would pick up some of these themes.

There was no ambiguity about Radclyffe Hall's 1928 novel The Well of Loneliness, written with the aim of exposing the cruelty of the prejudice against those who might today be classified as lesbian, gay, bisexual and transgender. The author was a devout British Catholic whose writing often took up religious themes and who was openly lesbian at a time when this met strong social disapproval. She addressed spiritual as well as wider social issues within a narrative grappling with broader themes of love, nature and sacrifice: indeed the hero is named Stephen after the first Christian martyr.

When Stephen is shocked by the self-destructiveness of some around her who have internalised the world's hatred and contempt, a wise Jewish gay man tells her, "Many die, many kill their bodies and souls, but they cannot kill the justice of God, even they cannot kill the eternal spirit. From their very degradation that spirit will rise up to demand of the world compassion and justice." At the end of the novel, Stephen prays, "Acknowledge us, oh God, before the whole world. Give us also the right to our existence!" Hall certainly succeeded in stirring up debate and the book was banned. However it played a part in a gradual shift of attitudes.

The furore over this novel also highlights the problem with a view sometimes expressed by senior clergy, that attitudes to sexuality have changed in wider culture and the church must respond. But 'the church' is, first and foremost, a community or movement made up of people, rather than a set of institutions, important as these are. So the church – through Christians seeking to follow Christ while pursuing their callings, including as writers and campaigners – has been centrally involved in this process of cultural change, alongside people of other faiths and none.

'Love, and usually love of the most complete kind, is the substance of the vast majority of homosexual relationships, and where the love is sincerely mutual it is immoral to devalue it,' wrote English Anglican theologian Archibald Kenneth Ingram [7] in his 1940 work *Sex–Morality Tomorrow*. [8] A barrister by profession, he also wrote on faith and ethics for a wide readership, for instance in *The Spectator*.

His 1944 booklet Christianity and sexual morality [9] systematically examined the prevailing views of his day and argued that an ethic based on love (understood not as temporary infatuation but rather as a deeper, usually faithful, relationship in which the beloved is treated as a person, not an object for one's own gratification) was more compatible with the Gospels. His work also sought to take account of the complexities of sexual orientation and human relationships and i included the challenging of widely-held misconceptions about homosexuality and bisexuality.

However, such opinions were still far removed from mainstream church thinking, in part because it was widely assumed that the Bible clearly forbade same-sex physical intimacy. In addition, such relationships were commonly thought to be fleeting or miserable, unable to promote emotional fulfilment and psychological maturity, while 'experts' held out the hope of a 'cure'. Hence even compassionate fellow-Christians did not want to encourage what they thought of as ultimately frustrating and harmful.

However, by the 1950s and 1960s, such views became difficult to sustain, in part because of the boldness of LGBT campaigners who promoted a more realistic understanding of their experience, as did their heterosexual allies. In addition, dedicated biblical scholars who were willing to try to set aside what they thought the texts said and study them afresh (which is harder than it sounds), helped to lay the foundations for radical change.

Beyond the sin of Sodom
By the mid-twentieth century, many Christians – including theologians and senior church leaders – had come to believe that contraceptive use was sometimes acceptable and that one partner in a marriage did not have to be superior to the other. This opened the door to further questions about when, and how, sexual relationships might be a source of good to the partners and to wider society.

In addition, churches in many countries had less prestige than in the past and were more willing to question the status quo. Though the Church of England, for instance, kept certain privileges, some of its theologians were willing to ask searching questions about society and its treatment of the poor and of minorities.

Harsh social, and in some countries legal, penalties had led many lesbians and gays to stay 'in the closet', hiding their feelings from most people around them and being secretive. In the

UK, for instance, gay sex was an imprisonable offence, and gays often struggled to change their sexuality, including undergoing drastic forms of medical treatment or getting married, which frequently led to disappointment and damage to all involved. When two men or two women did enter into a sexual relationship, all too often this was in part shaped by fear and internalised negativity. But campaigners called for change.

Senior clergy came to recognise the injustice of jailing gay men while, for instance, men who cheated on their wives faced no legal penalties, and helped to change the law. But most continued to believe that sex between men or between women was always sinful.

The Rev Dr Derrick Sherwin Bailey [10] of the Church of England's Moral Welfare Council played an important part in making a coherent case for decriminalisation. However he went further in his 1955 work Homosexuality and the Western Christian Tradition. Examining Scripture, tradition, reason and experience, he argued that the sin of Sodom described in Genesis 19 was inhospitality rather than homosexual practice, prohibitions in Old Testament law were not valid for Christians today and references in the Epistles did not apply to people who were, by nature, homosexual.

With regard to "moral judgements upon the sexual conduct of the genuine invert", he suggested that "Christian tradition... has at best but an indirect and dubious relevance". [11] Though he avoided endorsing same-sex relationships, he demonstrated that the biblical case against acceptance was far from clear and laid the foundations for ongoing re-evaluation.

Debates have continued over just what St Paul thought about human sexuality and how this should influence Christians today. However, many have come to accept the view that the story of Sodom, involving an attempted mob attack on two strangers who are in fact angels, is intended to show the dire consequences of mistreatment of the outsider and of injustice in general. This interpretation fits the immediate context (it is contrasted with the generous hospitality and compassion of Abraham, which bring rich blessings), and other Scriptural references to Sodom.

It is a sobering thought that what church leaders may confidently claim is God's view set out in the Bible may in fact represent their own biases or those of a particular society and over the past sixty years, many theologians addressing sexuality and other issues have acknowledged this risk.

In 1963 *Towards a Quaker View of Sex*, [12] written by several Quakers, put forward the view that a sexual act was immoral if it involved exploitation, whether of the same or opposite sex. In *The Ethics of Sex*, published in 1964, German Protestant theologian Helmut Thielicke [13] argued that while homosexuality was less than ideal and those so inclined should seek healing or try to be celibate, if this was not successful, entering into a faithful same-sex partnership might be an ethical path. Also in 1964, in *No new morality: Christian personal values and sexual morality,* [14] Douglas Rhymes, a Church of England cleric, called for a re-evaluation of attitudes to homosexuality.

Norman Pittenger, [15] an Anglican academic teaching in Cambridge University, urged acceptance of loving and responsible gay and lesbian relationships in his *Time for Consent* in 1967.

This was an issue that triggered powerful feelings, as Anglican theologian Hugh Montefiore found to his cost when he suggested that Jesus, whose unmarried status was most unusual in that age and culture, might have been homosexually inclined, though celibate. [16] The furious reaction was a reminder that grappling with the theology of sexuality was a risky business.

Questioning assumptions

Growing numbers of Christians were taking the view that theology at its best was not done by people in relatively privileged positions pretending to be detached from the struggles, joys and sorrows of those facing hardship and marginalisation. Increasingly, theologians writing on homosexuality, if not lesbian or gay themselves, knew people who were, some of whom led reasonably happy, well-adjusted lives with their partners. And the gay or lesbian orientation of pastors and teachers such as Harry Williams, [17] whose writings on Christian spirituality enriched the faith of many, was becoming more widely known.

In wider society, the West was marked by students' and workers' protests, anti-racist and anti-war struggles. Anti-imperialist movements in Asia, Africa and Latin America switched their focus from opposing direct colonial rule (now uncommon) to the more subtle use of economic and political power which led to a global imbalance in power. Philosophers such as Michel Foucault [18] encouraged people not to take for granted what seemed 'normal' and 'natural'.

While some in the church sought to defend the status quo, others were active in struggles for change and reflected on faith-related issues in the midst of conflict and danger. In the civil rights movement in the USA, which confronted racism in society with non-violent direct action, one of the most important leaders was Quaker peace and justice activist Bayard Rustin, a brilliant organiser, who once wrote, "When an individual is protesting society's refusal to acknowledge his dignity as a human being, his very act of protest confers dignity on him... It is this dignity that our Divine Creator has called all of creation towards. It is my honor to be a voice in this choir. We must be courageous and unafraid as we know that the truth of God is justice and to be afraid is to behave as if the truth were not true."19 Despite the law and social prejudice at the time, he was openly gay.

The lawyer and Episcopalian (Anglican) theologian William Stringfellow, [20] who lived and worked among the poor in Harlem, New York, taught that "The incarnation is not a mere theological abstraction... the church and the Christian people are not simply involved in public affairs of all sorts because of the nature of politics by which all are involved and abstention is a fiction, but because they honour and celebrate God's own presence and vitality in this world, because they know that the world – in all its strife and confusion, brokenness and travail, contention and controversy – is the scene of God's work and the focus of God's love." [21] He too was gay, as was Episcopalian priest and anti-racist campaigner Malcolm Boyd, [22] whose book of prayers in the everyday language of young people became a bestseller.

Chapter Four

A turning tide

Justice, love and discipleship

By the 1970s, a number of eminent thinkers from various church backgrounds were making a case for an approach to ethics in sexual relationships which would apply to lesbian and gay as well as heterosexual people. The importance of grounding discussions of Christian sexual ethics in the real-life situations of men and women striving to follow Christ was emphasised not only in theological journals and books, but also through other means such as the spiritual autobiography of Troy Perry, [1] founder of the Metropolitan Community Church, The Lord is my Shepherd and He Knows I'm Gay, published in 1972,

Patrick Henry, a lay Presbyterian and associate professor, drew on his experience of living alongside and teaching lesbian, gay, bisexual and trans (LGBT people) as well as on his understanding of the Bible and church tradition when he argued that "For centuries Christians have identified each other not with a question: 'Are you a Jew or a Greek? slave or free? male or female? straight or gay?'; but with a declaration: 'The Lord is risen!' to which the response is a reaffirmation, 'He is risen indeed!' The church is the outpost of the world transformed in the world as it is. For the church to declare homosexuality an offence against God is for the church to look back, to use 'the old leaven, the leaven of malice' (I Corinthians 5:8)." [2]

Biblical scholarship and exploration of church tradition were yielding new insights. In 1976 Jesuit scholar John J McNeill's book The Church and the Homosexual systematically addressed arguments from Scripture, tradition and philosophy. [3] The Second Vatican Council, held in the 1960s, had led to a climate of greater openness in the Roman Catholic Church, though later his work was suppressed.

In an article on Homosexuality and the Church, [4] James B

Nelson took as his fundamental principle in interpreting the Bible the assumption "that Jesus Christ is the bearer of God's invitation to human wholeness and is the focal point of God's humanising action; hence, Jesus Christ is the central norm through which and by which all else must be judged". He argued that for everyone, heterosexual or homosexual, "the central biblical message regarding sexuality is clear enough. Idolatry, the dishonouring of God, inevitably results in the dishonouring of persons. Faithful sexual expression always honours the personhood of the companion."

Is the Homosexual My Neighbor?, [5] by evangelical writers Letha Dawson Scanzoni and Virginia Ramey Mollenkott, which was first published in 1978, also made a strong Biblical case for greater acceptance. [6] (This is different from a later piece of the same name, also highly readable, containing a dialogue between Tony and Peggy Campolo. This illustrates how Christians with similar views may come to different conclusions on the theology of sexuality, while opposing homophobia and remaining in fellowship with one another. [7])

"We should take seriously the evidence that so many homosexuals, feeling condemned by contemporary society to lives of isolation and loneliness, see most clearly the positive value of fidelity and commitment," suggested Basil and Rachel Moss in *Humanity and Sexuality*, [8] a booklet published by the Church of England's Church Information Office in 1978 to promote discussion which took a brief but thoughtful look at the theology of sexuality as a whole: "If both marriage and celibacy have their public pledging of fidelity, why should this possibility be denied to that 5 per cent or so of the population who are homosexual by unalterable constitution?"

Feminism and other movements for justice deeply influenced theologians such as Carter Heyward. [9] In a 1979 article she argued that "historically the predominant effect of cultural conditioning has been to squeeze all humanity into a single large box labelled 'heterosexual'... The moment a boy child learns that little boys don't cry, the instant a girl child learns that little girls don't fight, the child takes a step further into the heterosexual box." In contrast "Sexuality, which finds its most intimate expression between lovers, moves us into an active realisation, and great relief, that we are not alone; that we are, in fact, bound up in the lives of others; and that this is good. That is why, I think, many (but too few) Christians speak of love and justice together; justice is the moral act of love." [10]

It is important, in considering homosexuality and Scripture, to look beyond a handful of verses, Walter Wink pointed out in an article that year: "The fact is that there is, behind the legal tenor of Scripture, an even deeper tenor, articulated by Israel out of the experience of the Exodus and brought to sublime embodiment in Jesus' identification with harlots, tax collectors, the diseased and maimed and outcast and poor. It is that God sides with the powerless, God liberates the oppressed, God suffers with the suffering and groans toward the reconciliation of all things. In the light of that supernal compassion, whatever our position on gays, the gospel's imperative to love, care for, and be identified with their sufferings is unmistakably clear." [11]

The influential ethicist Beverley Wildung Harrison [12] has also emphasised the importance of justice in theology, including sexual ethics, in her work.

Meanwhile, working parties set up by mainstream churches were beginning, after in-depth study, to conclude that same-sex relationships might in some instances be acceptable. This included a Task Force set up by the Presbyterian church in the USA, which reported to General Assembly in 1978, [13] and a Church of England Working Party chaired by John Yates, the Bishop of Gloucester. [14]

However, these conclusions proved too challenging for their denominations as a whole, which continued to insist that the only proper place for sex was in a marriage between a man and woman.

Love and grace

In the 1980s, through into the 1990s and the early twenty-first century, the work of social and natural scientists continued to throw light on the diversity within creation. This included scholarship on same-sex love and partnership in history and across cultures, including those of Asia, Africa and Latin America. Not surprisingly there was considerable debate – interpreting beliefs and practices is not always easy – but it was becoming apparent that things were not as clear as they had at one time appeared.

Historian John Boswell [15] revealed examples of loving same-sex friendships in the early church, some of which involved blessing ceremonies. While not suggesting that these always involved physical intimacy, he called into question the assumption that the fierce hostility towards homosexuality which took hold in the Middle Ages was the only attitude which had ever existed among pre-modern Christians. Alan Bray also delved deeply into the issue of same-sex friendship and commitment in history. [16] Bernadette J Brooten, another historian, examined women's lives and intimate friendships in the ancient world, and their theological implications. [17]

An increasing number of eminent theologians were engaging with the issue of lesbian and gay relationships, including Rowan Williams, [18] at that time professor of Divinity at the University of Oxford. In *The Body's Grace*, a lecture at a Lesbian and Gay Christian Movement event in 1989, he suggested that "if we are looking for a sexual ethic that can be seriously informed by our Bible, there is a good deal to steer us away from assuming that reproductive sex is a norm, however important and theologically significant it may be. When looking for a language that will be resourceful enough to speak of the complex and costly faithfulness between God and God's people, what several of the biblical writers turn to is sexuality understood very much in terms of the process of 'entering the body's grace...' A theology of the body's grace which can do justice to the experience, the pain and the variety, of concrete sexual discovery... depends heavily on believing in a certain sort of God – the trinitarian creator and saviour of the world – and it draws in a great many themes in the Christian understanding of humanity". This led to much discussion on the theological significance of sexual intimacy in general, not just for LGBT people. [19]

Others too had been grappling with the complexities of the

Bible's approach to human sexuality overall. These included Victor Paul Furnish in his 1979 work (later revised) on *The Moral Teaching of Paul* and Robin Scroggs, whose 1983 book *The New Testament and Homosexuality* had argued that the epistles did not clearly address non-exploitative same-sex relationships. Another New Testament scholar who studied the subject in depth was L William Countryman. In 1988 in *Dirt, Greed, and Sex*, [20] he examined the changing notions of purity and property in the Old and New Testaments, and argued that writing off a large part of humankind as 'impure' went against the core teaching of the Gospels and Epistles. The Bible offers profound insights into love and faithfulness in committed relationships for both opposite-sex and same-sex partners, the Old Testament scholar Bruce C Birch suggested in 1992 in *To Love as We Are Loved*.

Gregory Baum [21] (who had been a theological advisor to the Second Vatican Council) pointed out in 1994 that "for the first time in history we have personal witnesses and an extended literature in which homosexual men and women make known the hidden aspects of their personal lives, offer critical reflections of their own experiences and reveal the ethical orientation that guides them in their attitudes and actions... There seems to be no a priori reason why one should reject the thesis that God who creates the majority of humanity as heterosexual, creates a minority as a natural variant defined by a homosexual orientation. If that were true, homosexual love would be in perfect keeping with the natural law." [22]

The view put forward in 1994 by the Welsh Anglican theologian Jeffrey John [23] that *Permanent, Faithful, Stable* same-sex partnerships should be accepted in the church, was increasingly widely held.

Sexuality, liberation and "queerness"
In Latin America and other parts of the world, liberation theology [24] had become influential. This emphasised the Biblical themes of justice and freedom, especially for the poor and marginalised, and built on earlier Christian social thinking as well as on contemporary attempts to analyse oppressive systems and

structures.

Indeed, some spoke and wrote of liberation theologies, since this approach took different forms in different parts of the world and focused on a variety of forces – not simply economic – that hampered fullness of life. Such theologies often met with considerable opposition from powerful figures in society and the church.

Unsurprisingly, some theologians in Asia, Africa and Latin America perceived the mistreatment of gays and lesbians in the light of the numerous ways in which ordinary people suffered under repressive governments, powerful elites and an unjust international order. According to the Statement of the 1992 Assembly of the Ecumenical Association of Third World Theologians, held in Kenya, "The Third World cry for life is one multi-tonal cry. It reflects the various ways oppression assaults Third World life. It carries the cries of countries protesting economic indenture to IMF [the International Monetary Fund] and the World Bank...

> "It carries the cries of refugees, children, displaced people and those afflicted with AIDS, the cries against the discrimination of homosexuals, of those who suffer from economic oppression, women forced into prostitution, victims of drug abuse and the unjust politics of health care. It carries the cries of Blacks against apartheid. It carries the cries of the Dalits against the apartheid of caste oppression. It carries the cries of women against patriarchal dominance and sexual violence... following the Jesus of faith means following one who was dedicated to feeding the hungry, clothing the naked and fighting for the liberation of oppressed people... God is present to us in him." [25]

'Black theology' was one of the forms that liberation theology took in the West. Some African-American theologians such as Cornel West [26] and Dwight N Hopkins [27] took the view that sexism and homophobia, as well as racism and economic oppression, needed to be challenged in developing communities of mutual love and freedom.

Some LGBT theologians in the West also drew on the approach of liberation theology to explore their experience and calling, for example Richard Cleaver in the USA, who drew on Scripture in addressing issues of identity, community and justice. [28]

Among the theologians who openly identified as LGBT were some influenced by the 'queer' movement. This sought to reclaim a word used to insult people who did not fit society's notions of sexual 'normality', instead proudly affirming what some had dismissed as 'deviant'. Sometimes the celebration of 'queerness' was linked with radical political activism for greater equality. [29] Some 'queer theorists' questioned whether any form of identity was natural, emphasising instead the human-shaped aspects of gender and sexuality. [30]

'Queer theology' embraced a range of different perspectives, [31] but in general challenged the notion that patriarchal heterosexual households were especially blessed by God while all other ways of life were spiritually inferior. Some questioned whether monogamy was necessary. Robert E Goss, [32] for instance, the author of *Jesus ACTED UP: A Gay and Lesbian Manifesto* (1993), while acknowledging the value of pair-bonding, argued that other relationships too might embody something of God's love. [33] Others identified with queer theology have included Mona West, [34] Chris Glaser, [35] Ken Stone [36] and Nancy Wilson. [37] Elizabeth Stuart, [38] a UK-based theologian who has also been influential in this field, later argued that it had not gone far enough in exploring the essentially queer nature of the church, in which barriers are broken down and identity remade in Christ. [39]

Some academics exploring the theological implications of 'queerness' such as Gerard Loughlin [40] and Graham Ward [41] have drawn heavily on queer theory. *Que(e)rying Religion*, [42] a 1997 anthology edited by Gary David Comstock (earlier the author of *Gay Theology Without Apology* [43]) and Susan E Henking, ranged from the sociology of religion and history of sexuality to theological reflection. In 2001 Grace M Jantzen, a distinguished philosopher of religion, explored 'Contours of a queer theology'. [44]

Omnigender [45] by V R Mollenkott (who in the 1970s had co-written *Is the Homosexual My Neighbor?*) was especially relevant to trans and intersex people. It also generally questioned the neat division of humankind into males and females behaving in ways characteristic of their gender.

There was an overlap between queer and liberation theologies, perhaps most notably in the work of the late Marcella Althaus-Reid, [46] an Argentinian who worked among the poor in Buenos Aires and later became a theology professor in the University of Edinburgh. She put the case for "indecent theology" which broke free from the constraints of "proper" behaviour and acknowledged the "excessiveness of our hungry lives: our hunger for food, hunger for the touch of other bodies, for love and for God". [47]

There were however, other openly LGBT theologians who were more socially and theologically conservative. For example Peter J Gomes, Plummer Professor of Christian Morals at Harvard University and Baptist minister to its Memorial Church, [48] was an African-American scholar who became one of the USA's most celebrated preachers and delivered a sermon at the inauguration of President George Bush. His 1996 bestseller *The Good Book: Reading the Bible with Mind and Heart* made a case for thoughtful reading of Scripture [49] and was described by former Archbishop of Canterbury Robert Runcie as "Easily the best contemporary book on the Bible for thoughtful people." [50]

It was not only 'liberal' theologians who especially emphasised current scientific knowledge and contemporary experience who were exploring what it meant to be LGBT and Christian, but also thinkers from a wide theological spectrum. Prominent evangelicals who came out as gay and prompted others to question their assumptions about 'Bible-believing' Christianity included Mel White, who had worked with some of the USA's most famous evangelists, [51] UK academic Michael Vasey, whose book *Strangers and Friends: A New Exploration of Homosexuality and the Bible* [52] appeared in 1995, and the well-known preacher and writer Roy Clements, also in the UK. [53]

Not everyone engaged in theological debate on sexuality was

convinced by such writings, [54] and some refused even to consider the case for greater inclusion. But many were prompted at least to recognise that fellow-Christians who were lesbian or gay might, in good faith, enter into same-sex partnerships.

Theological reflection in fiction and film

Throughout the latter half of the twentieth century and beyond, theological reflection continued to take place not only in articles, books, talks and other direct forms (for instance documentaries such as For the Bible tells me so [55]), but also in poetry, fiction, feature films, literary criticism and other imaginative formats. Sometimes theologians have worked in more than one genre, for example Nicola Slee, who is also a poet. [56] But at other times, artists and critics addressing homosexuality in various ways have touched on theological themes.

Sometimes this was not overt, as in the 1961 film *Victim*, [57] directed by Basil Dearden and starring Dirk Bogarde, released at a time when gay sex was still illegal in the UK, and blackmailers often took advantage of this law (which the film has been credited with helping to change). Religion is not often mentioned explicitly (though in one telling scene a police officer who prides himself on being a puritan is gently challenged by a wiser colleague), but themes such as love, sacrifice and mercy are prominent.

'Blessed Assurance', a short story by African-American writer Langston Hughes published in 1963, also offered a sympathetic portrayal of gays, this time in the context of a black-led church, and the complex interplay of spirituality and the desire for human intimacy. [58]

Some measure of eroticism in human yearning for the divine is by no means uncommon in Christian spirituality. But a poem by James Kirkup published in the UK in Gay News in 1976, 'The Love That Dares To Speak Its Name', describing a gay Roman centurion's fantasies about Jesus, resulted in a furore, and the paper and its editor were successfully prosecuted for 'blasphemous libel'. [59]

By this time, there was a growing volume of fiction that did not always end in tragedy or loneliness for the main characters and in which same-sex as well as opposite-sex relationships could take place against a background of community, among LGBT people and also increasingly with accepting heterosexuals. For instance, Patricia Nell Warren's [60] 1976 novel *The Fancy Dancer* explores the experience of a Catholic priest who grows in emotional and spiritual maturity when he falls in love with another man. The lesbian and gay characters in her 1978 work The Beauty Queen, partnered and single, Christian and non-Christian, are forced to respond to a homophobic backlash against growing social acceptance, in which contradictions are exposed and secrets come to light.

The gay African-American novelist James Baldwin [61] continued to explore spiritual as well as political themes, for instance in his 1979 novel Just Above My Head. The healing power of love and struggle for human liberation from varying forms of oppression and alienation again featured in a very different novel, Alice Walker's The Color Purple, published in 1982, which won the Pulitzer prize for fiction in the following year. [62]

Antonia Bird's 1994 film about a young Roman Catholic – *Priest* [63] – who is forced out of the closet tackled the wider issue of clerical celibacy, though fine acting by Linus Roache, with strong support from Tom Wilkinson, Cathy Tyson and Robert Carlyle, helping to make it far more than an 'issue' movie.

Likewise Sigourney Weaver's powerful performance in *Prayers for Bobby*, [64] a 2009 film directed by Russell Mulcahy and based on a true story, helps to make it both moving and thought-provoking.

The spiritual implications of same-sex attraction and love continue to be explored in poetry, fiction and film. Sometimes this is understated, elsewhere it is explicit, as in the fiction of Michael Arditti, [65] , for example, in his moving and often funny novel *Easter*, in which clergy and laity celebrating Holy Week in a North London parish find their lives changed in unexpected ways.

Literature has in turn prompted some theologians to explore sexuality more deeply. For instance, Roger A Sneed drew on the work of black gay writers in his 2010 book *Representations of Homosexuality: Black Liberation Theology and Cultural Criticism.* [66]

Chapter Five

Change and resistance

Debating sexuality in the church

By the late twentieth century and beginning of the twenty-first, theological debates on homosexuality were taking place within a number of churches and traditions. Though some theologians still insisted that same-sex partnerships were unacceptable, or at least so controversial that churches should discriminate against those in such relationships to avoid offending the 'faithful', many others were taking a different stance.

The notion that same-sex love was necessarily unstable and led to unhappiness, in stark contrast to heterosexuality, was increasingly difficult to uphold in light of the evidence – though there was also a backlash, reflecting some people's feeling that too much was changing too fast in the modern world. Theologians found themselves in the midst of such debates. Some – especially those with the gift of being able to communicate in relatively simple ways – were able to make a valuable contribution, encouraging thoughtful responses and sometimes demonstrating how even the most learned could be humble enough to study, listen and re-examine their views.

Against the background of controversy among Presbyterians in the USA, Choon-Leong Seow's [1] reflection on the Wisdom tradition in 1996 in a chapter in Homosexuality and Christian Community examined the connections between Scripture and present-day experience, including the way in which he had come to revise his own views. He also edited the book, in which contributors reflected different viewpoints, but sought to promote mutual listening.

The well-known Anglican theologian John Austin Baker, when Bishop of Salisbury, had led the Church of England's House of Bishops in arguing against celebrating same-sex relationships. But in 1997 he publicly changed his position, taking the view that faithful and self-giving love, gay or straight, could enable people to grow in likeness to Christ. [2] "Persons living in faithful heterosexual and homosexual partnerships, can through sharing sexual love be 'the grace of God to each other'. The fruit of the Spirit can grow in that soil," he wrote. "I have seen the face of Christ in the sacrificial support of gay men for their lovers right to the end."

The 1998 Lambeth Conference exposed deep international divisions among Anglicans over homosexuality, and fierce resistance on the part of some bishops to even considering the possibility of greater acceptance. [3] Though this has sometimes been portrayed as a split between the 'traditionalist' South and more 'liberal' West, the reality was more complex. [4] South African Archbishop Desmond Tutu for instance, had taken a strong stance in favour of inclusion, [5] while some US bishops had been vigorously campaigning against this. [6]

Indeed, not only in Anglican circles but also the wider church, a number of prominent right-wing Christians in the USA worked hard to build alliances and extend their influence throughout the world, especially in Africa. As the Zambian priest and researcher Kapya Kaoma later pointed out, LGBT Africans found themselves at risk of becoming "collateral damage in the US culture wars". [7]

By the early twenty-first century, it was generally far less risky for a theologian to suggest that same-sex relationships could sometimes be helpful to spiritual growth than it would have been in the mid-twentieth century. Yet some remained under pressure to avoid voicing such views.

For instance, Rowland Jide Macaulay described the ongoing discrimination faced by LGBT people in many parts of Africa and how this affected Christians seeking to grasp the way to articulate and live out their faith. [8] In other countries where the state continued to punish people for being gay, theologians were also cautious about taking what might appear to be a subversive stance.

The marginalisation of LGBT people in many parts of the world was intensified by the tendency of some Western church leaders not to acknowledge diversity of views and experiences among Christians in the global South. "Although Asian cultures do exhibit diverse views on homosexuality, conservative Asian churches have regarded homosexual relation as sinful and shameful", wrote Kwok Pui-lan in 2000. But recently "feminist theologians in Asia have become more outspoken on the issue of the diverse sexual orientations of women." She called for an eco-centred feminist spirituality which challenged oppression of all kinds, combined social action with contemplation, challenged consumerism and celebrated diversity. [9]

In an article on the relevance of Dalit theology to exclusion in the Anglican Communion, Winnie Varghese (an Indian living in the USA) has suggested that in the missionary era, "The strategy in the colonies was to convert the powerful, or to cause the converted to become powerful... I wonder if much has changed today ... We are still in conversation with a supposed elite, many of whom we have trained in our seminaries and placed in power with international support. We don't know how to find or hear voices around the world, minority groups of all kinds, including groups as mild mannered as church women's groups, writing and speaking out, aghast at the presumption and/or hypocrisy of those in power who claim to speak for them." [10]

Within various denominations, tensions were running high. But in the Anglican diocese of Toronto, those with different views on this issue were able to relate warmly to one another while taking forward the debate, [11] a process later reflected on in a book Living Together in the Church: Including our Differences, edited by Chris Ambidge of Integrity Toronto – a key figure in enabling dialogue and fellowship – and Greig Dunn.

Catholic theologians and the Vatican

The Vatican had become increasingly heavy-handed in enforcing the line set out in a 1986 letter to bishops signed by conservative theologian Joseph Ratzinger (later to become Pope Benedict XVI), head of the Congregation for the Doctrine of the Faith, and backed by Pope John Paul II. [12] According to this, "Although the particular inclination of the homosexual person is not a sin, it is a more or less strong tendency ordered toward an intrinsic moral evil; and thus the inclination itself must be seen as an objective disorder", though "It is deplorable that homosexual persons have been and are the object of violent malice in speech or in action".

However, many theologians were unconvinced, as was reflected for instance, in David Matzko McCarthy's 1997 examination of what was beneficial in the experience of married or partnered life. [13]

In a widely publicised case, a priest and nun, who for many years had engaged in pastoral work with LGBT people and their families, were forbidden in 1999 to continue their work because they did not uphold this teaching. [14] This disciplinary measure was criticised by many in the Roman Catholic church, including Lisa Sowle Cahill, [15] a distinguished ethicist. [16]

While careful scholarship is much prized in the Roman Catholic church, some in the hierarchy reacted strongly against even considering the possibility that same-sex partnerships might be morally acceptable in some circumstances. This was perhaps connected to a deeper unease about gender and sexuality. Mark D Jordan, whose book The Silence of Sodom: Homosexuality in Modern Catholicism came out in 2000, argued that "The Roman Catholic church has long been both fiercely homophobic and intensely homoerotic." [17]

It should be possible to discuss complex issues of human sexuality, and the day-to-day challenges faced by those who are of lesbian or gay orientation in making ethical choices, in an atmosphere of mutual respect and without fear of reprisal, argued the theologian James F Keenan. [18]

In A Question of Truth: Christianity & Homosexuality, published in 2003, Gareth Moore drew on Scripture, theology and reason to counter the Vatican's arguments against accepting same-sex unions, [19] taking forward some of the themes in his earlier work The Body in Context: Sex and Catholicism. In his view, church teaching was only authoritative if it was true: it was not enough simply to command obedience without making a convincing case. This powerful and carefully-argued work, which systematically considered the main arguments against acceptance and found them wanting, was published after the author's death from cancer. [20]

The widely acclaimed Roman Catholic gay theologian James Alison [21] has explored how, through God's grace, humans can relate to one another without either victimising others or acting as victims. Christ's self-giving love "completely relativises all anthropological structures and ways of being together which depend on identity derived over against each other, on comparison, on rivalry, and ultimately on death", [22] enabling reconciliation and spiritual growth.

Inclusive theology and the challenge of difference

A number of scholars in other denominations were also reexamining the Bible and tradition and drawing radical conclusions. Much of the earlier work on the Bible and sexuality had examined a handful of passages possibly relating to sex between men, including their precise meaning and significance, and some theologians had looked at the creation story, considering what it did and did not imply.

Now however, it was also being argued by some that those who did not fit in with the norms of the time, which heavily emphasised marriage and childbearing, were unusually positively depicted, especially in the New Testament. Even today in certain societies, those who are past adolescence and unmarried or childless experience pity or disapproval: in Jewish society in Jesus' day, there was huge pressure to conform. Yet there are many, including Jesus himself, who do not fully fit in with expectations of masculine or feminine roles.

In 2000, in The Subversive Gospel: A New Testament Commentary on Liberation, Tom Hanks [23] argued that a close reading of the New Testament often offers positive images of sexual minorities. (The author is an academic based in Latin America who also sometimes writes as Thomas D Hanks, and is not the famous actor of the same name, though he too is a Christian who supports greater acceptance of LGBT people.)

Important work was published on good and bad ways of reading the Bible, a matter of great importance for Christians.

For example, a short book published in 2002, Struggling with Scripture, [24] contained chapters by Walter Brueggeman (perhaps the world's most eminent Old Testament scholar), William C Placher and Brian K Blount. [25] Drawing on the Reformed tradition, this emphasised the authority of the Bible, but argued that this required careful reading rather than crude literalism.

Controversially, in The man Jesus loved: homoerotic narratives from the New Testament in 2003 and Jacob's wound: homoerotic narrative in the literature of ancient Israel Theodore W Jennings Jr. [26] argued in 2005, that the Bible contains far more that is positive about same-sex intimacy and eroticism than is usually recognised. This was an approach later taken by Keith Sharpe in 2011 in The Gay Gospels. [27]

Jo Ind heavily emphasised the role of experience and self-awareness in her 2003 work Memories of Bliss: God, Sex and Us. [28] Eugene F Rogers Jr. took a different tack in 2004, arguing that for those not called to monasticism, marriage – whether between members of the opposite sex or same sex – can be a place of growth in holiness, of putting on the "wedding garment" of Matthew 22. In his view "Sexuality, in short, is for sanctification, that is, for God. It is to be a means by which God catches human beings up into the community of God's Spirit and the identity of God's child. Monogamy and monasticism are two ways of embodying features of the triune life in which God initiates, responds to and celebrates love." [29] Drawing on Scripture and tradition, Rogers later also made the point out that complementarity between partners need not be confined to biologically male-female couples. [30]

While biblical scholars, ethicists and other theologians studied the Bible, tradition, reason and experience, debate was intensifying in church circles.

The Episcopalian Charles W Allen wrote of the value of authentic engagement between those with differing theological views and personal experiences. [31] Within the Anglican Communion, debate had become more heated after the consecration of an openly gay and partnered bishop in the USA, and the adoption of a liturgy for same-sex blessings in a Canadian diocese, followed by calls from some other member churches for firm reprisals. The Episcopal Church and the Anglican Church of Canada were asked to explain their theological reasons, which they did in To Set Our Hope on Christ and the St Michael Report respectively. [32]

While some international Christian bodies heatedly debated sexuality, others played such issues down, perhaps afraid of igniting controversy. In an 'Open letter to the World Forum on Theology and Liberation' after this met in Brazil in 2005, the gay Brazilian theologian André Sidnei Musskopf argued that liberation theology should be rooted in the concrete experiences of poor people. "It seems to me that those who are in danger of losing their jobs, threatened of being thrown out of their families and communities, live on the streets and are forced into prostitution, commit suicide, are assassinated and suffer all kinds of violence constantly because of their sexual orientation are not counted among them. Why are we so afraid of really looking at the streets of our cities and see the poor who are living and dying there, without ignoring that they are sexual beings? There are not more urgent things to do than to reflect and fight for the liberation of the poor, the question is: are we ready to acknowledge who the poor are and what are the reasons that make them become poor and marginalised?" he wrote. [33]

A booklet written in 2005 by L William Countryman (author of Dirt, Greed and Sex) on Love Human and Divine: Reflections on Love, Sexuality and Friendship drew on the Song of Songs, as well as on the writings of the 17th-century mystic Thomas Traherne, to examine the place of the erotic in Christian spirituality. [34]

In addition to official publications and writings by individual theologians, a number of anthologies were published offering useful insights from theology and other disciplines on the sexuality debate, the situation of LGBT people and the nature of Christian fellowship and communion. Many contributors were well-known in academic circles and sometimes beyond, so that it was becoming increasingly difficult to argue that there was a single position in any denomination on sexual ethics.

For example Gays and the Future of Anglicanism, edited by

Andrew Linzey and Richard Kirker, came out in 2005, [35] with contributions from a number of distinguished theologians such as Keith Ward, Vincent Strudwick, Marilyn McCord Adam, Rowan Greer, George Pattison, Thomas Breidenthal, Elaine Graham, Martyn Percy and Adrian Thatcher. [36]

Other Voices, Other Worlds: The Global Church Speaks Out on Homosexuality, edited by Terry Brown, at that time the Bishop of Malaita, a thoughtful and informative study of attitudes to sexuality in various parts of the world and the implications for the church, was published in 2006. [37] It included chapters by Winston Halapua, Bishop for Polynesia (later to become an archbishop), Aruna Gnanadason from India, retired bishop David Russell from South Africa, Charles Hefling, a professor of systematic theology in the USA, and Brazilian theologian Mario Ribas. He examined the impact of colonialism on attitudes to sexuality, and described Brazilians as "still struggling with the institutionalised guilt we inherited in the colonisation process, which disciplined the country and colonised its bodies." [38]

In 2006, the publication of Jesus, the Bible, and Homosexuality: Explode the Myths, Heal the Church, [39] by Jack Rogers, who has served as Moderator of the General Assembly of the Presbyterian Church in the USA, which urged greater inclusion, caused something of a stir. Five years later, presbyteries were allowed, if they so chose, to ordain partnered gays and lesbians.

Respected New Testament scholar Deirdre J Good [40] suggested in her 2006 work Jesus' family values that the prevailing vision of family in the New Testament was far more inclusive than that put forward by many 'pro-family' Christians, while challenging kinship loyalties that might displace commitment to bringing about God's reign on earth. [41]

The Inclusive God: Reclaiming Theology for an Inclusive Church [42] by Hugh Rayment-Pickard and Steven Shakespeare, published in 2006, argued (drawing heavily on Scripture) that an inclusive vision of God is at the heart of Christian theology.

Also in 2006, in Sex and the Single Savior: Gender and Sexuality in Biblical Interpretation, [43] Dale B Martin undertook a radical questioning of whether there is a single 'correct' meaning of a range of Biblical passages, and explored the importance of the imagination in understanding and responding to Scripture.

In 2007, An Acceptable Sacrifice? Homosexuality and the Church, [44] edited by Duncan Dormor and Jeremy Morris, with chapters by Maggi Dawn, Andrew Mein and Jessica Martin among others, focused particularly on the Church of England. [45]

In a lecture on Being Biblical? Slavery, Sexuality, and the Inclusive Community, [46] Richard Burridge [47] discussed how the Bible should properly be approached, and emphasised the importance of learning from Jesus' actions as well as teaching. This was based in part on the experience of South Africa, where supporters of apartheid claimed it was biblically mandated. Key issues were explored in more depth in his 2007 book Imitating Jesus: An Inclusive Approach to New Testament Ethics Today. [48]

The theological implications of baptism were highlighted by some theologians, for instance Louis Weil [49] in a 2007 talk on 'When signs signify – the Baptismal Covenant in its sacramental context'. [50] Giles Goddard's 2008 work Space for Grace [51] explored St Paul's image in 1 Corinthians of the church as a body in which all members are honoured, and what this meant in practice in the experience of an inner-city church with a diverse congregation and parishioners.

In evangelical circles in particular, the influence of the 'ex-gay' movement, [52] which sought to change people's orientation (often with disastrous results) has been powerfully challenged by those who have been through this process and found out the hard way that for them, and many others, it did not work. Jeremy Marks' [53] highly readable and thought-provoking 2008 book Exchanging the truth of God for a lie examined the experience of those wanting to become heterosexual, and the theological issues. (Over the years, various other former leaders of 'ex-gay' organisations have also admitted that their activities often did considerable emotional and spiritual damage. [54])

Also in 2008, the South African scholar Yolanda Dreyer questioned Reformed Church attitudes towards gays and lesbians, in the context of Scripture and history. [55]

The Mennonite theologian Ted Grimsrud, whose main focus is peace and nonviolence but who has also done considerable work on sexuality, [56] wrote in 2008 that "the best and most respectful straightforward reading of the Bible supports the inclusive perspective – in my opinion. One can be relatively conservative in one's view of the Bible and still come to inclusive conclusions. I will argue for the inclusive perspective because of, not in spite of, the Bible." [57]

In the Summer 2008 issue of Anglican Theological Review, Margaret A Farley [58] (responding to a piece by Richard A Norris Jr. [59]) explored 'Same-Sex Relationships and Issues of Moral Obligation'. [60] She argued that "what emerges from attention to traditional sources is that none of them provides grounds for an absolute, incontestable condemnation of same-sex relations; neither do they provide grounds for an absolute blessing", and that "the norms for human relationships in the sexual sphere are more like than unlike the norms for human relationships in other spheres, such as the social, economic, or political... In short, these norms include at least: do no unjust harm, free consent, mutuality, equality, commitment, fruitfulness, and social justice."

In 2009, the Roman Catholic theologian James B Nickoloff critically examined the church hierarchy's teaching that gay and lesbian sexuality is "intrinsically disordered". [61]

Reflecting on an Indian court verdict striking down a colonial-era law criminalising gay sex, George Zachariah, an Indian theology professor and member of the Mar Thoma church, called for Christians to "re-imagine our theological and ethical methods from the perspectives of the excluded." He argued that "Christian faith that affirms one body, one spirit, one hope, one lord, one faith, one baptism, and one God is not a rejection of diversities; rather it is an affirmation of the reconciliation of all diversities in Christ." [62]

Also in 2009, the Chicago Consultation, an organisation made up largely of US Anglican theologians and committed to increasing inclusion of LGBT people, published "We Will, with God's Help": Perspectives on Baptism, Sexuality, and the Anglican Communion, [63] with an introduction by Ruth Meyers and chapters by Fredrica Harris Thompsett, William H Petersen and A Katherine Grieb. [64]

Reasonable and Holy, a clear and readable book by Tobias Haller, was also published in 2009. [65] Drawing on earlier posts on his blog In a Godward Direction, [66] Haller systematically considered issues surrounding same-sex partnerships, including the arguments used by theologians opposing greater acceptance, in particular Robert A Gagnon, and made a strong case that such relationships could be compatible with being a faithful Christian.

Papers from various perspectives were published to accompany the Anglican Church of Canada's Galilee Report. [67] Examples included Paul Jennings' work on being in love in The Grace of Eros and Walter Deller's piece The Bible, Human Sexuality, Marriage and Same-Sex Unions, which has sought to identify key Biblical themes and to consider relationships in this context.

In 2010 a study document was presented to the House of Bishops of the Episcopal Church which summarised arguments against and in favour of accepting Same-Sex Relationships in the Life of the Church. [68]

Ethical reasoning – how Christians make their minds up about moral issues – is of great importance both in this and wider contexts. For instance, drawing on the experience of Asian LGBT people, Patrick S Cheng argued the need for a Christological rather than legalistic approach to sin and grace. [69]

A 2010 paper by the South African theologian Jeremy Punt examined the complexity of notions of 'Family in the New Testament: Social location, households and "traditional family values"', pointing out the frequent undermining of patriarchal values. [70]

However, many throughout the world continued to assume that the Bible was clear on the unacceptability of same-sex relationships and sometimes on LGBT identities. "Even though believers perceive the Bible as the supreme authority, they almost always want and have to interpret it," wrote Masiiwa Ragies Gunda in a 2010 examination of the use of the Bible in debates on homosexuality in Zimbabwe, in the context of wider struggles over power and responses to social change. [71]

Chapter Six

Beyond certainty

A diversity of views

Werner G Jeanrond's wide-ranging 2010 work *A theology of love* [1] traced the development of Christian thinking about love through the ages. The author touched on the possibility of "broadening of the concept of marriage beyond the traditionally heterosexual framework", and took the view that "as in heterosexual partnership, the point is the faithful and committed opening towards God's gift of love... just offering a mere blessing to this or that form of lifelong partnership will never suffice either to do justice to the depth of ecclesial interconnectedness between all forms and institutions of love in Christ or to stress the obligation to relate a couple's praxis of love intimately to the mystery of Christ's emerging body."

The Roman Catholic hierarchy continued to exert pressure on those seeking to explore the theology of sexuality, but this was proving increasingly ineffectual. For instance, the Irish priest Owen O'Sullivan was banned from publishing further articles without prior Vatican approval after a piece in 2010 in which he challenged the official church position on homosexuality. [2] This prompted protest in Ireland. The German Roman Catholic theologian David Berger came out as gay in 2010 after many years of secrecy, stating that his theological writings had sometimes been edited to conform to the church leadership's teachings. [3]

In February 2011, over one hundred and forty theology professors at Catholic universities in Germany, Austria and Switzerland wrote an open letter calling for major changes by the Vatican, including allowing married priests and giving laypeople greater authority. [4] The authors included distinguished scholars such as Peter Hünermann and Dietmar Mieth of the Catholic Theological Faculty of Tübingen University. "The deep crisis of our Church demands that we address even those problems which, at first glance, do not have anything directly to do with the abuse scandal and its decades-long cover-up," they urged.

Absolute respect for every person, regard for freedom of conscience, commitment to justice and rights, solidarity with the poor and oppressed: these are the theological foundational standards which arise from the Church's obligation to the Gospel. Through these, love of God and neighbour become tangible...

Respect for individual conscience means placing trust in people's ability to make decisions and carry responsibility. It is the task of the Church to support this capability. The Church must not revert to paternalism. Serious work needs to be done especially in the realm of personal life decisions and individual manners of life. The Church's esteem for marriage and unmarried forms of life goes without saying. But this does not require that we exclude people who responsibly live out love, faithfulness, and mutual care in same-sex partnerships or in a remarriage after divorce. [5]

More theologians subsequently added their names as signatories, [6] including eminent figures such as Gregory Baum in Canada and Jon Sobrino in El Salvador. [7] Large numbers of laypeople also expressed their support.

In a radio interview in February 2011, the 94-year-old theologian and writer on spirituality Sebastian Moore, a Benedictine monk, described the change in attitudes towards same-sex love and desire as "a huge anthropological shift", while also highlighting the value of learning from tradition, including the blessing of same-sex friendships. [8]

Later that year, the politician Kristina Keneally (who has a master's degree in theology) reflected in the Australian media on "Why I support gay marriage". [9] "A Catholic conscience must give attention and respect to Church teachings, but is also bound to consider science, reason, human experience, scripture and other theological reflection," she explained. Her view "is formed by prayer, reading, and reflection. It gives me no relish to be at odds with my Church. But it also gives me no joy to see people who are created in God's image unable to fully express their humanity, or live with the rights and dignity that heterosexual people are afforded."

Work on sexual ethics also continued among theologians of other church backgrounds . Ancient views on gender and sex can be helpful in re-examining the theology of sexuality, Adrian Thatcher (one of the contributors to Gays and the Future of Anglicanism) suggested in 2011. [10] Drawing on the thought of the 4th century theologian Gregory of Nyssa among others, Sarah Coakley examined how desire could be rightly directed. [11] A book by Susannah Cornwall examined current Controversies in queer theology. [12]

In different churches and across the world, debates on sexuality have prompted many theologians to make the case for a more open approach than that which is dominant in some denominations. However, there are some who regard church unity as a greater good than acceptance of partnered gays and lesbians and have maintained that discrimination should continue until there is greater consensus on inclusion. [13] There are also some who do not believe that same-sex relationships are right but who want the church to be more inclusive, believing that being judgemental is wrong and that God is constantly at work enabling church members – gay or straight – to outgrow what is not spiritually helpful. [14]

A report to the Church of Scotland's General Assembly in May 2011 by a Special Commission on Same-Sex Relationships and the Ministry examined some of the theological and pastoral issues and acknowledged differences of opinion and the need to continue a "process of prayerful discernment". [15]

Likewise in July 2011, a national convention of the Evangelical Lutheran Church in Canada agreed [16] a thoughtful ELCIC Social Statement on Human Sexuality, [17] produced over several years by a task force. This did not reach clear conclusions on the issue of same-sex relationships,but identified various important issues relevant to the theology of sexuality, and pointed out that Christian unity did not require agreement on all matters, saying instead, "When we feel tension around matters of morality, sexuality and interpretation of scripture, and hear threats to divide, Word and Sacrament remind us to turn to God, the true source and provider of our unity."

Sometimes theologians have come to think differently about inclusion of sexual minorities when studying a quite different topic. The retired professor of worship Arlo D Duba, former Director of Admissions and Director of Chapel at Princeton Theological Seminary and former Dean of University of Dubuque Theological Seminary, was doing research on baptism when he came to believe that the account in Acts of Philip's conversion of the Ethiopian eunuch might have more far-reaching implications than he had previously recognised, and that "when the church does not open itself to 'the other,' it deprives itself of the leadership and power that the Holy Spirit can turn loose." [18]

Drawing on the history of the evangelical movement, Jonathan Dudley pointed out in 2011 that "love cannot only require holding others accountable to systems of morality; it requires reconsidering systems of morality too. Part of 'loving the sinner' must be making sure that legitimate desires are not classified as 'sin.'" [19]

Creating space for discussion and reflection

A survey undertaken in the USA in August 2011 found much higher levels of support among young adults than among older people. [20] for allowing same-sex as well as opposite-sex couples to marry The following month, commenting on the fact that 44% of white evangelicals aged 18–29 favoured marriage equality, Dean Snyder (a Methodist) argued that this was the result of "reading their Bibles with fresh eyes and insight. For those who do their theological and ethical thinking, as Karl Barth reportedly advised us to do, with a Bible in one hand and a newspaper in the other, it is hard to maintain a biblically based opposition to marriage equality... The Bible has a way of not remaining hostage to a culture or ideology. Its revelatory focus on liberation, justice, reconciliation and inclusion has a way of liberating it from repressive cultural assumptions that some try to use it to reinforce." [21]

The debate on marriage equality has prompted much discussion on whether church recognition of same-sex partnerships is desirable and, if so, whether this constitutes marriage or something fundamentally different. Christian Scharen, an assistant professor at Luther Seminary, was one of those who argued that the marriage of same-sex couples could be a source of blessing to heterosexual people too. [22]

Even among senior clergy, some have openly questioned whether their institutions have given sufficient recognition to the potentially valuable aspects of committed partnerships.

Jeffrey John, who by 2012 was Dean of St Alban's and in a civil partnership (albeit celibate), explained in an interview why he believed that "same-sex monogamy seems to me to be spiritually indistinguishable from a marriage between two people who are unable to have children together." [23] Meanwhile the retired Australian Roman Catholic bishop Geoffrey Robinson was making a thoughtful case for a wide-ranging reconsideration of sexual ethics. [24]

Even in parts of the world where equal marriage seemed a distant prospect and where Christians sometimes formed a minority, theologians were reflecting on the experiences of LGBT people in the light of the Bible and tradition. For instance, in 2012 in Malaysia, using insights from queer theology, Joseph Goh reflected on the experience of mak nyahs, male-to-female transsexuals. [25]

In Love Lost in Translation: Homosexuality and the Bible in 2013, Renato Lings carried out an extremely detailed examination of biblical texts related to sexuality and argued that later prejudices had often been read into ancient texts. [26]

In response to a 2013 Church of England Faith and Order Commission document which argued that 'complementarity' based on male-female difference was central to being married, Charlotte Methuen described the varying models of marriage in the Bible and church history. She suggested that "extending the definition of marriage to include same-sex couples might in fact be a redemptive step. For it might allow the institution of marriage to transcend the profound inequalities between men and women which have too often shaped it." [27]

Another Church of England publication in 2013 (albeit reflecting a working party's view, rather than an official line) recognised the lack of consensus over sexuality and included a biblical argument for inclusion by David Runcorn, as well as a piece from a contrary perspective. [28] One bishop who went further, arguing the case for equal marriage in the 2014 book More Perfect Union, was Alan Wilson. [29] Simon V Taylor, canon chancellor for Derby, prepared a tightly-argued paper on 'An invitation to the feast: A positive Biblical approach to equal marriage'. [30]

The Belgian Roman Catholic Bishop Johan Bonny of Antwerp, did not go as far but towards the end of 2014, he called for "formal recognition of the kind of interpersonal relationship that is also present in many gay couples. Just as there are a variety of legal frameworks for partners in civil society, one must arrive at a diversity of forms in the church." [31] A couple of months earlier, in preparation for an international bishops' gathering, he had produced a paper 'Synod on the Family: Expectations of a Diocesan Bishop', [32] reflecting theologically on the experiences and moral issues confronting present-day families.

Even in denominations where dissent has long been frowned on, theological arguments for acceptance of same-sex partnerships are increasingly being voiced, though it is still risky in some circles to speak out for greater inclusion.

The Bible re-read, evangelicalism transformed

Perhaps the most prominent trend in recent years has been among evangelicals, growing numbers of whom have made biblical arguments for acceptance. The role of social media , along with face-to-face networking, has also been prominent; theologians have sometimes initially shared theories online, in blogs or the web versions of news media, before these found their way into print. Videos have sometimes been used along with the written word, a phenomenon which some theologians in other fields have also embraced.

One young writer seeking to make his work accessible to a broad public was Justin Lee, founder of a Gay Christian Network which has sought to promote respectful conversation among people with different views on the acceptance of sexuality. His

2012 book *Torn: Rescuing the Gospel from the Gays-vs.-Christians debate* [33] combined theological argument with autobiography. Similarly Matthew Vines, creator of the Reformation Project, in 2014 put forward a biblical case for equality in God and the Gay Christian, [34] while also drawing on his own experience as an ardent believer who came to find certain interpretations of the Bible increasingly unconvincing.

Taking an inclusive position has sometimes been met with a strong reaction. For instance, when the Baptist minister, entrepreneur and popular evangelical speaker Steve Chalke argued in Christianity magazine in 2013 that same-sex relationships were not necessarily sinful, he emphasised that he had formed his view "not out of any disregard for the Bible's authority, but by way of grappling with it and, through prayerful reflection, seeking to take it seriously." [35] Nevertheless the Oasis Trust, a charity he led, ended up being expelled by the Evangelical Alliance.

The fear of negative reactions did not deter some established evangelical scholars from publicly changing their minds on sexuality. One of these was James V Brownson, a professor at Western Theological Seminary in Michigan and Reformed Church minister, who in 2013 re-examined the biblical passages commonly cited in debates on homosexuality, seeking to understand the moral logic behind these. [36] The following year, David P Gushee, also a professor and an influential evangelical ethicist, produced a book examining various options in the sexuality debate and the biblical evidence for each, emphasising the ethical importance of responding to suffering and concluding that the church should affirm committed same-sex partnerships. [37]

Created and redeemed

Differences on sexuality among Christians are still sometimes treated as an example of the tension between 'liberal' thinkers who emphasise experience and 'evangelicals' or 'traditionalists' who give more weight to the Bible. However this distinction is increasingly hard to sustain.

In late 2014, an original and carefully-argued book by yet another professor, Robert Song, was published. *Covenant and*

Calling: Towards a Theology of Same-Sex Relationships [38] examined the purpose of marriage and centrality (or otherwise) of procreation in the light of Genesis, and of New Testament accounts of the significance of Jesus' coming. Looking critically at self-centred and consumerist sexual and social norms in today's world, he suggested that covenant partnerships could be ethically positive. Like many other books, articles and talks emerging during the course of the sexuality debate, it touched on matters of importance to human relationships in general and the nature of Christian calling and hope.

Theological reflection on the nature and purpose of human existence and the wider cosmos can assist Christians in addressing the question of whether same-sex as well as opposite-sex love can indeed be 'good' and if so, in what circumstances. To be truly credible, this should take seriously the complexity of the universe in which we live, and learn from the ways in which Christians through the ages have misinterpreted God's will, for instance to try to justify racial oppression, misogyny or ecological destruction.

What on Earth did God create? Overtures to an ecumenical theology of creation, [39] by the South African theologian Ernst M Conradie, highlighted the value of an adequate theology of creation, one that takes into account Christ's saving work and avoids the shortcomings of earlier such theologies which legitimised Nazism, apartheid or other oppressive ideologies, including domination on grounds of gender or sexual orientation. He argued that "the Christian confession that God the Father is the 'Maker of heaven and Earth', that through Jesus Christ 'all things were made' and that the Holy Spirit is the 'Giver of life'" is a "deeply counter-intuitive claim given the tension that we as humans experience between the grandeur and the misery of our existence", involving learning to see afresh "in the light of the Light of the world."

Looking back and forward

This chapter is far from comprehensive, and does not claim to be objective. Nevertheless I think it is evident that, especially since the 1950s, when Derrick Sherwin Bailey began to re-examine Christian responses to same-sex relationships, much important work has been done by theologians on this and related issues.

Some writings are relatively well-known, such as Rowan Williams' The Body's Grace and Gareth Moore's A Question of Truth, while other publications, despite their quality, are probably less commonly read today – for example Bruce C Birch's To Love as We Are Loved and Bishop John Austin Baker's Homosexuality and Christian ethics. Some work, for instance Tobias Haller's Reasonable and Holy, covers a spectrum of issues, while other writings, such as 'An argument for gay marriage' and 'Same-sex complementarity' by Eugene F Rogers, have a more specific focus. In some instances, as in Robert Song's Covenant and Calling, marriage and partnerships overall are considered in the broader context of Christian calling and the fulfilment of creation. It is noteworthy that many theologians with very different backgrounds and perspectives, while taking different routes, have reached the same destination of acceptance.

Yet there are some Christians today – both for and against full inclusion of partnered LGBT people – who have little awareness of the debates that have taken place in theological circles over the past century, and the process by which so many theologians today have come to support greater inclusion. Some seem to believe that calls for acceptance in the church are based on embracing society's values (at least in parts of the world where same-sex relationships are by and large accepted) and ignoring those aspects of the Bible and church tradition that do not fit. This is regarded as a mark of either faithlessness or progress, depending on people's own views on the subject.

However this does not do justice to the efforts of most theologians who have argued the case for greater inclusion, drawing on the witness of the Bible and the church through the ages, to discern how God has been and is at work in a complex and constantly changing world. Moreover, it makes it harder to find common ground to enable fellowship and dialogue among those with different views, and to promote mutual understanding even if disagreement persists.

Making such works more accessible, especially to those of us not academically trained in theology, might help – though some of the theologians mentioned above write quite clearly and simply, at least some of the time! The internet has also opened up new possibilities for exploring and discussing theological issues.

Life-stories of LGBT Christians and their families too can help to clarify how the theology of sexuality is embodied in concrete situations. Many people find it hard to think in purely abstract terms.

Opponents of change may be dismayed by the growing number of theologians who believe that some same-sex unions can be spiritually fruitful, or may dismiss this as a passing trend. Yet other people may see the journey towards acceptance as an example of the way the Spirit of truth continues to guide followers of Christ (John 16.12–14).

Part 2: Conflict and change: snapshots from the churches

Some people may think of change in the church as a matter of gradual progress, based either on deepening moral sensitivity or the wish to keep up with society and stay relevant. The reality is messier and more interesting.

I have written extensively for various publications on debates among Christians over sexuality. This part of the book contains a selection of articles published in Ekklesia, generally with only minor stylistic changes (except occasionally when two short pieces have been merged or an extract taken from a longer piece). Chapters 7 and 8 look back to incidents in the earlier part of the twentieth century which raise important issues about how churches do, and should, handle difficult questions. Chapters 9–25 deal with what was taking place at the time of writing, though sometimes set in historical context.

The question being addressed was not simply whether "gay is just as good as straight", to quote a popular slogan, but also what sexual relationships are about, at their best – a question which affects heterosexual people as well as those who are lesbian, gay, bisexual or transgender (LGBT). To earlier generations, this may have seemed more clear-cut, when the economic benefits of having many children and male domination in family and society were taken for granted. A different approach, based on pleasure and convenience, has also been tried but found wanting. Christians and other people of faith may believe that ancient wisdom has something to offer but differ on what this is.

The aim here is not to give a comprehensive account of all that was happening in churches but rather snapshots which together, make up an album portraying the upheaval taking place. As is perhaps inevitable, the pictures were taken from a particular angle, but I hope they may have something to offer even to those who view life through a different lens. Likewise, while the focus is more on some denominations and countries than others, there were ma-

jor similarities with what was taking place elsewhere.

While outwardly the debates taking place were about right and wrong in sexual relationships, politics in the church and beyond also played a part, as did different assumptions about the Bible, unity, justice and other topics.

Nor were these arguments taking place only in church conferences and assemblies: they also happened in all kinds of places where Christians met and talked, from kitchens and living-rooms to the Houses of Parliament. While there were instances of bad behaviour, there were also occasions when well-meaning, caring people found themselves on opposite sides while others were left bewildered, as can also happen during wider social change. At the same time, people with strongly opposing views on this matter can often be found praying together or volunteering for a credit union or foodbank. Even those of us who are Christians belonging to local congregations and long involved in these discussions can sometimes be left confused.

In time, I expect, these matters will be resolved and perhaps future generations will be surprised at the intensity of feeling aroused by controversies over same-sex partnerships. Meanwhile, the church and wider communities continue to wrestle with issues of human sexuality.

Chapter Seven

Prayerfully seeking justice and mercy

More than forty years ago, the UK Parliament agreed to decriminalise sex in private between men over the age of 21 in England and Wales. This was due in part to the efforts of the Archbishop of Canterbury at the time, Michael Ramsey. He was in some ways an unlikely champion of law reform. The previous archbishop had reportedly advised against his appointment, thinking him too unworldly: "Dr Ramsey is a theologian, a scholar and a man of prayer. Therefore, he is entirely unsuitable as Archbishop of Canterbury".

But those very qualities led Archbishop Ramsey to work for the welfare and rights of immigrants from the Commonwealth and, perhaps even more controversially, for gays facing harsh discrimination.

Contemplation, care and righting wrongs

To Ramsey, who was theologically far from radical, the incarnation and cross were of great importance. "To Jesus, God is everywhere at work," he said in a lecture in 1963. "Nature is the perpetual scene of the providential actions of His intimate fatherly care, and the disciples are bidden to have their eyes open to God's graciousness and God's demands thereby conveyed. No less vividly is God at work in history, especially in the history and the scriptures of the chosen people." To him, Christ's glory was not cut off from the world of human suffering but "bound up with the divine love and leading on to the Cross".

Later, in The Christian Priest Today, he emphasised the importance of worship and prayer – "In contemplation you will reach into the peace and stillness of God's eternity, in intercession you will reach into the rough and tumble of the world of time and change" – and of caring: "nothing that is human and nothing that is created lies outside the compassion of God".

Christian concern was "with a divine order embracing heaven

and earth, and with its reflection in every part of human affairs", though it was important to keep a sense of perspective about particular causes. Clergy should study and learn in partnership with lay people, who would sometimes "have knowledge which you have not", and not downplay the personal: "the very few, the one man, the one woman, the one child are of infinite worth to God".

At that time, most Christians disapproved of gay and lesbian sex in any circumstances, and Ramsey was no exception. While a huge amount of research and debate on sexuality took place in later decades, far less had been published in the fields of the natural and social sciences and history than is currently available, and few theologians (Derrick Sherwin Bailey was one notable exception) were giving systematic attention to the issues involved. Stark prejudice and ignorance were extremely common.

But even by the mid-1950s, there was growing recognition that there was a significant minority of people attracted mainly to members of the same sex who could face considerable hostility and, in the case of men, imprisonment if they acted on their feelings. They could not talk freely with doctors and other professionals. Many lived in fear and were easy prey for extortionists.

One account which helped to raise awareness of the human cost of the law as it then stood was written by one of its victims who was a journalist, Peter Wildeblood. In Against the Law he described his gradual discovery of his sexuality – "I suppose I must always have known that I was different from other children, but it took me years to find out in what way I differed", his realisation that "I could not prevent myself from being attracted towards other men, however hard I might try not to be", and the diversity among gays, who included men who were in faithful and loving relationships despite the risks that this involved.

Shortly after he was arrested, Wildeblood was surprised and impressed to read a "broad-minded" and "clear-headed" Church of England Moral Welfare Council report calling for decriminalisation, especially since he "had always thought of the Church as the last bastion of prejudice and had never found an occasion for praising it for its courage in controversial matters". Adultery was after all not a crime, despite its human cost, let alone fornication: there were certain matters in which it was widely recognised that the criminal law should not interfere.

In 1957, the government-appointed Wolfenden Committee recommended that the law be changed. Ramsey carefully considered the evidence and was persuaded. But there were long delays in legislating on this potentially vote-losing issue, and the passage of the Sexual Offences Bill through Parliament was stormy.

Upholding morality

Michael Ramsey was by no means the only prominent Christian to argue for the Bill during parliamentary debates. Indeed, the leading Methodist Donald Soper was bolder: unlike many others in the House of Lords, "I should myself not feel nearly so much ease and confidence in pronouncing whether certain homosexual practices are necessarily sinful." But Ramsey's leadership of an established Church with a huge membership gave extra weight to his support – and made him a target for those inside and outside Parliament who felt angry or hurt at what they saw as an abandonment of the Church's duty.

The emotions aroused by the issue, whether conscious or unacknowledged, made disagreement all the more intense. "I want to make it quite clear that I am wholly against the Bill," the Earl of Dudley declared. "I cannot stand homosexuals. They are the most disgusting people in the world, and they are, unfortunately, on the increase. I loathe them. Prison is much too good a place for them."

But there were others, less ferociously hostile, who were concerned that what had seemed fixed moral standards might be called into question by changing the law. "I find a great many Church people who are rather surprised at the attitude of the leaders of the Church of England, who appear to be in favour of this relaxation" of the law, said Lord Brocket.

"Some 60 or 70 years ago I was instructed, by men who were an ornament to that Church, to which I belonged, in their doctrine, in their service book, in their ritual and in their moral code," Lord Saltoun told the House of Lords. Gradually these had been abandoned, and "I am sorry to say that the moral code set by the Church now is one that I have ceased altogether to agree with. I feel like a shipwrecked mariner who has taken refuge on an iceberg which has carried him to calmer and warmer waters and then melted and left him foundering in the waves."

Ramsey did not relish the controversy, but to him the matter had to be addressed if justice was to be done and unnecessary harm prevented, even if some of the disapproval and dislike commonly experienced by an unpopular minority ended up being directed at him.

Lord Arran, a sponsor of the Bill, mentioned anonymous letters, "full of the most fearful condemnation", often quoting Deuteronomy and Leviticus, and sometimes obscene, and observed that, "No doubt others of your Lordships have had similar communications. These we can laugh off but others, more serious, are also more wounding and make one wonder sometimes whether one is doing the right thing." But "just as one is thinking of chucking it, one gets another of those ghastly letters from some man who is being blackmailed, or who is facing criminal prosecution, or from parents who are terrified on behalf of their homosexual son", and in the face of such suffering "one has to go on".

Ramsey too persisted, and eloquently argued the case for reform. In the House of Lords in October 1965, he criticised "what I can only call a really lopsided presentation of morality" which "takes the line that sexual sins are apparently the worst of all sins, and that homosexual sins are invariably the worst sort of sins among sexual sins." But in the teaching of Christ, those "sins which defile a man" were "acts of fornication, theft, murder, adultery, ruthless greed, malice, fraud, envy, slander, arrogance". While some were sexual, others were not, and "among the sexual sins there is not apparently an isolation of homosexuality as being more cardinally sinful than are the others. I believe that it is a presentation of morality, balanced, Christian and rational, that can win the respect and the allegiance of the younger generation, hard task though it is."

Through the persistence of Ramsey and Arran in the Lords, Leo Abse in the Commons and others within and outside Parliament, the Sexual Offences Act was passed in 1967. While decriminalisation was not complete, and social attitudes were still often hostile, it was a major achievement.

Spirituality in a turbulent world

At a Jubilee Group conference in 1977, Michael Ramsey warned against too easy an identification of any social programme with the Kingdom of God, given "the corruption of humanity, and the human ability to corrupt good things", as well as "the relativity of the human grasp of God's purpose in different historical situations" and uncertainty about the extent to which it could be realised on earth. Yet it was an important concept; and "we may speak of the divine sovereignty in terms of the reflection of some of God's own attributes in human life: God's compassion perfectly imitated by human creatures in their dealings with one another, and God's justice reproduced in human creatures in imitation of the justice of God."

Spirituality and social engagement are sometimes seen as disconnected. Worse still, leaders of faith communities sometimes give way to the temptation to use their position and talents to offer easy answers to complex questions, shying away from deep study and any questioning of their own preconceptions, or to bolster their own power by exploiting people's prejudices and fears. But for Michael Ramsey, humble openness to God, attentiveness to the reality of people's lives, compassion in the face of suffering and boldness in seeking justice were closely intertwined.

[This article was first published in February 2007]

Chapter Eight

Christian heritage and a marriage of inconvenience

Not so long ago, in the year my sister was born, the then Bishop of London was faced with a dilemma. A couple were due to have a wedding ceremony at a church in Kensington, and this was arousing intense anger and fear.

Quite apart from the fact that there were some who would regard such a marriage as unnatural and immoral, a breach of Biblical teaching which in some parts of the world would be illegal, there was heavy pressure from certain African leaders not to allow it. These included a devoutly religious prime minister who had at one time been a pastor, who declared it 'disgusting'. There was the risk of a diplomatic incident, the chance that Britain's interests would be affected.

The Bishop bowed to pressure and refused the couple permission to marry in church. What was later described as a 'marriage of inconvenience' went ahead in a registry office.

Though at first the young couple had hard times, some of those who had most vehemently condemned the relationship were later reconciled to it. He was later to become the first president of an independent Botswana, where she was held in high regard.

It is perhaps hard now to imagine that the 1948 marriage of a white British woman, secretary Ruth Williams, and an African man, law student Seretse Khama, could have been so controversial. Yet a couple of decades later many Christians in some parts of the world still believed passionately that segregation was ordained by God, and in Britain it was common for immigrants to be persuaded to stay away from 'mainstream' churches because of the genuine anguish it caused some white people in their congregations.

Even in modern Europe, there is an undercurrent of subtle racism, punctuated by surges of far-right extremism, linked often with the notion of preserving a Christian heritage. Even people who are quite liberal are often unaware of the ways in which minority groups are excluded, and the damage done to those who internalise a sense of inferiority or who feel permanently unwanted or unsafe.

While the debate around 'racial mixing' is not identical to current controversies affecting mainstream churches, there are certain parallels. Though it is no longer respectable to claim that humans are of different 'races' who should be kept apart, there is still sometimes an echo of the view of the Dutch Reformed Church under apartheid that "The Christian calling lies in acceptance of the place which God has given", or at least that it is unchristian vigorously to resist being excluded.

At one time, church leaders had a lot to say about justice, but now there tends to be an emphasis on the virtues of unity and a refusal to assert oneself. If some people feel contaminated by the presence of other 'types', especially if those trying to maintain 'purity' can quote verses from the Bible to rationalise this, should not those who it is feared might 'pollute' the church keep a low profile for the time being? Sooner or later, change will of course occur; cannot those already on the inside who feel unsettled by the presence of the 'other' be gently persuaded to rethink, rather than pressured? It can be tempting to go to great lengths to avoid offence to those whose privilege is threatened.

Patience is of course needed, and the wisdom to choose when to move slowly and when to move fast. Yet there are serious risks in accepting the human-made barriers and hierarchies which keep people apart. Apart from the harm done to those who are excluded, the spiritual harm people do to themselves when they marginalise or stereotype others should be considered, given the close connection between love of God and love of neighbour. All of us have perhaps benefited at one time or another by being jolted into recognising a common humanity with those whom we would at one time have looked down on or barely noticed.

Greater understanding may arise from observing a previously unimagined reality. For example, people who disliked the notion of 'interracial marriage', when given the opportunity to see how love could flourish between a couple one of whom was black and the other white, could be prompted to rethink their assumptions. This only became possible because some people were bold enough not to hide what others at first found offensive.

And church unity is of questionable value if the church does not strive, however imperfectly, to witness to and embody the realm of God, where the lion lies down with the lamb and all live in peace (Isaiah 65.17–25). If the church does not offer good news to the poor and marginalised but instead perpetuates social divisions, it may become like salt that has lost its savour (Matthew 5. 13).

I would not wish to condemn the Bishop of London in 1948 for making what seemed an expedient choice. However it cannot always be assumed that those refusing the norms of their family, community and church are just being rash and selfish. Perhaps this may be the case, but perhaps they are helping to point to a glorious future where, through the gracious outpouring of the Holy Spirit, humans recognise God's image in one another and relate with mutual respect and love.

[This article was first published in October 2007]

Chapter Nine

Will Anglicans learn the lessons of Jamaica?

The Anglican Consultative Council is currently in the middle of a fortnight-long meeting in Kingston, Jamaica. Made up of representatives from member churches throughout the world, it includes laypeople as well as bishops and other clergy. This gathering will be a test of its ability, amidst organisational politics, to hold on to its ideals and to balance unity with other values. These include justice, mercy and involvement by ordinary Christians as well as senior clergy in making decisions.

Kingston has a rich but troubled history, marked by slavery and colonialism as well as by resistance to these and other forms of oppression. Over 30,000 people filled the newly built National Stadium in 1962 when independence was declared. There were high hopes of creating a truly independent and just society, but gradually these were blighted and – as in many other ex-colonies – Western economic dominance kept its grip.

Though Kingston was a major cultural centre, high unemployment and poverty remained. Frustration was sometimes violently expressed and gays and lesbians became a convenient target.

Violent homophobia in Jamaica has destroyed people emotionally and sometimes physically and has taught others to hate their gay, lesbian, bisexual and transgendered neighbours. During a prison riot in Kingston in 1997, warders failed to protect supposedly gay prisoners, several of whom were stabbed or burnt to death. Horrific violence continues and is sometimes justified on supposedly religious grounds.

International Anglican gatherings have repeatedly announced their commitment to human rights for all, including lesbian and gay people. Thirty years ago, the ACC called on member churches and individuals to "rigorously assess their own structures, attitudes and modes of working to ensure the promotion of human rights within them" and "involve themselves in all possible ways with the struggles of people who are denied human rights".

Some Christians in the Caribbean (including senior Anglican clergy) have sought to promote greater acceptance and justice. Yet leaders such as the recently-retired Archbishop of the West Indies, Drexel Gomez, have had other priorities.

For over a decade he has been a crusader against the acceptance of 'liberalism' in the Anglican Communion, in particular openness to the possibility of 'out' gay or lesbian bishops and orders of service to bless same-sex couples. In 2001 he helped to draw up proposals to discipline national churches which took acceptance too far. These would have given archbishops unprecedented international power. The proposals were rejected, but he was later put in charge of preparing a 'Covenant' which would supposedly bring about greater unity.

Though not in favour of extreme homophobia, Archbishop Gomez – along with many other church leaders elsewhere – helped to foster the notion that accepting same-sex partnerships was far more problematic for Christians than failing to challenge abuse and hatred.

There were strong reactions by some churches against earlier drafts of the Covenant and a new version has been produced, to be discussed by the Anglican Consultative Council in Kingston. Though this takes on board some of the concerns voiced earlier, the emphasis is still heavily on reining in those provinces which might do something 'controversial'. In practice, this is more likely to affect pro-inclusion churches than those where leaders have refused to enter into dialogue with lesbian, gay and transgendered people and their families, or to uphold their human rights.

It remains to be seen whether the Anglican Consultative Council, which has previously resisted attempts to over-centralise authority in the Communion, will give way in the interests of persuading 'conservative' churches to stay. Many members of the Council have taken a bold and sometimes prophetic stance on respect and justice for all, caring and campaigning for the poor and marginalised, yet they face huge pressure.

Perhaps those attending the ACC gathering could spend a

few moments remembering the many gay, lesbian, bisexual and transgendered people in Kingston who have been terrorised, raped, beaten or murdered, or learnt to hate themselves, as well as the families and friends who mourn them, and the children who have been taught hatred rather than love of neighbour. There are no easy answers, but with thought and prayer, maybe the Council can develop an approach that recognises the evil of homophobia.

[This article was first published in May 2009]

Chapter Ten

US Anglicans forty years after Stonewall

The Stonewall riots in June 1969 in New York helped to transform society in the USA and beyond. The General Convention of the Episcopal Church being held in California in July 2009 is far more sedate. Topics for discussion range from 'Liturgical Materials for Pastoral Care in the Adoption of Children' to 'Climate Change and the Millennium Development Goals'. Yet, once again, media attention is focused on attitudes to, and behaviour towards LGBT people, in the context of their families and communities. In several other Christian denominations too, LGBT issues are still especially controversial. The spiritual challenges faced by US Christians in the 1960s have helped to set the context for today's debates.

Human sexuality and the Episcopal Church
The Anglican Communion has traditionally avoided over-centralising authority. Leaders of member churches throughout the world can, and often do, ignore the numerous resolutions passed at international gatherings without facing any sanctions. There are also various matters on which Anglicans strongly disapprove of one another's beliefs and actions while outwardly remaining united. There is however one exception: consecrating a partnered lesbian or gay man as a bishop, or authorising a liturgy for blessing same-sex partnerships, is widely regarded as exceptionally serious.

The Episcopal Church (TEC), mainly based in the USA, and the Anglican Church in Canada, have been under particular pressure. A few years ago, moves within these churches towards greater acceptance of LGBT people were condemned by many senior Anglican clergy elsewhere. These included people who believed there was a strong theological case for greater equality but who feared that taking action now was divisive. From their point of view, it would be better to wait until there was broad agreement among member churches. Since Anglican leaders in some other countries refused to study the issue in depth or enter into dialogue with LGBT people in their midst, campaigning instead to have them imprisoned, this would clearly be a long wait.

TEC's last General Convention (a synod of representatives from different areas, including laypersons, bishops and other clergy) was in 2006. This passed resolution B033, calling on those choosing bishops "to exercise restraint by not consenting to the consecration of any candidate to the episcopate whose manner of life presents a challenge to the wider church and will lead to further strains on communion". The House of Bishops later agreed not to authorise orders of service for blessing same-sex unions.

This has been a cause of deep discomfort to many US Anglicans, even among those who have, for the sake of international unity, supported a moratorium on moves towards equal treatment of LGBT people in the church. Many at General Convention in 2009 have called for this to be set aside, describing the harm it has done. Instead they would like the same welcome to be extended to heterosexual and LGBT people and the same disciplines imposed. Anglican leaders elsewhere in the world would still be free to act differently within their own provinces but not to dominate others.

Some of those strongly opposed to TEC condemn such reluctance to treat LGBT people differently as a sign that it is too concerned with following society's trends rather than Biblical teaching and church tradition. Indeed some of those on both sides of the debate on sexuality are not critical enough of worldly values, and take cultural norms for granted. Yet much of the discomfort with resolution B033 is based on deep religious convictions.

The need for angelic troublemakers
There is a thread of spirituality running through US Christianity which has influenced numerous churchgoers of various denominations and has had a wider impact on society. This combines awe at God's greatness with a vivid sense of the presence of the

Word made flesh dwelling in our midst (John 1.14) and concern to seek and serve Christ in the least of his brothers and sisters (Matthew 25.31–46). From this perspective, those who do not love their fellow-humans are estranged from God too (1 John 4.16–21). However, Christ's death and resurrection offer the hope of a new life not bound by prejudice, lack of caring or legalism, but instead inspired by the Holy Spirit and filled with love (Galatians 2.20–3.4, 5.13–17).

Injustice is thus perceived not only as an affront to the mental and physical welfare of the oppressed, who are precious to God, but also to the spiritual welfare of the oppressor. Institutions and societies where oppression is routine need to be healed, however secure and orderly they might at first appear. All are made in the divine image. And all, not just those in authority, have a part to play in seeking justice and peace: however weak or insignificant they may be in worldly terms, God's strength can make up for what they would otherwise lack.

This was a belief held by many in the civil rights movement. It is easy to forget how disturbing it was at the time to many respectable citizens, not only those who believed that the inferiority of black people was ordained by the Bible, but also to more liberal people who believed in gradual change and not in large-scale disruption and confrontation.

'Injustice anywhere is a threat to justice everywhere. We are caught in an inescapable network of mutuality', wrote the Baptist minister Dr Martin Luther King Jr in Letter from a Birmingham Jail. "Like a boil that can never be cured so long as it is covered up but must be opened with all its ugliness to the natural medicines of air and light, injustice must be exposed, with all the tension its exposure creates, to the light of human conscience and the air of national opinion before it can be cured." He also took a strong stance against economic injustice, both in the USA and internationally.

Another leading figure in the civil rights movement was the Quaker peace activist Bayard Rustin, the key organiser of the 1963 march on Washington for jobs and freedom. He was perhaps even more controversial than King. An African-American

Quaker, openly gay and a former member of the Young Communist League, Rustin was inspired by the Gandhian movement in India, spent time there learning from its techniques and helped popularise the notion of non-violent direct action in the USA. He spent time in jail not only for protesting against racial injustice but also for breaking anti-gay laws, and in his later life he campaigned for greater equality for LGBT people.

"Loving your enemy is manifest in putting your arms not around the man but around the social situation, to take power from those who misuse it – at which point they can become human too", he argued. He believed that "We need, in every community, a group of angelic troublemakers."

Though some in the Episcopal Church were reluctant to get involved in such a controversial movement, others were drawn to it. They included Barbara Harris, an African-American community activist in Philadelphia, who was deeply involved in the Church of the Advocate. She would later be ordained and become one of the first Anglican women bishops, while remaining a keen supporter of further inclusion: "I would like to see the church come to some better understanding of what it means to be an inclusive fellowship, how to more fully exhibit the love of Christ in the world."

Many white people were drawn to the civil rights movement too, though they risked being branded as race traitors and were also subjected to violence. William Stringfellow was one of these, a Harvard-educated lawyer who put his skills at the service of slum dwellers in New York and who was one of the Episcopal Church's leading theologians. He argued that racism was not simply a social problem, "not an evil in human hearts or minds, racism is a principality, a demonic power, a representative image, an embodiment of death", yet a "power with which Jesus Christ was confronted and which, at great and sufficient cost, he overcame... The issue is the unity of all humankind wrought by God in the life and work of Christ. Baptism is the sacrament of that unity of all humanity in God." With his partner Anthony Towne, he sought to bear witness to his belief: "In the face of death, live humanly. In the middle of chaos, celebrate the Word." To him, prayer, Bible study and the sacraments were at the heart of resistance to violence and injustice.

Malcolm Boyd was a journalist who became an Episcopalian priest, adopted approaches to mission and ministry that appealed to young people and wrote a book of prayers which became a best-seller. He became a freedom rider and used his skills as a communicator to highlight the damage caused by racial segregation. He warned that the notion of the church as a reconciler could be "perverted to mean soft compromiser, meek agent of acquiescence in social evils, gently sentimental moderate, or apostate symbol of the status quo whose final allegiance is to society instead of God." In contrast "The church can act as a reconciler by scrupulously looking to the breakdowns in its own moral and intellectual integrity, listening before it speaks, not being afraid to speak at whatever human cost when it knows it must, and, at the core of everything, struggling to continue loving." Boyd later came out as gay.

Militancy grew within the anti-racist movement, especially after the murder of Martin Luther King Jr. Anti-war activists were protesting and feminists were organising to win greater equality for women. It was against this background that an apparently routine police raid on a bar in New York City turned into a riot.

Growing visibility and the call to do justice
In the 1950s and 1960s, LGBT people in the USA faced harsh social and sometimes legal penalties. For some years, courageous campaigners for greater equality had sought to change the law and public attitudes. Meanwhile those labelled criminals, perverts and sinners faced an often-harsh existence, especially if not shielded, even a little, by wealth, education or ethnic privilege.

Many of the patrons of the Stonewall Inn in Greenwich Village were African-American or Latino. Seventeen-year-old Sylvia Rivera was one of those present in the early morning of 28 June 1969. Her life had not been easy. Born biologically male in New York, to a Puerto Rican father who soon left, and a Venezuelan mother who committed suicide when the child was three, she was raised by her grandmother, a pieceworker in a factory, who often beat her. The femininity of Rivera, drawn to wearing make-up and attracted to boys and men at an early age, was a particular source of conflict. At the age of ten or eleven she ended up as a homeless prostitute. As she later explained, on the streets she found a new 'family' of transgender people who cared for one another. She took the name Sylvia and began to get politically active, becoming involved in the civil rights and anti-war movement.

She and her friends faced many hazards, from drug abuse (developing self-esteem and taking care of one's health in such circumstances could be hard) to violence, sometimes at the hands of the police. Beatings were common, even rape. But that night at the Stonewall Inn, when police raided, people in and outside the bar fought back, throwing coins and other objects. According to Rivera this started with street gays and drag queens and others joined in.

The Stonewall riots marked a greater assertiveness among LGBT people, though some still remained ashamed and secretive. Heterosexual people had to rethink what they had taken for granted and recognise that family members, workmates or fellow-students, people they socialised with, relied on and worshipped alongside, did not fit into society's norms of gender and sexual orientation. What is more, it became increasingly clear that LGBT lifestyles varied, as did those of heterosexuals and that some partners formed bonds of depth, stability and mutual love, providing a basis for mutual caring, emotional growth and joint service to the wider community.

Attempts had previously been common among psychiatrists, religious ministers and other figures of authority to try to change people's sexuality, or at least persuade them to pretend to be 'normal', often with damaging effects. More and more, however, this was called into question: might it be better to acknowledge that people were diverse in orientation, and help them find a path that fitted their own gifts and capabilities?

For many Christians, this meant acknowledging that some of those they sought to serve and minister to and who served and ministered to them, were LGBT. This might include anyone from a destitute person in a soup kitchen or troubled teenager in a youth club to a godparent, verger or bishop. There was no longer a neat dividing line between 'them' and 'us'.

Discrimination was not easy to overcome and even now, LGBT people can face exclusion, mistreatment and indeed, violence. Rivera became active in the Metropolitan Community Church of New York, where she ran a food pantry for the poor. She continued to campaign and organise, especially for the rights of trans people and for a better deal for homeless LGBT youth, until her death in 2002. To her, and many other US Christians, care for the destitute and downtrodden and struggles for justice could not easily be separated out into sets of issues or programmes, to be dealt with at different times.

In other countries too, as LGBT people became more visible, often in the context of resistance to oppression, churches were faced with a new challenge. Leaders responded in a range of ways, often linked with their wider beliefs about the nature of faith, the value of justice and the possibility that they themselves might have something to learn and gain.

Upholding the dignity of all
Though an increasing number of theologians in the USA and elsewhere came to believe that same-sex relationships were not necessarily wrong, some Episcopalians remained unconvinced. Yet for those who did come to accept that, ideally, the church should bless same-sex relationships under certain circumstances and choose the best candidates to be bishops whether heterosexual or otherwise, it was difficult to continue to discriminate, even in the interests of 'church unity'. Given the historical background, this seemed an affront not only to those treated as outsiders or second class citizens but also to their Creator, representing a failure to live as a follower of Christ, emboldened by the Holy Spirit to challenge unloving attitudes and structures.

The seeds sown four decades ago have continued to grow. At a Eucharist at General Convention on 10 July 2009 sponsored by Integrity, which seeks greater inclusion for LGBT people in TEC, Barbara Harris, now retired, preached a powerful sermon arguing against the "false peace" of resolution B033 and reminding those present that God has no favourites. B033, she said, "needs to be superseded by something positive that recognises the dignity of all God's human creation."

As debates continue among Christians of various denominations about human sexuality and diversity, the experience of US Anglicans will almost certainly remain in the spotlight. There are no easy answers. Yet for many people, and not just in the USA, the challenge remains of acknowledging the true spiritual as well as physical and emotional impact of the divisions caused by poverty and discrimination and of witnessing in deed and word to the hope – through divine grace – of a different manner of life for all.

[This article was first published in July 2009]

Chapter Eleven

The Anglican Communion's future and different approaches to unity

[Edited excerpts from 'A better future for the Anglican Communion?', first published in September 2009]

Rowan Williams, the Archbishop of Canterbury, recently published 'reflections' proposing major changes in the way the Anglican Communion is organised. Because of a growing willingness in the Episcopal Church (TEC) both to consider it possible that lesbians and gays, including those who are partnered, may be called to any kind of ministry within the church, and also to respond positively to requests to bless same-sex unions, he has suggested a "'two-track' approach. Provinces such as TEC would not be able to carry out certain functions such as representing the Anglican Communion in ecumenical circles, while those which signed up to a Covenant would have a more central position.

While the intention of the Archbishop's proposal is to promote Christian unity and spiritual growth, there is a strong possibility that the results will be the opposite. A different approach, less focused on institutional structures, might be more effective in addressing divisions and ultimately enabling Anglicans to move towards a deeper unity.

The Archbishop's thoughts on the development of Anglicanism

The Anglican Communion, made up of a number of provinces in various parts of the world, has been wracked by controversy in recent years. Though debate over human sexuality has been especially heated, divisions on this issue reflect deeper theological differences. [1]

For over a century the role of the Archbishop of Canterbury, as well as being primate (most senior bishop) of the Church of

England, has involved chairing a Lambeth Conference of bishops every ten years or so to strengthen fellowship and discuss important issues, though he has no power over Anglicans in other parts of the world. However, over the past decade , there has been intense discussion about the nature, structure and membership of the Anglican Communion and how it relates to other denominations. It is in this context that the Archbishop has produced this piece.

In it, he acknowledges TEC's concern for other churches in the Communion, suggesting however, that this is not enough to repair damaged relationships. He suggests that the human rights of LGBT people should be upheld more consistently by Anglicans, but argues that this is not a good enough argument to overturn the moratorium on consecrating partnered LGBT people and blessing same-sex unions.

In his view, for any province to undertake such an act would be a major break with the way that the church has consistently read the Bible for two thousand years, and would be unacceptable unless a strong theological case were to be made and a high level of consensus achieved among Anglicans and across denominations, which has not happened. He suggests a 'two-track' Anglican Communion, in which only those provinces willing to pledge mutual accountability and sign up to a Covenant can represent the Communion in ecumenical and interfaith circles, unlike those such as TEC who put local autonomy first.

"Authority of the Church Catholic"

Williams' emphasis on the need for any part of the universal church not to move forward on any matter unless there is consensus seems odd in the light of church history. To him, "a blessing for a same-sex union cannot have the authority of the Church Catholic, or even of the Communion as a whole" and thus cannot be supported.

Yet, from the outset, church leaders have moved forward on controversial matters without getting universal consent. Peter baptised members of a Gentile household without the approval of the rest of the church, upsetting many, and explained his reasons afterwards, according to the Acts of the Apostles. [2] In the letter to the Galatians, Paul showed little of the expected deference to the church hierarchy – "those who were supposed to be acknowledged leaders (what they actually were makes no difference to me; God shows no partiality)" – and described his willingness to challenge them in defence of inclusion for Gentiles. [3]

The founding of Anglicanism – with authority vested in a national church rather than the Vatican, a liturgy in the language of the common people and likewise the Bible made freely available to them in their own tongue – was, of course, a huge offence against the "authority of the Church Catholic" (in particular the Roman Catholic hierarchy). [4]

Considerable flexibility has persisted among, and sometimes within, Anglican churches around the world, permitting theological diversity and making it possible to explore difficult issues and try out new approaches to mission and ministry, although perhaps initially on a limited scale .

Older Anglicans may recall how controversial the use of contraceptives once was: when in 1930 a Lambeth Conference resolved that this could sometimes be acceptable, [5] it was a radical departure from what was regarded by both Protestant and Catholic churches as the teaching of the Bible and church tradition, [6] and from the former mainstream Anglican position.

As in wider society, moves towards greater inclusion have long been controversial. The consecration of the first black Anglican bishop, Samuel Ajayi Crowther, in 1864 was strongly opposed by some fellow-Anglicans. [7] Whatever the worth of a native bishop, it was argued, he could not command the necessary respect. This was a time when notions of racial inferiority were deeply ingrained. He continued to face opposition for the rest of his life, and many of the priests he ordained were suspended, despite his objections, for failing to lead exemplary lives. [8] Yet gradually the notion of bishops of African, Asian and Latin American descent became more acceptable. Moves to ordain and later consecrate women also met with objections, in part because it was argued that, even if theologically acceptable, there was no consensus on this matter. Yet many now benefit from women's ordained ministry, and even take it for granted, though some still object. [9]

Prayer, study and discussion on issues of human sexuality in various denominations has led to greater acceptance of LGBT people, including those who are partnered, and many of the churches in Europe with which the Church of England is in full communion already offer blessings to same-sex couples. [10]

"Mutual consultation" and "local autonomy"

There is certainly value in seeking others' views and seeking to understand their reasoning on difficult issues and in awareness of one's own fallibility and the possibility of benefiting from the wisdom of others in previous generations as well as one's own. Paul's advice to "love one another with mutual affection; outdo one another in showing honour," and "Live in harmony with one another; do not be haughty, but associate with the lowly; do not claim to be wiser than you are" is worth taking seriously. [11]

It is doubtful however, whether Williams is correct in his portrayal of TEC as having decided that "local autonomy had to be the prevailing value". Indeed it could be argued that TEC has shown greater commitment to the Anglican Communion than many of its accusers, whose enthusiasm for a Covenant is largely based on the belief (from the actions of the Archbishop of Canterbury, among others) that they themselves will be able to continue to do more or less as they please. [12]

Anglicans have, for centuries, sought to draw on Scripture, tradition, reason and often experience in grappling with contentious issues. Even the wisest person may get things wrong: as the 16th century theologian Richard Hooker put it, "such is the untoward constitution of our nature that we neither do so perfectly understand the way and knowledge of the Lord, nor so steadfastly embrace it when it is understood, nor so graciously utter it when it is embraced, nor so peaceably maintain it when it is uttered, but that the best of us are overtaken sometimes". [13]

The 1930 Lambeth Conference of Anglican bishops drew attention to the need for "a fresh insistence upon the duty of thinking and learning as essential elements in the Christian life." [14]

In 1958 the Lambeth Conference gratefully acknowledged "our debt to the host of devoted scholars who, worshipping the God of Truth, have enriched and deepened our understanding of the Bible," [15] as well as the work of scientists, calling on Christians "both to learn reverently from every new disclosure of truth, and at the same time to bear witness to the biblical message of a God and Saviour apart from whom no gift can be rightly used". [16]

This, combined with the freedom enjoyed by member churches to seek to understand and minister in their own contexts (international Anglican gatherings had repeatedly rejected the notion of centralised authority [17]), gave considerable scope for trying to disentangle prevailing norms from eternal truths, especially to those in post-colonial settings. If errors were made, they could be challenged and in time set right, with the aid of the Holy Spirit, who would guide those with open hearts into all the truth. [18]

The 1978 Lambeth Conference commended the "need for theological study of sexuality in such a way as to relate sexual relationships to that wholeness of human life which itself derives from God, who is the source of masculinity and femininity" and, while reaffirming heterosexuality as the "scriptural norm", recognised "the need for deep and dispassionate study of the question of homosexuality, which would take seriously both the teaching of Scripture and the results of scientific and medical research. The Church, recognising the need for pastoral concern for those who are homosexual, encourages dialogue with them. (We note with satisfaction that such studies are now proceeding in some member Churches of the Anglican Communion.)" [19]

This was reaffirmed at the 1988 Lambeth Conference, which urged "such study and reflection to take account of biological, genetic and psychological research being undertaken by other agencies, and the socio-cultural factors that lead to the different attitudes in the provinces of our Communion", and called on "each province to reassess, in the light of such study and because of our concern for human rights, its care for and attitude towards persons of homosexual orientation". [20]

By the time of the next Lambeth Conference, ten years later, however, it became apparent that, while provinces such as TEC had been conscientiously studying the issue for decades, in others, the process had not yet begun, nor was there any intention of acting on these resolutions.

After heated debate, Resolution 1.10 on human sexuality was passed at Lambeth 1998. It was mixed, and in parts somewhat confusing. While "rejecting homosexual practice as incompatible with Scripture" and stating that the Conference "cannot advise the legitimising or blessing of same sex unions nor ordaining those involved in same gender unions", it made a commitment "to listen to the experience of homosexual persons", and called "on all our people to minister pastorally and sensitively to all irrespective of sexual orientation and to condemn irrational fear of homosexuals". [21] It also both commended a report which recognised the difficulty of agreeing a common position on sexuality and noted the significance of the Kuala Lumpur Statement on Human Sexuality, which ruled out the possibility of accepting same-sex partnerships and indeed, the remarriage of divorced persons, though this was a practice accepted by some 'conservatives' adamantly opposed to LGBT relationships. [22]

It quickly became clear, however, that some bishops did not intend to take part in any process of genuine listening or dialogue. Strenuous efforts were made by the Anglican Communion Office to take forward the listening process but, as made clear in Reports from the Provinces, [23] some leaders made no effort even to pretend to listen to and learn from the experiences of their LGBT members, let alone consider the findings of eminent theologians and scientists who had engaged with the issue.

Meanwhile, in TEC, where the process of listening and study had begun in the 1960s, many church members wished to act on what they had come to believe was God's will for them.

If a genuine debate had been taking place in which leaders of 'conservative' provinces explained what they thought were the flaws in the arguments of leading theologians in TEC, while demonstrating their attentiveness to the views of LGBT people in their own societies, senior clergy could perhaps have persuaded those wanting greater equality to wait longer, in the hope of reaching some kind of consensus. However, this was not the case. It was in this context that an openly gay and partnered man was chosen as Bishop of New Hampshire in 2003.

The difficulty of following potentially contradictory advice from international Anglican gatherings, and the failure of several other churches in the Communion to abide by Lambeth Conference resolutions on sexuality and other matters, should be acknowledged before TEC is described as putting "local autonomy" before "mutual responsibility".

"Human dignity and civil liberties"

Williams states in his 'reflections' that "it needs to be made absolutely clear that, on the basis of repeated statements at the highest levels of the Communion's life, no Anglican has any business reinforcing prejudice against LGBT people, questioning their human dignity and civil liberties or their place within the Body of Christ. Our overall record as a Communion has not been consistent in this respect and this needs to be acknowledged with penitence." This is commendable. But it is not clear what, if anything, he intends to do about it.

Commitment to human rights has long been important to the Anglican Communion, based on love of neighbour and unwillingness to accept that any person or institution should usurp God's place. The 1948 Lambeth Conference endorsed the United Nations Universal Declaration of Human Rights, then still in its draft form. [24] (The drafting body was in fact chaired by an Anglican, though the Declaration appealed to people of all faiths and none. [25])

Time and again, international Anglican gatherings urged commitment to human rights. For instance, in 1973 the ACC urged member churches "to be sensitive to the violent dehumanisation of minority peoples in their midst", "to acknowledge the Church's vocation to side with the oppressed in empowering them to live their own lives in freedom, even at some sacrifice to itself, while at the same time seeking in the power of Christian love to bring about the true liberation of the oppressor" and "to seek for the education of the majority in these needs by confrontation with and participation in the suffering of the oppressed". [26]

In 1979, the ACC urged member churches to "rigorously assess their own structures, attitudes and modes of working to ensure the promotion of human rights within them, and to seek to make the church truly an image of God's just Kingdom and witness in today's world, and to "involve themselves in all possible ways with the struggles of people who are denied human rights". [27] The Lambeth resolution in 1988 supporting "Human Rights for Those of Homosexual Orientation" was discussed above, and the 1998 Lambeth Conference resolved that "its members urge compliance with the United Nations Universal Declaration of Human Rights by the nations in which our various member Churches are located, and all others over whom we may exercise any influence". [28]

This TEC has sought to do, but some provinces have done the opposite, especially when those denied human rights have been LGBT. Such violations were all too common in the twentieth century, including in the West, and persist even now. [29]

While the Archbishop of Canterbury is clearly uneasy about human rights abuses against LGBT people, he has generally been unwilling (along with many other Church of England bishops and other moderate Anglicans) to challenge church complicity in these directly, in contrast to repeated criticisms of TEC for moving forward on equality. This has reinforced the impression that civil liberties and human dignity are of relatively little importance – a grave departure from traditional Anglican social teaching.

"Not the end of the Anglican way"

Rowan Williams' deep desire for Christian unity has been at the heart of his actions in recent years, and there is little doubt that he sincerely hopes that these 'reflections' will bring this goal closer. The problem is that the approach which has been taken has encouraged threats and bullying, including warnings by certain provincial leaders that they will leave and thus split the Communion if people in other provinces do not obey their commands, rather than the mutual submission which Paul urges in

Ephesians. [30]

The value of unity is indeed emphasised in the Bible and Anglican teaching. Yet a different approach, drawing on Scripture and reflection in international Anglican circles, may be more fruitful.

To begin with, it may be useful to approach unity as a gift from God, an unearned grace, intimately bound up with how humans relate to the divine and thus to one another, rather than something to be achieved through institutional means. This is not to say that human effort is unimportant, but receptivity and generosity, an open heart, open mind and open hands, matter even more. This can be hard to grasp, being contrary to the way that society often approaches unity. Politicians seeking to strengthen unity in their party, community or nation may even focus on an external 'enemy' or local scapegoat to unite people more effectively, so that what draws a group together may also deepen separation at a broader level.

This may not be malicious: it may be thought that whatever is good for a particular corporation, state or party is ultimately good for the world, and occasional sacrifices may be necessary for this noble aim. Churches have sometimes operated in this way, for instance covering up cases of child abuse by clergy or members of religious orders in case exposure might undermine trust in the institution and thus its ability to take forward mission and ministry, though in the end this has proved counterproductive. But when, in Luke's gospel, Jesus turns to the poor, excluded and reviled, telling them that the kingdom of heaven is theirs and that they should seek to be like their Father in generosity and mercy, and assures his followers that God cares about each of them so much that "even the hairs of your head are all counted" (Luke 6.20–23, 35–36, 12.6–7), this is a radically different approach. He is willing to offend the pious and cause division as he ushers in a new community in which all are valued and learn to value one another (Luke 12.49–53, 14.1–6, 15.1–7).

John's gospel likewise depicts Christ as embodying God's love for all, and as willing to challenge religious leaders and disrupt communal unity in defence of the marginalised. Christ's followers are described as connected like branches of a single vine (John 15.1–5), brought together through him. "Just as I have loved you, you also should love one another," he tells them, later praying to the Father, "The glory that you have given me I have given them, so that they may be one, as we are one, I in them and you in me" (John 13.34, 17.22–23). Those drawn to One whose glory is shown in identification with the wretched, destitute, condemned and dying, and ultimately in the overturning of all systems which subjugate and destroy, will through him come to radiate love.

Sometimes, as in the Bible, authentically close relationships will only be achieved through openly confronting tensions and disagreements and wrestling with questions to which there are no easy answers. In the Old and New Testament, time and again families and communities are wracked by misunderstanding, betrayal and division, yet God does not abandon those involved and, in the end, they are reconciled, not through pretence or procedural means but divine grace.

Superficial unity based on tolerance but little real engagement, or power-wielding and use of disciplinary measures, is no longer adequate in the face of the challenges of Christian mission in today's world. Whatever institutional changes are made to the Anglican Communion, there are genuine differences which need to be tackled if Anglicans are to grow in faith, hope and love and more clearly discern what God is calling them to do.

It is not always easy to be aware of the divine likeness in those who are marginalised or with whom one passionately disagrees, to make the right decisions on complex matters and to follow Christ's example of love in deed as well as word. Humans inevitably make mistakes and fail to live up to their ideals. Yet through prayer, worship, study and sometimes struggle, Anglicans can hope, by divine grace, in time to "come to the full maturity of the Body of Christ".

Chapter Twelve

Dumping dubious remedies: 'curing' homosexuality

All too often, ineffective or dangerous remedies, no longer saleable in the West, are exported to Africa. The notion that homosexuality can be 'cured' is just one example.

Drug dumping – when unreliable, useless or dangerous pharmaceutical products are donated to countries in the South – can make bad situations worse. For instance, during emergency relief operations, "Expired drugs (at the time of their arrival) and drugs close to expiry still comprise a large proportion of donations from non-governmental organisations, corporations, pharmaceutical industries and associations," as pointed out in a World Health Organisation (WHO) Bulletin in 2008 by Cristina P Pinheiro.

Treatments now seldom used in the West may continue to be common in poorer countries. For instance, medicines effective against HIV but with dangerous, sometimes deadly, side-effects continued to be widely used in Africa years after they stopped being routinely administered to North American and European patients. Even when there are some benefits, it is questionable whether treatments no longer acceptable in the West should be regarded as good enough for people in other parts of the world.

Methods aimed at 'curing' homosexuality, which failed badly in the West, are now being peddled in Africa and elsewhere. And the discredited theories behind these methods are being used to try to justify harsh repression, for instance in Uganda, where parliament may pass a law inflicting life imprisonment on gays and lesbians and jailing heterosexuals, such as clergy who do not inform on members of their congregations.

Wrecking lives

In September 2009, the UK Prime Minister offered a posthumous apology to one of the greatest scientists of the twenty-first century: a mathematical genius whose code-breaking skills helped to defeat Nazi Germany during the Second World War and who laid the foundations for modern computer science. Alan Turing had the misfortune to be gay at a time when sex between men was illegal. He was arrested in 1952, his security clearance was withdrawn and he was offered a choice between prison and drug 'treatment', which he took. The side-effects were extremely distressing and in 1954, at the age of forty-one, he took his own life. Who knows what discoveries he might have gone on to make had he not been driven to suicide?

Attempts to 'cure homosexuality' were common in countries such as the UK and USA in the early to mid twentieth century. It was recognised that a minority of people were strongly attracted to the same, rather than the opposite sex, often from an early age. Having the 'wrong' sexual orientation was frowned on. The threat of being arrested for men, and of public scorn and loss of livelihood for both sexes, led many to try to make themselves 'normal'. Some got married, often disastrously. Doctors and psychotherapists used various methods to try to 'cure' homosexuality, from talking therapies to electric shocks, while ministers of religion prayed and offered 'spiritual guidance'.

But gradually it became clear that such 'treatments' seldom worked and often did great harm. Gays and lesbians might for a while convince themselves and others that they had changed, but in the longer term, the feelings they had would usually return. They might marry in the hope of changing, but this often led to a strained relationship, in which the partner too, might suffer greatly.

Extracts from interviews published in 2004 in the British Medical Journal (BMJ) revealed the lasting damage which some experienced. One man described his "feeling of a lack of self worth — I think that was a tremendous impact, because I shouldn't feel like that and I don't have any gay friends who do feel like that. I think that treatment had a lot to answer for in that respect."

Another personal account on a website set up by the BMJ researchers – Michael King, Glenn Smith and Annie Bartlett – described how "Increasingly I feel betrayed by the promises of treatment. After I left treatment, where was the back up? My deepest feelings, the very structure of my being had been torn apart in the name of science – like so many others perhaps – and left abandoned whilst the psychologists got on with building their own careers and lives."

However LGBT people in some European countries had an even worse experience. In Germany under Hitler during the 1940s, some were locked up in concentration camps. In Franco's Spain in 1954, gay relationships were declared illegal "with the purpose of collective guarantee and the aspiration of correcting those subjects fallen to the lowest levels of morality. This law is not intended to punish, but to correct and reform". Many men were sent to 'correction camps' for 'therapy'. Such state-sponsored repression continued until 1979.

Accepting gay and lesbian orientation

Meanwhile, historians and social scientists were uncovering more and more evidence that people experienced same-sex attraction and intimacy across different eras and cultures, though this had been understood in different ways. Naturalists also found examples of same-sex sexual behaviour among numerous animal species.

As more gays and lesbians grew bold enough to live openly, people increasingly came to recognise that they could live well-adjusted lives if they and others could come to terms with human diversity. Trying to 'cure' what was not an illness came to seem unnecessary. Though some people of faith still believed same-sex relationships to be less than ideal, many urged celibacy rather than to attempt in vain to turn gays into heterosexuals. Others however, took the view that faithful and loving relationships should be nurtured.

Some of the professionals who tried to change people's sexual orientation still try to justify what they did, to themselves and others, and a few still persist in trying. For some, perhaps, it is a defence against the guilt that might otherwise overwhelm them for using 'treatments' which did such physical, psychological and spiritual damage, including in some cases mental breakdown, loss of faith, despair and suicide.

Others feel ashamed. A clinical psychologist, interviewed for the BMJ admitted that "I feel a lot of shame. I don't think I've ever spoken about it since then apart from now." Three former leaders of the Christian 'ex-gay' movement made a public apology in 2007: "Some who heard our message were compelled to try to change an integral part of themselves, bringing harm to themselves and their families. Although we acted in good faith, we have since witnessed the isolation, shame, fear, and loss of faith that this message creates."

One of these, Darlene Bogle, confessed, "My heart breaks as I hear the many stories of abuse and suicide from men and women who couldn't change their orientation, regardless of what Exodus and other Christian ministries told them. One of our female attendees became so depressed over her inability to change that she jumped off a bridge rather than continue the struggle. I was told it wasn't my fault, but my heart knew better." Another, Michael Bussee, also from the USA and a founder of the 'ex-gay' organisation, Exodus International, reckoned that "not one of the hundreds of people we counselled became straight."

Exporting what is discredited in the West

Some in the West, especially in certain kinds of church circles, still promote such 'solutions'. They are unable to accept the fact that a large-scale human experiment over several decades, using multiple methods aimed at changing people's sexuality, seldom achieved the desired goal and far more often resulted in harm.

Such 'treatments' however, no longer have mainstream scientific credibility. In 2007, the UK-based Royal College of Psychiatrists stated that "There is now a large body of research evidence that indicates that being gay, lesbian or bisexual is compatible with normal mental health and social adjustment...

"A small minority of therapists will even go so far as to attempt to change their client's sexual orientation. This can be deeply damaging. Although there is now a number of therapists and organisation[s] in the USA and in the UK that claim that therapy can help homosexuals to become heterosexual, there is no evidence that such change is possible... we know from historical evidence that treatments to change sexual orientation that were common in the 1960s and 1970s were very damaging to those patients who underwent them and affected no change in their sexual orientation."

In 2009, an American Psychological Association task force reviewed scientific studies of sexual orientation change efforts (SOCE) and "found serious methodological problems in this area of research, such that only a few studies met the minimal standards for evaluating whether psychological treatments, such as efforts to change sexual orientation, are effective.

"...the results of scientifically valid research indicate that it is unlikely that individuals will be able to reduce same-sex attractions or increase other-sex sexual attractions through SOCE."

However 'treatments' of this kind are now being promoted in other parts of the world. For instance, Uganda's Anti Homosexuality Bill was proposed after three visiting Americans, presented as experts on the issue, gave a series of talks in March 2009 to politicians, teachers and police officers, among others. Scott Lively, Caleb Lee Brundidge and Don Schmierer graphically warned about the supposed threat posed by gays and lesbians to young people and wider society and promoted the view that those who wanted to turn heterosexual could do so. This helped to fuel fierce anger against gays and lesbians across the country.

Human rights activists, locally and internationally, have mobilised against the Bill. Ironically, some Ugandans now regard it as a matter of national pride to legislate on the basis of such claims, which have been thoroughly discredited in the USA itself. In effect, toxic 'treatments' are being 'dumped' on people in the South with the support of certain local leaders, though others are less than enthusiastic.

The debate over 'curing' gay and lesbian sexuality is sometimes portrayed as a source of tension between the 'liberal' West and the more socially conservative South. But much of the treatment of LGBT people in Europe and North America over the past eighty years or so has been far from liberal. It did however, become clear through bitter experience that attempts to change orientation were unlikely to succeed. Sooner or later, many of the Ugandans and others in the South who are keen to import such 'treatments' will find they do more harm than good. However, it is hard to estimate how many more people, both LGBT and heterosexual, will have had their lives wrecked.

[An earlier version of this article was first published in February 2010]

Chapter Thirteen

Debating same-sex partnerships and Christianity

In recent years, the relationship between faith and sexuality has been much debated in church and society. Growing numbers of LGBT Christians no longer hide their identity, and many heterosexual churchgoers are also openly accepting. However, some church leaders and congregations are strongly opposed to celebrating same-sex partnerships and there have been threats of schism in several denominations over the issue.

In the UK, disagreement over several questions has been widely reported in the media. Are same-sex partnerships against God's will? Should partnered LGBT people be chosen as elders or ordained as priests or bishops? Should civil partnerships be celebrated in religious buildings, if the faith communities in charge of these are happy for this to happen? Should the term 'marriage' be reserved for the relationship between husband and wife?

I believe such debates can take place without causing unnecessary divisions in local and faith communities. But this requires people to be willing to value and listen to one another and avoid dubious assumptions.

Scripture and tradition: views differ

To begin with, the disagreement among Christians is not a clear-cut division between those who value Scripture and tradition and others who put reason and experience first. This is a frequent error among both opponents and champions of greater inclusion, who sometimes write off those they disagree with as either 'liberal' followers of secular thinking or 'conservatives' stuck in an irrelevant past.

Even theologically 'liberal' supporters of the equality of LGBT people are often guided by values grounded in the Bible and tradition, in particular the example of, and relationship with, Christ. Though some might be rightly criticised for not arguing their case rigorously enough and acknowledging the wisdom of the past, many are more 'biblical' and 'traditional' than even they might admit!

And some who call for full acceptance put forward arguments that are grounded in deep appreciation of the Bible and the beliefs and practices of Christians through the ages, which are varied and sometimes complex.

Perhaps in reaction to the tendency during the nineteenth and twentieth centuries increasingly to question received beliefs, and rapid technological and social change, some Christians have tended to treat views on LGBT partnership as a test of one's general theological beliefs. While church positions on all kinds of other issues have shifted back and forth without the sky falling down, this topic is given a deep symbolic significance, the test of whether fellow-Christians are 'sound' or 'unsound'.

But every Sunday, throughout the world, Christians are getting through services without any reference to the theology of sexuality! Whether they are singing the Gloria and Creed in a more 'traditional' liturgy or praise songs, or are part of emergent networks with experimental forms of worship, the focus is actually quite different.

Favouring opposite-sex partnership is not necessarily homophobic

There is also a widespread but I believe, mistaken view that anyone who upholds human rights for LGBT people should automatically be in favour of equal marriage in society and the church. Those who believe that male-female partnerships should be privileged in some way are not all homophobic (though some undoubtedly are), and homophobia cannot be justified by appealing to religious beliefs about sexual morality.

Unsurprisingly, in a world full of prejudice of various kinds, as well as consumerism, indifference to the needy and many other flawed attitudes, Christians are not immune. From anti-gay comments in the classroom, factory and office to stereotyped presentations in the media, Christians can pick up, and pass on, unjust and hurtful views. Indeed churches can be as bad or worse, judging some people more harshly than others. If we admit our fallibility, we can learn and grow: "If we say we have no sin, we deceive ourselves, and the truth is not in us. If we confess our sins, he is faithful and just to forgive us our sins and to cleanse us from all unrighteousness" (1 John 1.8–9).

It is also less than impressive when certain Christians cannot be bothered to listen to, and seriously consider, theological and scientific arguments for greater acceptance of same-sex partnerships, while fiercely denouncing such relationships. This does not fit with Jesus' call to treat others as we would wish to be treated (Matthew 7.12).

Yet Christians who try to treat LGBT people justly and compassionately may nevertheless believe that lesbian and gay relationships do not create conditions which promote the emotional and spiritual growth of those involved. In my view, this may be based on a faulty reading of the Bible, or faulty data – for instance by assuming that the unhappiness of LGBT people not at ease with themselves is due to their sexuality and not society's pressures. But it is nevertheless a sincere belief which deserves to be taken seriously and met with courteous argument, not denounced in harsh terms.

In addition there are people (including some LGBT theologians) who believe that there are fundamental differences between heterosexual and same-sex relationships and who feel that marriage is not a pattern which LGBT people should seek to follow, nor that the term should be used for opposite-sex partnerships.

Indeed, the meaning of marriage for heterosexual people has also changed radically for many over the course of their lives, especially in the light of women's changing status, growing acceptance of use of contraception among Christians and longer average life-spans. A young man pushing a pram, or an elderly man caring for his frail wife, in some ways present as much of a challenge to certain notions of marriage prevalent just a few decades ago as do same-sex partners.

A sense of proportion is also important. For instance, UK newspapers reported in October that a housing manager's misgivings about same-sex partnerships in church, expressed privately to friends on the social networking site Facebook, resulted in demotion at work and a pay cut. Apparently, in commenting on a BBC news story 'Gay church marriages get go ahead' (actually referring to civil partnerships), Adrian Smith had stated that he did not really approve: "I don't understand why people who have no faith and don't believe in Christ would want to get hitched in church the bible is quite specific that marriage is for men and women if the state wants to offer civil marriage to same sex then that is up to state; but they shouldn't impose its rules on places of faith and conscience".

Some of his colleagues who read this took issue with his views and, since he had mentioned on his home page that he worked for Trafford Housing Trust, he was disciplined by his employer, since the comment could be regarded as homophobic. His remarks displayed a lack of understanding – no faith communities will be forced to host such ceremonies, and he did not seem to recognise the situation of LGBT Christians who want to get "hitched in church". But giving him a less responsible job and heavily cutting his pay might seem disproportionate and an infringement of freedom of speech.

Creating space for mutually respectful debate

Some churches have worked hard to create space where issues of sexuality can be discussed in an atmosphere of mutual respect. Others (at least at leadership level) are further behind.

It may be helpful for those trying to move the debate forward to recognise and challenge, however gently, the belief of some opponents of inclusion that anyone in favour cannot be a true believer, but also the more general tendency to resort to labelling others too easily.

Understanding more about human sexuality and relationships can be helpful to heterosexual as well as LGBT people. Prayerful reflection, study and discussion will not create instant consensus, but can at least help those with different perspectives to understand one another better, and the church to move forward in its mission and ministry.

[An earlier version of this article was first published in October 2011]

Chapter Fourteen

The Pope, 'the family' and Christmas

The foundations of family life and key aspects of humanity are under threat, the Pope has claimed, referring to the debate over marriage for same-sex couples. Yet the reasoning behind his warnings is weak, and his theology out of step with the message of Christmas.

Is women's status pre-ordained?

Addressing cardinals and Vatican officials, Pope Benedict XVI said that "the family is still strong and vibrant today. But there is no denying the crisis that threatens it to its foundations – especially in the western world".

Mentioning the situation in France, where some Roman Catholic and other religious leaders have opposed marriage equality, he warned that "the attack we are currently experiencing on the true structure of the family, made up of father, mother, and child, goes much deeper. While up to now we regarded a false understanding of the nature of human freedom as one cause of the crisis of the family, it is now becoming clear that the very notion of being – of what being human really means – is being called into question."

He appeared to take the view that questioning 'traditional' male and female roles, and the notion that there was only one valid type of family – father, mother and children – was rebelling against God.

He was critical of gender theorists who argued that "sex is no longer a given element of nature, that man has to accept and personally make sense of: it is a social role that we choose for ourselves, while in the past it was chosen for us by society... People dispute the idea that they have a nature, given by their bodily identity, that serves as a defining element of the human being."

But, said the Pope, "According to the biblical creation account, being created by God as male and female pertains to the essence of the human creature. This duality is an essential aspect of what being human is all about, as ordained by God." What is more, "if there is no pre-ordained duality of man and woman in creation, then neither is the family any longer a reality established by creation."

He warned that "When the freedom to be creative becomes the freedom to create oneself, then necessarily the Maker Himself is denied and ultimately man too is stripped of his dignity as a creature of God, as the image of God at the core of his being."

There are several flaws in his case against diversity in marriage and family life.

To begin with, even if some aspects of what it means to be a man or woman are based on biology, it is hard to deny that sometimes unjust claims have been made about what women are capable of, and how they should be treated, supposedly based on their 'natural' inferiority.

> "Unfortunately, we are heirs to a history which has conditioned us to a remarkable extent. In every time and place, this conditioning has been an obstacle to the progress of women. Women's dignity has often been unacknowledged and their prerogatives misrepresented; they have often been relegated to the margins of society and even reduced to servitude. This has prevented women from truly being themselves and it has resulted in a spiritual impoverishment of humanity. Certainly it is no easy task to assign the blame for this, considering the many kinds of cultural conditioning which down the centuries have shaped ways of thinking and acting."

These are the words not of a radical feminist but of Pope John Paul II, in 1995.

Secondly, even if most men and women are 'naturally' best suited to marrying members of the opposite sex and having children together, why should this apply to all? Some people are infertile, others are mainly attracted to the same sex from an early age. And if one pattern only is acceptable, does this not mean that arranging celibate orders of monks and nuns is encouraging rebellion against nature?

Indeed many LGBT people would claim that their sexual orientation and gender identity are not a matter of choice, but rather an intrinsic aspect of themselves. People of faith may assert, rightly or wrongly, that this is how God made them. So supporting equal marriage need not involve believing in "the freedom to create oneself".

Thirdly, given that various communities throughout history have found ways of institutionalising identities that today might be described as LGBT (e.g. two-spirit peoples in North America), is there evidence that this led to a diminishing of human existence? If not, why should this be the case today?

Fourthly, many people feel drawn to be part of committed heterosexual relationships in which children are conceived, and these often make an important contribution to society. But why (especially since the global population has grown dramatically in the past couple of centuries) is this form of family life more authentic than all others, for instance fostering, adoption or caring for sick adults?

Christ's coming and human identity
What is more, for Christians, Jesus' birth calls into question conventional approaches to family life and dualistic notions of identity.

At the beginning of the Gospels of Matthew and Luke,, Mary is able to do more through the Holy Spirit than would have seemed possible. Jesus is brought up by a mother and stepfather, a deviation from the narrow model described by the Pope.

"In the beginning was the Word, and the Word was with God, and the Word was God," declares the first chapter of John's Gospel. Those open to the living Word become part of a non-biological family: "to all who received him, who believed in his name, he gave power to become children of God, who were born, not of blood or of the will of the flesh or of the will of man, but of God. And the Word became flesh and lived among us, and we have seen his glory".

In the new family life celebrated at Christmas, according to the Epistle to the Galatians, it would appear that the duality of gender is not reinforced but overcome: "in Christ Jesus you are all children of God through faith. As many of you as were baptised into Christ have clothed yourselves with Christ. There is no longer Jew or Greek, there is no longer slave or free, there is no longer male and female; for all of you are one in Christ Jesus... when the fullness of time had come, God sent his Son, born of a woman, born under the law, in order to redeem those who were under the law, so that we might receive adoption as children."

While Christians should indeed examine social and cultural changes critically, the fearfulness of the Pope about shifting attitudes to gender and sexual orientation seems excessive. Christmas should be a time of celebration in response to God's generous love, through which barriers are broken down and humanity's potential fulfilled.

[An earlier version of this article was first published in December 2012]

Chapter Fifteen

The Evangelical Alliance responds unconvincingly to Steve Chalke

In January 2013 the Evangelical Alliance's general director Steve Clifford criticised the influential evangelical leader Steve Chalke for changing his stance on homosexuality. Chalke, a UK-based Baptist minister, now believes that the Bible does not rule out faithful, committed same-sex partnerships. While Clifford raises important issues, he is ultimately unconvincing.

In an article in Christianity magazine, Chalke had pointed out how easy it was to misread the Bible, as on the issues of the solar system, the role of women and slavery. Instead "thoughtful conformity to Christ – not unthinking conformity to either contemporary culture or ancient textual prohibitions" should be central to Christian ethical thinking.

He stated that the Bible is "a very diverse collection of books, written in many different times and cultures, containing an array of perspectives, not a few tensions, and even some apparent contradictions." He suggested that it should be read as "the account of the ancient conversation initiated, inspired and guided by God with and among humanity", through which knowledge grows of "the character of Yahweh; fully revealed only in Jesus", and which continues, "involving all of those who give themselves to Christ's on-going redemptive movement."

In this light he re-examined the passages often taken as forbidding same-sex relationships, and questioned their applicability to permanent faithful partnerships. He emphasised the damage caused by the church's historical "failure to provide homosexual people with any model of how to cope with their sexuality, except for those who have the gift of, or capacity for, celibacy. In this way we have left people vulnerable and isolated." It was time instead to "consider nurturing positive models for permanent and monogamous homosexual relationships".

Clifford's response, published on the EA website and in Christianity Today, starts by mentioning that he is a long-standing friend of Chalke, but expresses "sadness and disappointment" that he "has not only distanced himself from the vast majority of the evangelical community here in the UK, but indeed from the Church across the world and 2,000 years of biblical interpretation."

This is an exaggeration. There are plenty of evangelicals in the UK and beyond who broadly agree with Chalke or are undecided, and church tradition is rather more varied and at times ambiguous, though it is true that most Christians have disapproved of sex between two men or two women. But then, up to mediaeval times, most Christians believed that the Bible presented a very different picture of the cosmos from that which is now known.

Clifford appears to fall into the trap of conformity other than to Christ. While he accuses Chalke of taking an approach to biblical interpretation which "allows for a god in the likeness of 21st century Western-European mindsets", he fails to recognise that hostility to same-sex relationships may also be culturally influenced. Clifford seems reluctant to acknowledge that if theologians of the calibre of Martin Luther could sometimes be wildly wrong, so might he. Certainly the work of the many eminent theologians calling for acceptance, some of them evangelical, should not be so dogmatically dismissed.

Likewise, Clifford criticises Chalke for undermining the many Christians attracted to the same sex who make "courageous lifestyle decisions" to be celibate. But what of the many others who end up in despair, sometimes even losing their faith?

> "We all come to the gospel in our brokenness, with an attachment to things, self-centeredness, addictions, fears and pride. We all need a saviour in every area of our lives, including our sexuality," declares Clifford. "The radical inclusiveness of the gospel means we are all welcomed. In a wonderful grace-filled process we find repentance and forgiveness... God doesn't leave us on our own, He promises to work in us, to bring us into our ultimate goal which is His

likeness."

But surely this applies just as much to heterosexual as to lesbian, gay, bisexual and trans (LGBT) people, and there is considerable evidence that committed loving partnerships can be a space in which spiritual growth takes place.

However he is correct in urging that "Jesus requires us to disagree without being disagreeable. We must listen honestly and carefully to one another, being courteous and generous."

[An earlier version of this article was first published in January 2013]

Chapter Sixteen

Christians divided as Parliament debates equal marriage

[A version of this chapter was first published in June 2013; based on two articles. In the UK Parliament, bills are debated in both the House of Commons and House of Lords]

What happens when we debate marriage equality in the House of Commons?

Differences are evident. Some Christian MPs strongly support marriage equality while others are strongly against it. In the UK and beyond, parliamentary debates on celebrating same-sex partnerships have revealed that whatever top clerics or elders say, opinion within the churches is divided.

Many theologians now take the view that committed loving relationships should be valued, though not all regard these as equivalent to heterosexual marriage.

In numerous congregations and among those who identify as Christians in many countries, there is a similar range of opinion, as debates in the House of Common have shown. Lay people whose consciences are developed in the context of their faith – though other factors also influence their choices – can be found in all walks of life. Debates on marriage in Westminster offer insights into the reasons why people who worship together often have conflicting positions on marriage.

Shifting views among Christians on marriage equality

Both Church of England and Roman Catholic church leaders have vigorously campaigned against the Marriage (Same Sex Couples) Bill, which would bring about equal marriage in England and Wales. Separate legislation is planned for Scotland.

Though a few smaller faith groups are in favour or neutral, such active opposition may give the impression that the mainstream church position is strongly against opening up marriage to same-sex couples.

But at grassroots level, the story is very different, though there are congregations in which few would dare to voice their support for marriage equality.

For example, the results of a YouGov poll commissioned for the Westminster Faith Debate were published in April 2013. This found that half of all religious people in Britain were in favour of allowing same-sex marriage, and that those who identified as Anglican and Catholic supported it by a small margin.

Among regular churchgoers, support was slightly lower. 40 per cent of Anglicans were in favour and 47 per cent against, while 42 per cent of Catholics were in favour, 48 per cent against. This mixture of opinions was nevertheless extraordinary, given the negative public stance of the hierarchy of both churches (with a few exceptions).

MPs did not simply divide along party lines on this issue. For instance, opponents included Conservative Edward Leigh and Labour Stephen Timms; supporters Labour David Lammy and Conservative Peter Bottomley. And speeches when the Bill had its second reading and (after Committee stage discussions) third reading, highlighted differences in theological as well as wider ethical reasoning.

Upholding the importance of procreation

Some of the speeches on 5 February and 20 and 21 May 2013 took the view that Christian views on marriage ruled out any possibility of it being opened up to same-sex couples.

For instance, according to Gainsborough MP Edward Leigh:

The catechism of the Roman Catholic Church beautifully describes the institution. Anybody of any faith or no faith who supports traditional marriage could echo these words. The catechism says that marriage is a "covenant" in which "a man and a woman establish themselves in a partnership" for "the whole of life", and that marriage is "by its nature ordered towards the good of the spouses and the procreation and education of offspring...

The Bill is not evolution, but revolution. It is true that I am blessed with six children. I realise that not every married couple is able to have the gift of children, and that some married couples may not want it, yet that does not change the fact that the concept of marriage has always been bestowed with a vision of procreation.

East Ham MP Stephen Timms likewise argued that:

[T]he Church of England was the custodian of marriage in Britain for hundreds of years. For many people, it still is...

The 1662 version of the Church of England service, which has been in use for the past 350 years, sets out three reasons for marriage. The first is that it was "ordained for the procreation of children, to be brought up in the fear and nurture of the Lord.

The central problem with the Bill is that it introduces a definition of marriage that includes the second and third reasons but drops that first one. The result is something that is a good deal weaker than the original.

This led to an amusing exchange when West Ham MP Lyn Brown commented that, "at my wedding, I was not young when I got married, and unless I had been blessed like Elizabeth, it was highly unlikely that I was going to be able to procreate after all that time. Is he telling me that my marriage is less valid than anybody else's?" (This was a reference to Luke 1.5–25, in which Elizabeth, who was barren and getting on in years, conceived through God's intervention.)

Removing barriers and loving one's neighbour as oneself
In contrast, the black Tottenham MP David Lammy argued that the Bill:

[C]ommands the support of the country, because it respects religious freedom and tradition by permitting, rather than mandating, religious organisations to conduct the ceremonies, and because it is the end of an organic journey from criminalisation to equality for the gay community that began over half a century ago. This change is right and necessary and the time is now.

There are still those who say it is unnecessary. "Why do we need gay marriage", they say, "when we already have civil partnerships?" They are, they claim, "Separate but equal." Let me speak frankly: separate but equal is a fraud... It is the same naivety that led to my dad being granted citizenship when he arrived here in 1956, but being refused by landlords who proclaimed, "No blacks, no Irish, no dogs"...

Separate is not equal, so let us be rid of it... As long as our statute book suggests that love between two men or two women is unworthy of recognition through marriage, we allow the rot of homophobia to fester and we entrench a society where 20,000 homophobic crimes take place each year and where 800,000 people have witnessed homophobic bullying at work in the past five years.

I am a Christian. I go to Mass. I recognise how important this is...

When I married my wife, I understood our marriage to have two important dimensions: the expression of love, fidelity and mutuality over the course of our life together; and a commitment to raise children. Gay men and women can now raise children – this House made that decision – so let us not hear any further discussion about having a family as if gay men and women cannot have that.

The Jesus I know was born a refugee, illegitimate, with a death warrant on his name, and in a barn among animals. He would stand up for minorities. That is why it is right for those of religious conviction to vote for this Bill.

Sir Peter Bottomley, MP for Worthing West, also supported the Bill on faith-related grounds:

The primary commandment is to love the Lord my God with

all my heart, soul, mind and strength. I have been reminded by one ordained constituent that that should be used as a way of defining the second great commandment, which is to treat my neighbour as myself. Essentially, we are asking whether we can remove the barriers that stop same-sex couples enjoying the commitment – the "at one" meaning – of marriage. That is what the Bill comes down to. It does not redefine marriage; it just takes away barriers...

A man called Tribe, in a book from 1935 called "The Christian Social Tradition", stated: "The problem of society is the finding of unity in diversity, and to reconcile freedom with order."

I think that is loving my neighbour as myself, and that what I have experienced, good or bad, others should have a chance of choosing or avoiding. I have not experienced discrimination. I have watched others who have. I hope that when this matter is concluded those who have spent their time writing messages saying that we are all wrong will realise, as people did with the creation of civil partnerships, that maybe they can see life differently in the future.

House of Lords debate

The House of Lords too backed a Bill to allow same-sex couples in England and Wales to marry, by 390 votes to 148. After a long debate in which Christians argued for and against the Marriage (Same-Sex Couples) Bill, a bid by opponents to block a second reading was heavily defeated.

In the Bill "Marriage is abolished, redefined and recreated," the Archbishop of Canterbury Justin Welby warned. "The concept of marriage as a normative place for procreation is lost. The idea of marriage as a covenant is diminished. The family in its normal sense," he claimed, "is weakened."

He argued that, "rather than adding a new and valued institution alongside it for same-gender relationships, which I would personally strongly support to strengthen us all, the Bill weakens what exists and replaces it with a less good option that is neither equal nor effective." This was "not at heart a faith issue. It is about the general social good."

But other peers, including clergy and lay Christians, highlighted the flaws in these arguments. They included retired Bishop of Oxford Richard Harries, now Lord Harries of Pentregarth, who became an honorary theology professor at King's College London. He pointed out that many gay and lesbian people "want to enter not just into a civil partnership but a marriage: a lifelong commitment of love and fidelity, for better, for worse, for richer, for poorer, in sickness and in health."

He believed, "with the Jewish rabbi of old, that in the love of a couple there dwells the shekinah – the divine presence; or, to put it in Christian terms, that which reflects the mutual love of Christ and his church. I believe in the institution of marriage and I want it to be available to same-sex couples as well as to males and females."

Another former senior cleric supporting the Bill was Baroness Richardson of Calow, a minister who once served as president of the Methodist Conference and later moderator of the Free Church Council.

Lay Christians also spoke out for marriage equality, including Baroness Brinton, who outlined the shift in theological thinking on sexuality and other issues, quoting the Bishop of Salisbury (not a peer), who supports marriage equality.

Lord Jenkin of Roding questioned exaggerated fears about the Bill's impact, pointing out that it was hardly likely to harm the quality of his sixty-year marriage, nor that of younger couples. He described a scenario: "A young man poses the question to his intended, 'Will you marry me?' and she replies, 'Oh no. This Bill has made it all totally different. It's for gays and lesbians – I can't possibly marry you'. That is pure fantasy and I do not think we should pay too much attention to it."

Instead the Bill would "to put right at the centre of marriage the concept of a stable, loving relationship." To him, "The character of love which marriage reflects – that it is faithful, stable, tough, unselfish and unconditional – is the same character that most Christians see in the love of God. Marriage is therefore holy, not because it is ordained by God, but because it reflects that most important central truth of our religion: the love of God for all of us."

"I am a Christian and I believe we are all equal in the eyes of God, and should be so under man's laws," said Lord Black of Brentwood. To him, the debate was not simply about abstract principles: "I am gay. I am in a civil partnership with somebody with whom I have been together for nearly a quarter of a century. I love him very much and nothing would give me greater pride than to marry him."

Baroness Morgan of Ely, "a committed Christian, an active member of the Church in Wales and the daughter of a much-loved priest" and wife of an ordinand, spoke movingly of her belief that "equal marriage is in the best interests of my children and everyone else's children." She warned that "We risk making marriage into a stone idol, rather than a living, life-enhancing experience, by denying it to same-sex couples."

To her, "Marriage is a vocation, a response to a divine call rather than a set of dusty, ancient rules. For those who celebrate their Christian faith, marriage is far more than a legal contract. Marriage is a response to God's call to love, and I see no reason why that should be limited to being between women and men."

She agreed with the Archbishop of Canterbury that the quality of gay relationships could be "stunning" (a point he had made in an interview). "My gay friends are not beating down my door demanding that we recognise their 'stunning' relationships as marriage. It is people like me – mothers, sisters, friends – who look at their relationships and recognise the vocation of marriage when we see it, and are demanding that we should recognise and celebrate their calling and not try to hide it in some dark corner by calling it something else."

Among other faiths too, differing views were apparent. Keen supporters of equal marriage included Lord Alli, a Muslim, and Jewish peer Baroness Neuberger, a rabbi.

The large majority in favour of the Bill, in free votes in the Houses of Commons and Lords, indicates a major shift in public opinion and also in Christian thinking over recent decades.

Chapter Seventeen

The Pilling Report and theological diversity

The Church of England working party report, the Pilling report on sexuality (Winter 2013), suggests that clergy be allowed to hold public services to mark same-sex partnerships. Some critics have complained that allowing too much flexibility might seem to affirm what the church still officially regards as wrong.

For instance, one of the criticisms made by the evangelical group Fulcrum was that, "Although the church's teaching is upheld, its theological and biblical basis is not clearly articulated and there appears to be a willingness to separate teaching and practice in a way which threatens incoherence and charges of hypocrisy."

Yet what happens in worship is often at odds with official policy, and somehow the Church of England manages to cope.

There are varying views among evangelicals on how Christ saves, as well as on sexuality (many are now in favour of celebrating same-sex partnerships). Some preach the doctrine of penal substitutionary atonement, in opposition to official church teaching.

The notion of "propitiation as the placating by man of an angry God is definitely unchristian," declared the Church of England Doctrine Commission in 1938. I and many others would agree, and point out that it is at odds with much of what the Bible teaches.

This was emphasised again in 1995, when the Doctrine Commission pointed out that "the traditional vocabulary of atonement with its central themes of law, wrath, guilt, punishment and acquittal, leave many Christians cold and signally fail to move many people, young and old, who wish to take steps towards faith. These images do not correspond to the spiritual search of many people today and therefore hamper the Church's mission." Instead, the Cross should be presented "as revealing the heart of a fellow-suffering God."

Yet, thankfully, the Church of England does not hunt down priests whose sermons put forward this notion. In fact, they may even be allowed to become bishops. When there is widespread disagreement, reasoned debate can be a more effective means of seeking the truth than trying to eradicate 'heretical' practice.

Likewise, the 39 Articles of Religion state that "The Romish Doctrine concerning Purgatory, Pardons, Worshipping and Adoration, as well of Images as of Relics, and also Invocation of Saints, is a fond thing, vainly invented, and grounded upon no warranty of Scripture, but rather repugnant to the Word of God."

The 39 Articles no longer carry the force they once had and it has been acknowledged, for instance at general synod in February 2008, that there are Anglicans who ask for the prayers of Mary and other saints. Hence some Anglo-Catholics worship in ways that could be said to depart from formal church teaching.

Similarly, there is a growing number of people within the Anglican Communion who embrace, or have been influenced by, Anabaptist ideas, or who are pacifists, despite the condemnation of two other Articles which oppose the notion of holding goods in common (contrary to Acts 2) or of refusing military service "as some Anabaptists do falsely proclaim".

There are times when it is right for church leaders to take disciplinary action, for instance against racism, which is generally agreed to be contrary to the good news of Christ.

But where sizeable numbers have disagreed on particular theological matters, attempted crackdowns on practice which did not conform with official church teaching have usually not worked very well.

In the Church of England and some other churches, many benefit from the fact that strict discipline is not enforced on them. Yet not all of these are willing to extend the same courtesy to others.

It is important to examine the theological rationale behind different approaches to worship and pastoral care, and to continue to study and reflect on sexuality along with other controversial issues.

However, until something approaching consensus is reached, practice may not consistently be in line with official teaching, or uncertainty about what is right may have to be openly acknowledged. Following Christ is not always about having definite answers.

[An earlier version of this article was first published in December 2013]

Chapter Eighteen

Learning from the social and natural sciences

[Excerpts from 'Edging towards accepting diversity: the Pilling Report on sexuality', first published in January 2014]

A Church of England working party on sexuality, chaired by Sir Joseph Pilling, has called for a more welcoming approach to lesbian and gay people, though not for full inclusion. It recognises the current lack of consensus on the theology of sexuality, including what the Bible has to say, and recommends that clergy be free to hold services, though not weddings, for same-sex couples.

The report [1] is a small step forward, though it is over-cautious and its handling of historical and scientific evidence is weak.

Evidence on sexual attitudes and practices

Part 2 of the Pilling report, 'Summarising the evidence', states that "Whatever problems the Church may have with issues of sexuality, we believe that the wider culture is much more confused about sexuality than is often recognised,", rightly pointing to the problems arising from the commercialisation of sex and the risks of abuse of power.

However, there are questionable assumptions made about modern sexual mores, for instance the claim that "Even though the idea of covenantal relationships is not by any means dead, it is increasingly counter-cultural. For all the contemporary social commentary on sex and relationships, there is remarkably little about making things work for life." In contrast, "Permanence, fidelity and openness to the nurturing of family life provide the essential context for a Christian ethic of sexual relationships, for the simple reason that they are a reflection of God's love for us."

But recent sociological evidence indicates that, while young people are more relaxed about same-sex relationships than previous generations, they tend to value fidelity in committed partnerships.

Findings from the Third National Survey of Sexual Attitudes and Lifestyles (NATSAL) appeared in *The Lancet* [2] at around the same time as the Pilling report, and are based on interviews with adults across Britain in 2010–12. These indicate that about half of all men aged 16–44, and two-thirds of women of the same age, believe that same-sex partnerships are not wrong at all. The proportion of men in that age-group who report having had at least one same-sex experience was 7.3% (4.8% involving genital contact) while for women it was 16% (7.9% involving genital contact).

Compared with two decades ago, disapproval of non-exclusivity in marriage has risen among both men and women (from 44.7% to 62.5% and 53.2% to 69.8% respectively) in the 16–44 age-group. Only 20.2% of men see nothing wrong in 'one-night stands', much the same as in 1990–91; the number of women with this view has increased from 5.4% to 13.0%, still a small minority. So young people's disapproval of church attitudes to same-sex partnerships may have more to do with perceived injustice, and the perversity of discouraging LGBT people from forming loving relationships, than an 'anything goes' attitude.

With regard to the prevalence of various sexual orientations, the report cites Integrated Household Survey figures. Of NATSAL participants aged 16–74, 97.1% of men and 97.3% of women identified as heterosexual/straight (96.7% of men and 95.9% of women in the 16–24 age-group), 1.5% of men and 1% of women as gay/lesbian, 1% of men and 1.4% of women as bisexual and 0.3% of both men and women as other. In addition, as this and other surveys indicate, a higher proportion of people have reportedly had a same-sex experience, and in one English survey in 2007, [3] 5.3% of men and 5.6% of women reported they were not entirely heterosexual. In surveys on sexual orientation and practice, slight differences in methodology can noticeably affect the findings.

Science and pseudo-science

The next section, on science, disappointingly appears to give equal weight to a major national scientific institution, the Royal College of Psychiatrists (which broadly agrees with the American Psychiatric Association on sexuality) and the Core Issues Trust, which describes itself as "a non-profit Christian ministry supporting men and women with homosexual issues who voluntarily seek change in sexual preference and expression", and which is currently at odds with the UK Council for Psychotherapy over the ethics of attempting to change clients' sexual orientation.

This is rather like equating the Royal Institution with a local science club: the possibility that the scientific establishment has got it wrong should not be ruled out but, in general, leading organisations and top scientists are more likely to be right.

There are currently two company directors for the Core Issues Trust – Mike Davidson, an 'ex-gay', [4] and Lisa Nolland, who believes that the drive for marriage equality is part of a "social engineering project" which will undermine public morality and end up legitimising bestiality and paedophilia. [5]

The report's coverage of trans issues is superficial and, dubiously, it is suggested as evidence of the fluidity of sexual orientation in some people at least, that they "move from being 'gay' to being 'straight' and vice versa. So, at least for some people, sexual attraction is not immutable. They may not necessarily self-identify as 'bisexual', if bisexual is understood as attraction to people of both sexes at the same time." That is not my definition of bisexuality. Bisexual people, like heterosexuals, may sometimes faithfully love a particular person and feel little attraction to others

Across cultures and throughout history, there has been a minority attracted largely or mainly to the same sex and/or not fitting prevailing gender norms, but how people have lived out such identities has varied widely. There may also be a minority of people whose sexuality alters somewhat in the course of a lifetime.

However, attempts to change sexual orientation intentionally have rarely succeeded. In Europe and beyond, during living memory, numerous gay and lesbian people – motivated by fear of imprisonment, ostracism or job loss or by religious beliefs – have tried to 'go straight' and failed, though a handful may have shifted their feelings to some degree. In Nazi Germany, gays and lesbians were even put into concentration camps, but this did not eliminate homosexuality. [6]

Various explanations were put forward for why a minority of people turned out to be gay or lesbian. These often involved defective upbringing (leaving many parents feeling guilty) or wilful misbehaviour. In the hope of being 'cured', people tried prayer, willpower, aversion therapy involving vomiting or electric shocks, psychotherapy or marriage to the opposite sex. Trans people also found themselves under pressure to suppress their identity.

While people trying to become heterosexual could sometimes temporarily persuade themselves that they were 'better', rather as adrenaline and wishful thinking can result in apparent 'miracles' by faith healers on stage, after a while the old feelings tended to return, leading to f a sense of guilt, inadequacy and despair. Gradually, internationally [7] and in the UK, [8] society woke up to the fact that being attracted to the same sex was not a sin or sickness, and that therapeutic attempts to bring about change carried too high a risk of damaging the client to be ethically acceptable.

Some people still did not accept same-sex relationships on religious grounds but focused on encouraging gays and lesbians to try to stay celibate, with varying degrees of success. Understanding of the complexities of gender identity also grew.

A few faith-based ministries however, kept insisting that those truly wanting to turn heterosexual in orientation would have a good chance of doing so with appropriate support, [9] despite mounting evidence of high rates of failure, psychological and spiritual harm. [10]

Prejudice and wellbeing
Swayed by the Core Issues Trust, the report suggests "that a

causative link between social prejudice and health issues among gay and lesbian people is neither proven nor ruled out by the evidence. But the alternative possibility that homosexual orientation 'and all it entails cuts against a fundamental, gender-based given of the human condition, thus causing distress' is likewise neither proved nor ruled out by the available scientific evidence."

However, this is a direct contradiction of the earlier acknowledgement that "Gay people have been attacked and sometimes murdered by strangers, solely on grounds of their sexuality (or assumptions about their sexuality) and many gay and lesbian people have been driven to depression, and sometimes suicide, by homophobic treatment." Indeed, it is a very odd assertion: for instance homophobic murders have an evident impact on health.

Unsurprisingly, research findings from the UK [11] and internationally [12] confirm that lesbian and gay people are more likely to experience mental health problems if they have encountered hostility – though, of course, many are resilient and lead generally happy and healthy lives.

It is however true that there is some evidence that society's negativity is not the only reason for above-average levels of distress among LGBT people. This does not necessarily mean that being LGBT is the cause of the distress: it is a basic tenet of research that correlation does not imply causation. [13] Indeed, a Swedish study in 2010 [14] found that "Rates of depression, generalised anxiety disorder (GAD), eating disorders, alcohol dependence and attention deficit hyperactivity disorder (ADHD) were increased among men and women with same-sex sexual experiences. Adjusting for perceived discrimination and hate crime victimisation lowered this risk whereas controlling for familial (genetic or environmental) factors in within-twin pair comparisons further reduced or eliminated it." It is to be hoped that scientific work in years to come will test how robust this theory is.

With regard to the notion that a clear-cut division between males and females, and opposite-sex relationships, are the only 'natural' pattern for humans and maybe for other mammals, t would have been useful for this section of the report to mention the extensive research in recent decades on same-sex coupling or pair-bonding, and behaviour uncharacteristic of male-female roles in various species. [15] Though human ethics cannot be based entirely on other species' activities, understanding something of the diversity among living things and the possible evolutionary advantages of different sexual patterns, can be informative.

Research in recent years indicates that more widespread social and legal recognition may be enhancing wellbeing among LGBT people. For instance, a study from California published in the American Journal of Public Health in 2012 [16] found that "Same-sex married lesbian, gay, and bisexual persons were significantly less distressed than lesbian, gay, and bisexual persons not in a legally recognised relationship; married heterosexuals were significantly less distressed than non-married heterosexuals... Being in a legally recognised same-sex relationship, marriage in particular, appeared to diminish mental health differentials between heterosexuals and lesbian, gay, and bisexual persons." Some people may regard this as welcome news.

[An earlier version of this article was first published in December 2013]

Chapter Nineteen

Gay people hunted in Russia: a challenge for churches

A powerful British television documentary on Channel 4, 'Hunted' (broadcast in February 2014), shows the level of homophobic hatred and violence in Russia. As the Winter Olympics begin in Sochi, the United Nations Secretary-General and writers from many countries have condemned the human rights abuses taking place. Churches should consider their stance.

Negative treatment of LGBT people has been fuelled by Russian Orthodox church leaders, who more generally have supported president Vladimir Putin in violating human rights. While there are varying views among Christians about sexual ethics, persecuting a vulnerable minority is unjust, unloving and a rejection of Christ.

Gays are "basically serving the devil", Sergei Rybko, a senior cleric, told the documentary-makers led by investigative journalist Liz MacKean. The consequences of promoting such attitudes were graphically shown on Dispatches on 5 February 2014.

Gangs track down, beat and torture gays, videoing the attacks to be shared online in order to further humiliate and 'out' the victims.

"If it's constantly drilled into people that we are... scum and perverts, I understand why these guys shot at me," said 25-year-old Dima, who had been blinded in one eye; "a hunting season is open and we are the hunted."

A law against pro-gay 'propaganda' blocks people of goodwill from effectively countering prejudice and misinformation. Nevertheless, as the documentary showed, some human rights defenders in Russia are courageously putting themselves on the line.

Internationally, people in various walks of life have taken a stand against the hate-mongering and repression.

"Many professional athletes, gay and straight, are speaking out against prejudice. We must all raise our voices against attacks on lesbian, gay, bisexual, transgender or intersex people," UN Secretary-General Ban Ki-moon told the International Olympic Committee. "We must oppose the arrests, imprisonments and discriminatory restrictions they face."

He said that "Hatred of any kind must have no place in the 21st century."

Over two hundred writers (some of them Russian) signed an open letter published in the Guardian on 6 February 2014, pointing out that "during the last 18 months, Russian lawmakers have passed a number of laws that place a chokehold on the right to express oneself freely in Russia."

"Three of these laws specifically put writers at risk: the so-called gay 'propaganda' and 'blasphemy' laws, prohibiting the 'promotion' of homosexuality and 'religious insult' respectively, and the re-criminalisation of defamation," they stated. They urged the Russian authorities to repeal these laws and create "an environment in which all citizens can experience the benefit of the free exchange of opinion." Signatories included Günter Grass, Salman Rushdie, Margaret Atwood, Wole Soyinka and Ariel Dorfman.

Churches which disapprove of hunting LGBT people, in Russia or anywhere else in the world, might wish to consider whether they have made clear their reasons for believing in human rights for all, as well as educating their own members on this issue.

At ecumenical events, Russian Orthodox leaders have been blunt in criticising other churches for being too soft in their attitudes to same-sex partnerships, using alarmist terms. "Militant secularism" includes "the straightforward destruction of traditional notions of marriage and the family", as witnessed by "the new phenomenon of equating homosexual unions with marriage and allowing single-sex couples to adopt children," Metropolitan Hilarion of Volokolamsk told the World Council of Churches in November 2013.

"Unfortunately, not all Christian Churches today find within themselves the courage and resolve to vindicate the biblical ideals by going against that which is fashionable and the prevalent secular outlook", claimed Hilarion, chairman of the department for external church relations of the Moscow patriarchate.

However it is contrary to Gospel values to victimise the vulnerable and teach people to loathe their neighbour. Perhaps churches committed to compassion and justice for all should do more to make this clear.

[An earlier version of this article was first published in February 2014]

Chapter Twenty

The Church in Wales considers the issue of same-sex partnerships

A pastoral response is vital when considering same-sex partnerships, according to a thought-provoking report by the Standing Doctrinal Commission of the Church in Wales (Spring 2014). The Church in Wales and same-sex partnerships may also be useful to other churches grappling with sexual ethics.

Against the background of a change in the law allowing lesbian and gay couples to get legally married, the Commission examined the issue of same-sex partnerships, listening to people with a range of views. The seriousness with which they approached the task is reflected in the report.

It outlines the history of marriage in the west from Roman times and examines relevant scientific evidence. It then sets out a theological case for each of three options: a) marriage between a man and a woman is the only type of sexual relationship which should be blessed, b) blessing for same-sex partnerships should be offered but not marriage, c) marriage is a union of loving equals, irrespective of sexual difference. It ends by emphasising the importance of a pastoral response which takes account of lived experience.

The report recognises that "defining marriage is exceptionally difficult" and outlines some of the ways in which understanding of its meaning has shifted. The mediaeval Christian belief that "The ministers of the sacrament were the couple themselves", which "meant that, strictly speaking, no ceremony or blessing was necessary" is mentioned, though the possible implications for current controversies are not fully explored.

The section on science acknowledges that "Scientific evidence gathered to date supports the perspective that homosexual orientation should not be regarded as a pathology but as a natural characteristic which, for a small but significant proportion of the population, is acquired before birth"; though this "does not in itself clinch the argument of whether or not same-sex acts are morally or theologically acceptable."

More on the history of attempts to change people's sexual orientation, with often deeply damaging results, would have been useful. Nevertheless, these sections set the scene for three different but powerfully-made arguments, (positions a), b) and c)), all drawing heavily on the Bible but focusing on "the search to recognise holiness." This also has implications for attitudes to gender identity, though this is not covered in detail.

The concluding section focuses on the need for a pastoral approach:

"And the Word became flesh and lived among us, and we have seen his glory, the glory as of the Father's only Son, full of grace and truth. John 1.14 (NRSV)

"The Gospels bear witness to a Saviour who is fully God and fully human, who chooses the way of humility and sacrifice, and who calls all people into a pattern of life-giving relationship exemplified in God himself. As such, Christianity is an incarnational faith which does not begin with dogma or doctrine but with people and call."

The pastoral needs of "those for whom these questions are not merely theory but bound up in a deeply personal way with their own experience and identity" are highlighted. But there is also mention of the "pastoral needs of those who would be appalled by the thought of their church countenancing same-sex partnerships at all." To me, however, how these should be met is by no means obvious.

If someone does not just disagree with the idea of blessing same-sex relationships but reacts strongly against even considering the possibility, this may be a symptom of prejudice or insecurity. Shying away from greater inclusion in such instances may be a disservice not only to those excluded but also, less obviously, to those whose barriers against 'the other' are reinforced.

The report suggests that "it may be possible in some sense to hold together a range of convictions in order to create space for genuinely new insights to emerge." When the Church in Wales governing body meets later in April, it is to be hoped that clergy and parishes could be given freedom to choose among the three positions described above as part of a discernment process which may take some years.

While neutrality on sexual ethics is hard to achieve, a genuine effort is made to acknowledge something of the breadth of views among churchgoers in Wales and beyond. Though the report is not perfect, it is far better than most other Anglican publications on the subject, including those by the Church of England in recent years, and could be a valuable resource for other denominations too.

* The report can be found on http://cinw.s3.amazonaws.com/wp-content/uploads/2013/10/1404-GB-SS-Partnership-ENG-LISH.pdf, with other papers on http://www.churchinwales.org.uk/faith/doctrinal-commission/

[An earlier version of this article was first published in April 2014]

Chapter Twenty-One

Free to marry

Pastors may, if they wish, marry same-sex couples in areas where this is legal, the Presbyterian Church (USA) decided in the Summer of 2014. The general assembly also called for a change in how marriage is defined, if a majority of presbyteries agree.

Many have been delighted by this decision though some object strongly. It reflects a shift in many denominations internationally in which the theology of partnership has been freely discussed. Growing numbers of worshippers have come to believe that celebrating same-sex partnerships is right, though views differ.

Increasingly, such churches are allowing some freedom to ministers or elders and congregations – a middle ground which allows people with varying views to remain in fellowship.

"Worship is a central element of the pastoral care of the people of God", the assembly resolved, and "freedom of conscience in the interpretation of Scripture" has "deep roots in our Reformed tradition and theology." Where the civil authorities allow same-sex couples to marry, teaching elders may – but do not have to – "participate in any such marriage they believe the Holy Spirit calls them to perform."

The Assembly also recommended a change of language in the Book of Order to indicate that "marriage involves a unique commitment between two people, traditionally a man and a woman."

"The Church affirmed all its faithful members today. This vote is an answer to many prayers for the Church to recognise love between committed same-sex couples," said Alex McNeill, executive director of More Light Presbyterians, which has campaigned for change.

In time, Christians may hope that the Holy Spirit, who is believed to guide followers of Christ into all truth (John 16.13), will bring about consensus on this issue. Until then, recognising diverse perspectives while upholding the dignity and safety of lesbian, gay, bisexual and transgender people offers a wise way forward.

LGBT Methodists may get married, Conference agrees

Clergy and laypersons should not get into trouble for marrying their same-sex partners, the Methodist Church in Britain agreed. For the time being, only opposite-sex couples will be allowed to marry in church. But a two-year period of study and discussion will examine whether this should change.

Equal marriage became law in England, Wales and Scotland this year. After a consultation, a report exploring the issues raised was presented at the 2014 Methodist Conference, held in Birmingham. This recognised the range of views and the need for further listening, reflection and discernment.

The Conference resolved that there was no reason per se to prevent anyone within the Church, ordained or lay, from entering into or remaining within a legally contracted same-sex marriage. Same-sex couples should be welcomed and treated with respect, the report urged. Guidelines will be produced on how to deal with homophobia.

Ministers have been asked to respond with pastoral sensitivity to requests for prayers by same-sex couples, without going against their own consciences, while taking account of current teaching. Church weddings will only be offered to heterosexual couples.

This will be disappointing for some, the report acknowledges: "There will be many who would see the Church's unwillingness to revisit its definition of marriage at this time as a denial of our commitment in 1993 'to combat repression and discrimination, to work for justice and human rights and to give dignity and worth to people whatever their sexuality."

However, it will be reviewed in 2016, after further reflection on living with contradictory convictions and the nature of biblical authority. The report helpfully recognises that it is possible to take the Bible seriously while also supporting marriage equality.

Full inclusion is still some distance away. Nevertheless, the willingness to take differing views seriously, and the decision not to discipline LGBT church leaders who get married, are welcome steps forward.

The move will encourage those in other churches who want to move towards greater acceptance of theological diversity on sexuality and gender identity. This includes Methodists overseas and members of various denominations.

In particular, it will have an impact on the Church of England, which has a covenant with the Methodist Church in Britain promoting a close relationship. This is likely to be strengthened this year (2014).

There too, discussion on sexuality is taking place. But the bishops have so far avoided engaging with the theological case for opening up marriage to same-sex couples, and clergy who marry risk being punished.

One of those who responded to the consultation was "a supernumerary Methodist minister in a committed relationship of 33 years and in a civil partnership since they became possible. I hope that in my lifetime I will be able to have that converted to marriage and know that what I believe is blessed by God might be blessed by our church."

[Material from this article was first published in June and July 2014, based on two news and comment pieces]

Chapter Twenty-Two

The Archbishop of York challenged over discrimination against married gay chaplain

In October 2014, protesters at Southwell Minster criticised the Archbishop of York John Sentamu for discriminating against a married gay chaplain, Jeremy Pemberton. This meant that he could not take up a job at a local NHS trust.

Pemberton had been selected by Sherwood Forest Hospitals NHS Foundation Trust as chaplaincy and bereavement manager. But he was refused a licence by acting Bishop for Southwell and Nottingham, Richard Inwood, who consulted Sentamu.

House of Bishops guidance issued in early 2014 stated that marrying a same-sex partner went against church teaching and would not be appropriate for clergy. But in some dioceses the penalties are far less severe . Pemberton remains a chaplain at United Lincolnshire Hospitals.

He has filed an employment tribunal claim but his case is complicated by the fact that the NHS is generally an equal opportunities employer. What is more, if he had been a layperson (as some chaplains are), official church policy would have been to accept his conscientious decision.

The archbishop was reopening the recently refurbished Archbishop's Palace, home to some of his predecessors. These included Cardinal Wolsey, right-hand man to Henry VIII, founder of the Church of England.

One of the notable differences from the Roman Catholic past was that priests were allowed to enter into legal marriages. Those not called to celibacy had previously struggled or, in some cases, had secret relationships – a less than ideal situation.

Heterosexual clergy as well as laypersons have, since the reformation, been allowed to enjoy the intimacy and companionship of marriage and to face its challenges.. But this has been denied to those in love with members of the same sex.

Now that the law has changed to allow equal marriage, some feel it is right to make this pledge. Many theologians today believe that committed same-sex partnerships are morally acceptable and most church members agree. People who are not lesbian, gay, bisexual or transgender (LGBT) themselves often have friends or relatives who are.

However, senior clergy in the Church of England have been afraid of upsetting the minority passionately opposed to letting clergy and congregations act in line with their own consciences, as happens on various other matters.

The bishops are also under pressure from leaders of certain other provinces, some of whom are opposed even to basic human rights for their own LGBT members, and are unwilling to consider interpretations of the Bible which differ from their own. However, Church of England leaders are increasingly aware that their stance is undermining mission and ministry.

Those who took part in the protest included Peter Tatchell, Davis Mac-Iyalla, Tracy Byrne and the Rev Christina Beardsley. Changing Attitude, the Lesbian and Gay Christian Movement (to which I belong) and the Peter Tatchell Foundation were represented.

Tatchell urged Sentamu to repent since "discrimination is not compatible with Christian values." The archbishop responded that he could not comment since legal action was pending.

Whatever the outcome of the tribunal, controversy over harsh treatment of LGBT clergy such as Pemberton is undermining the church's ability to witness to the good news of God's love for all.

It might be wise for the Church of England to return to the official position set out in the Thirty-Nine Articles of Religion during the reformation: "Bishops, Priests, and Deacons, are not commanded by God's Law, either to vow the estate of single life, or to abstain from marriage: therefore it is lawful for them... to marry at their own discretion, as they shall judge the same to serve better to godliness."

[An earlier version of this article first appeared in October 2014]

Chapter Twenty-Three

After Synod, the Catholic debate on sexuality continues

A statement issued at the end of a Synod on the Family in the Autumn of 2014 pulled back from a bolder stance on including divorced and lesbian, gay, bisexual and transgender (LGBT) people. However, in a major advance, sexuality is now being debated more openly in the Roman Catholic church.

In recent decades and in many countries attitudes have shifted considerably on sexual ethics both in the pews and among theologians. Although less obviously, the emphasis has also changed to some extent in official doctrine.

The two-week discussion among bishops is the start of a build-up to a broader Synod in a year's time. Over the next few months, amidst a greater openness under Pope Francis, calls for a more just and welcoming attitude will be widely heard.

Too far or not far enough?
The official position of the Roman Catholic church has long been that the only right place for sex is within marriage, which cannot be dissolved and in which sex should always be open to conception if possible. However, some marriages are annulled. Also couples can still marry although unable to have babies, or if they use timing to reduce the chance of conceiving for the purposes of family planning.

Many theologians argue for a very different approach to sexuality and, in practice, this is favoured by numerous parishioners. Many today use contraceptives and want people who have experienced marital breakdown to be treated mercifully. Increasing numbers also welcome lesbian, gay, bisexual and transgender (LGBT) people and often support committed loving partnerships.

However, the hierarchy has been far from encouraging to those expressing dissenting views, sometimes using disciplinary measures to stifle debate. And the language used has on occasions been cold and off-putting.

An example was a 1986 Vatican letter which stated that "Although the particular inclination of the homosexual person is not a sin, it is...ordered toward an intrinsic moral evil; and thus... an objective disorder", though it added that "It is deplorable that homosexual persons have been and are the object of violent malice in speech or in action."

The election in 2013 of Cardinal Jorge Mario Bergoglio of Argentina, who became Pope Francis, marked a shift of tone. He had already spoken out in favour of a less legalistic, more pastoral approach.

While he did not himself propose any major doctrinal change, those senior clergy in favour of greater inclusion were given greater scope to put their case. What is more, especially in a church where reason is valued along with the Bible and tradition, pastoral encounters with people in diverse settings help provide a store of knowledge about what helps or hinders holiness. This can influence ethical thinking.

After Catholics internationally were asked about their views and experiences – itself a breakthrough – he convened a gathering of bishops in Rome to talk about family life.

A Relatio *post disceptationem* (report after debate) on the discussion issued halfway through the Synod surprised some people by its warm tone towards those long treated frostily in official pronouncements. This included cohabiting couples, divorced and remarried people excluded from communion and lesbians and gays.

It stated that, "Homosexuals have gifts and qualities to offer to the Christian community" and asked if it might be possible to value their sexual orientation. It even noted, with regard to same-sex unions that "there are cases in which mutual aid to the point of sacrifice constitutes a precious support in the life of the partners."

Not surprisingly, there was a backlash by some 'traditionalist' bishops. The final draft watered down some of the more radical proposals and certain paragraphs failed to get the required two-thirds majority because some participants thought they went too far, others that they did not go far enough.

Nevertheless, debate has been opened up on key issues in a way which has not happened since the Second Vatican Council in the 1960s. This is likely to intensify in the run-up to another, wider, Synod in a year's time.

Francis himself sounded far from discouraged in his closing speech, pointing out that "we still have one year to mature, with true spiritual discernment, the proposed ideas and to find concrete solutions to so many difficulties and innumerable challenges that families must confront."

Cardinal Vincent Nichols, the Archbishop of Westminster and one of the bishops who has promoted a more pastoral and inclusive approach, also struck a positive chord when he was interviewed by BBC radio. He emphasised the new openness: "people expressed themselves freely and frankly, which is exactly what the Pope asked them to do." To him, "this Synod is the first movement of a rather long concerto."

He pointed out that there was some encouragement for people in second marriages. But he felt that even the final draft did not go far enough in making a commitment to respect, welcome and value lesbian and gay people, and expressed the hope that the church will continue to move forward through dialogue and discernment.

This is likely to be a broad process drawing in the laity as well as clergy. In a talk in October, Cardinal Walter Kasper emphasised that the Pope wanted "the People of God, every single one them, to participate in the church", the National Catholic Reporter stated. Francis is a "gift of God", he said.

Tradition and change
The Roman Catholic hierarchy has a (sometimes deserved) reputation for inflexibility – or, as some would regard it, praiseworthy persistence in doctrine and practice. However, in reality, there have been huge shifts, for instance from a rather anti-sexual stance where celibacy was favoured, and in attitudes to women.

In recent decades, even 'traditionalist' popes helped to re-orientate the emphasis on marriage being mainly for the purpose of procreation, highlighting the importance of a couple's love.

In a series of lectures by John Paul II on the theology of the body, given from 1979 to1984, he suggested that the relationship between spouses was of great importance, linking this with key theological themes including the Holy Trinity.

Revisiting the beginning of Genesis, he wrote that the human "becomes the image of God not so much in the moment of solitude as in the moment of communion. Right 'from the beginning,' he is not only an image in which the solitude of a person who rules the world is reflected, but also, and essentially, an image of an inscrutable divine communion of persons."

In a 1994 'Letter to families', he added that "In the light of the New Testament it is possible to discern how the primordial model of the family is to be sought in God himself, in the Trinitarian mystery of his life" (emphasis in original).

Benedict XVIII's 2005 encyclical 'God is love' went further, locating married love in the wider context of the loving nature of God and affirming that the erotic could be positive.

Referring to the Song of Songs, he suggested that "Love is indeed 'ecstasy', not in the sense of a moment of intoxication, but rather as a journey, an ongoing exodus out of the closed inward-looking self towards its liberation through self-giving, and thus towards authentic self-discovery and indeed the discovery of God: 'Whoever seeks to gain his life will lose it, but whoever loses his life will preserve it' (Luke 17:33), as Jesus says throughout the Gospels."

However, love cannot be confined to a family unit but must go further: "The rich man (cf. Luke 16:19–31) begs from his place of torment that his brothers be informed about what happens to those who simply ignore the poor man in need. Jesus takes up this cry for help as a warning to help us return to the right path. The parable of the Good Samaritan (cf. Luke 10:25–37)" clarifies that "Anyone who needs me, and whom I can help, is my neighbour."

He highlighted the need for the church to take up the work of love more widely through charity, seeking justice and acting with compassion. "Love is the light – and in the end, the only light – that can always illuminate a world grown dim and give us the courage needed to keep living and working. Love is possible, and we are able to practise it because we are created in the image of God", he wrote.

Revisiting the theology of sexuality

'The ways of love', an international Catholic conference on the pastoral care of LGBT people, was held in early October 2014, just before the Synod on the Family met. Speakers included Geoffrey Robinson, a now-retired auxiliary bishop who served in Sydney, Australia.

"There is no possibility of a change in the teaching of the Catholic Church on homosexual acts unless and until there is first a change in its teaching on heterosexual acts," he suggested.

The official position is "that God created human sex for two reasons: as the means by which new human life is brought into being (the procreative aspect) and as a means of expressing and fostering love between a couple (the unitive aspect... the use of sex is 'according to nature' only when it serves both of these God-given purposes, and that both are truly present only within marriage, and even then only when intercourse is open to new life", he explained.

He questioned the assumptions this involved about nature and God and whether the teaching was based on assertions rather than evidence. While "the unitive and procreative elements are foundational aspects of marriage as an institution of the whole human race", he asked why these had to be present in every marriage and act of sexual intimacy.

For instance a "couple might decide that they already have several children and that they are both financially and psychologically unable to add to their family. On what basis is it claimed that they would be acting against God's will?" There are "problems when human beings claim that they know the mind of God."

Attention to "the experience of millions of people in the very human endeavour of seeking to combine sex, love and the procreation of new life in the midst of the turbulence of human sexuality and the complexities of human life" was important, he argued.

This applied also to lesbians and gays: "Why should we turn to some abstraction in determining what is natural rather than to the actual lived experience of human beings? Why should we say that homosexuals are acting against nature when they are acting in accordance with the only nature they have ever experienced?" Such a claim "brings the whole concept of natural law into disrepute."

Sexual ethics should be more deeply rooted in the teaching of Jesus, he argued. He suggested a "move to an ethic that:
1. sees any offence against God as being brought about, not by the sexual act in and of itself, but by the harm caused to human beings;
2. speaks in terms of persons and relationships rather than physical acts;
3. draws its ideas of what is natural from reality rather than abstractions;
4. draws consciously and directly on the gospels,
5. and then builds an argument on these foundations rather than on unproven assertions."

This was not simply about embracing the prevailing culture. "In its simplest terms, the Church is saying that, because love is all-important in human life and because sex is so vital a way of expressing love, sex is serious, while modern society has become more and more accepting of the most casual sexual activity, even when in no way related to love or relationship", he wrote. "On this basic point I find myself instinctively more in sympathy with the views of the Church than with those of modern society."

He suggested that "we must take the harm that can be caused by sexual desire very seriously", and raised the question: "Are we moving towards a genuinely Christian ethic if we base our sexual actions on a profound respect for the relationships that give meaning, purpose and direction to human life, and on loving our neighbour as we would want our neighbour to love us?"

Many others in the Roman Catholic church also have been reflecting on how Gospel values may be reflected more truly in approaches to sexuality, and the Synod on the Family has encouraged greater openness about the diversity of views and experiences.

What is more, Catholics are part of a wider Christian community where numerous others have been thinking seriously about sexual ethics. Moving beyond the use of depersonalising language and mere assertions which fail to convince, while remaining true to what is richest in the Christian heritage, is a challenging task for the churches as a whole.

[An earlier version of this article was first published in October 2014]

Chapter Twenty-Four

No rejoicing here: the Scottish Episcopal Church's marriage guidance

Many Christians regard their wedding day as one of the most joyful, and spiritually significant, in their lives. Those preparing to celebrate marriage are part of the body of the church, whose other members may wish to rejoice with and support them as they make a costly, as well as fulfilling commitment.

In Scotland, for the first time same-sex as well as opposite-sex couples will be able to get legally married. The new law takes effect on 16 December 2014, with weddings booked from 31 December.

In many churches there, as elsewhere, opinion is divided and discussions are taking place on how best to honour different views of what conscience demands. Meanwhile institutional churches need to provide pastoral care to those who feel called to pledge their love publicly to their life-partner, as well as to those opposed.

There is little sense of this in the Scottish Episcopal Church's College of Bishops' Guidance for Clergy and Lay Readers in the light of the Marriage and Civil Partnership (Scotland) Act 2014. This document is perhaps even more grim and threatening than the Church of England bishops' February 2014 'pastoral' guidance.

It begins by explaining that the guidance applies while the church is "currently in a period of discussion regarding its understanding of same-sex relationships" and, for the time being, marriage is regarded as "a physical, spiritual and mystical union of one man and one woman..."

What is more, within the new legal framework, "Pending any decision on the part of the SEC to 'opt in', our clergy are not able to solemnise same-sex marriages or register religious civil partnerships." This is true enough.

The tone then descends from the factual to the dismal and doom-laden. If any priest holds a marriage ceremony for a same-sex couple which might lead them to believe they are legally married, this would be "a criminal offence."

Grudging permission of sorts is given to clergy who wish to give an informal blessing to couples entering a marriage or civil partnership, provided they consult their bishop, though "The Church cannot give official sanction to informal blessings."

But clergy and lay readers, and those who wish to apply or are training for such roles, are warned against getting married, and instructed to talk to their bishop if considering such a move.

The document then underlines the legal freedom "to hold and impart views, including opposition to marriage of same-sex couples", provided such "comments or behaviour do not incite hatred and are not intended to cause public disorder". There is no mention of freedom of conscience within the church itself for those in favour of equal marriage.

Such a negative and forbidding tone might be understandable if almost all members of SEC believed that same-sex relationships were morally wrong. But in reality, opinion has shifted, both among theologians and in the pews. Many Scottish Christians – Anglicans included – believe it would be wrong to discourage faithful, self-giving, lifelong relationships through which partners can better understand, and reflect, divine love.

The bishops could have issued a very different document recognising the variety of views and experiences within the church while highlighting the legal situation, and advising clergy that some congregations might react negatively if they were married. That they did not do so perhaps reflects a habit of fear of those most opposed to inclusion, combined with pastoral insensitivity to those in favour.

Pouring a bucket of cold water over couples in love and their families and friends is not the best approach to mission and ministry. Once again, Christians seeking a more just and welcoming church will be left with the challenge of trying to limit the damage done by official statements.

* The College of Bishops' guidance can be found here: http://www.thinkinganglicans.org.uk/uploads/College%20of%20Bishops%20Gui

[An earlier version of this article was first published in December 2014]

Postscript: In June 2015, the General Synod of the Scottish Episcopal Church agreed to begin a process that could lead to the opening up of marriage to same-gender couples by 2017.

Chapter Twenty-Five

Better understanding of international church conflicts over sexuality

In various denominations, debates on sexual ethics and the treatment of minorities have sparked heated international controversy. This is sometimes seen as a conflict between a 'liberal' west and 'conservative' south. But the reality is more complicated.

Both acceptance of, and hostility towards, LGBT people can be found across continents and cultures. And, while those most opposed to celebrating, or even allowing, same-sex partnerships sometimes claim to be protecting their people from the influence of the west, their actions serve to reinforce global power imbalances and western domination.

International divisions and a show of independence

In January 2014, the Nigerian president Goodluck Jonathan signed into law draconian legislation targeting an already criminalised LGBT minority, along with their families and friends. A mother who let her gay son live with his partner under her roof, or a theologian putting forward a biblical case for accepting same-sex relationships, risked being jailed for ten years.

This was praised by various church leaders. The decision "not to bow to international pressure in the promotion of unethical and immoral practices of same sex union and other related vices is indeed a courageous one," declared Catholic Archbishop Ignatius Kaigama.

He commended the president for resisting a "conspiracy of the developed world to make our country and continent, the dumping ground for the promotion of all immoral practices, that have continued to debase the purpose of God for man in the area of creation and morality, in their own countries." Human rights defenders in Africa and internationally had pointed out that the new law would violate fundamental principles and persuaded western governments to distance themselves.

Later however, at an international Synod on the Family in October, Kaigama distanced himself from the criminalisation of LGBT people while still resisting recognition of same-sex partnerships. Though over 200,000 Nigerians die of AIDS each year, he condemned international organisations which "give us condoms and artificial contraceptives. Those are not the things we want. We want food, we want education, we want good roads, regular light, and so on" – as if these were mutually exclusive, and Nigerian anti-HIV activists had not sought affordable protection.

Several other supporters of the law remain unrepentant, including the Anglican Archbishop Nicholas Okoh, who also praised the president, stating that those opposed to this law were rebelling against God. Okoh had earlier helped to whip up support for the bill, for instance spuriously claiming in 2010 that Nigeria was at risk from an "invading army of homosexuality, lesbianism and bisexual lifestyle" and that "The church in the west had vowed to use their money to spread the homosexual lifestyle in African societies and churches."

In Uganda too, Anglican leaders had backed a punitive anti-homosexuality bill, after it had been amended to remove the death penalty and the requirement that clergy and professionals inform on LGBT people in their care. A spokesperson told the Christian Post in 2014 that "we support Uganda's national sovereignty and our right to self-determination in establishing this law, and will not bow to international pressure to change that part of our culture that aligns with our biblical convictions."

Such leaders have expressed unwillingness to be in fellowship with those who treat LGBT people equally, and the Archbishop of Canterbury Justin Welby told a Times interviewer in December 2014 that there may end up being "a sort of temporary separation" in the Anglican Communion,

While many opponents of full inclusion are less extreme, in other denominations such as the United Methodists, international tensions have arisen over the issue of same-sex partnerships. Some explain such differences as the result of a cultural and spiritual rift between the south, especially Africa, and more liberal (especially western) countries.

"Revulsion against homosexuals is ancient, deep and, in its way, sincere, even if some of the politicians leading the backlash do so for cynical reasons," according to an Economist leader on 'The gay divide'. "Emerging countries in Asia and Latin America have generally grown kinder to gay people as they have grown richer, more open and more democratic. The hope is that as Africa and the Arab world catch up, they will follow suit... For those who cling to the notion of progress, it is hard to believe that tolerance will not spread."

Yet almost half a century ago, UK parliamentarians were pondering why their own part of the globe was so much less tolerant than others such as the Arab world.

Homosexuality "is not a thing of advanced decadence, or something which has come to light only lately, in societies which have become over-civilised. It is something which all history has known," the Earl of Huntingdon pointed out in May 1965, as the House of Lords debated whether gay sex should be decriminalised. "Some societies, such as the Arab or the Eastern, accept it; others react strongly against it." This is a reminder of how quickly attitudes can change, both positively and negatively.

At that time, LGBT people in the UK could be evicted or sacked and if male, locked up, or pressured into undergoing one of the 'therapies' which were usually ineffectual and often deeply damaging. Extortion was rife: the law was nicknamed the 'blackmailer's charter'. Elsewhere in the west, things had got even worse.

Just twenty years before in economically advanced, technologically sophisticated Germany, gays and lesbians had been herded into concentration camps in terrible conditions, where some died. Those in charge thought this represented the pinnacle of science and morality.

Meanwhile, in much of the world, people tended to be indifferent to same-sex relationships provided these were discreet or even, in some cultures, created space for those whose sexuality or gender identity was different from that of most others. (Examples include the 'yan daudu among the Hausa of Nigeria and hijras of India.)

148

Some of these parts of the world have since become hostile. Elsewhere attitudes have become more accepting, but a vocal minority continues to promote discrimination in secular as well as religious settings, at home and abroad.

Social change, clashes and a colonial legacy

Over the past few centuries, the forces of modernity wrought huge changes across the world, some life-enhancing and others destructive. A number of prominent figures championed freedom and dignity for all, while others sought to exploit their neighbours more scientifically, devising elaborate theories to justify social inequality and sometimes violence. There were also people who looked back nostalgically to a more predictable, less impersonal world – even if this perpetuated feudal privilege – or to a more distant romanticised past.

Unsurprisingly Christians could be found on different sides of various conflicts taking place, and the number of churches grew rapidly. There was a sense of liberation in the message some conveyed that ordinary Christians no longer had to rely on clergy or rulers to tell them about God but could read this themselves in the Bible, translated into their own language. But new tyrannies rose when leaders demanded that their own selection of biblical verses, sometimes questionably translated, represented ultimate truth on particular topics.

Even as sexual minorities were becoming more visible, repression of those with same-sex partners became more systematic, often at the same time as other forms of discrimination such as anti-semitism.

As Europeans conquered large swathes of the world, they were often shocked at the 'immorality' of the 'natives'. The versions of Christianity which accompanied expanding empires reflected their founders' cultural assumptions and reinforced the legal frameworks they introduced.

This generally included criminalising 'sodomy', sometimes described as the 'Oriental vice'. In Africa there were diverse traditions, some of which openly permitted sexual relationships between partners of the same biological sex, but this did not fit the new norms. The Bible was also quoted in attempts to justify racism and even the slave trade, though some Christians in the west opposed the worst excesses of colonial rule.

Colonial education "was a project of social engineering which aimed to inscribe superiority on sexual formations which aligned with colonial notions of 'good' identity. Civilized and 'proper' men were expected to behave like European men in everything including sexual conduct. Civilized and 'proper' women were those whose sexual conducts were in line with Victorian codes", wrote C Otutubikey Izugbara in 'Patriarchal Ideology and Discourses of Sexuality in Nigeria, African Regional Sexuality Resource Centre, 2004. So "homosexuality, same-sex erotic desire, and relationships that do not clearly reinforce male control of life spheres" were treated "as 'improper' if not dangerous."

Yet Christian faith was inevitably reinterpreted to some extent wherever it took root: laws were not always enforced and repression met not only with conformity but also resistance. On the one hand faith, was often entwined with the rigid notions of masculinity, femininity and propriety prevalent in the west, sometimes combined with local patriarchal traditions. On the other hand, it could inspire struggles for justice and freedom.

In the early-mid twentieth century, anti-colonial movements gained ground across Asia, Africa and Latin America, often leading to ostensible independence. A generation of church leaders from these continents faced the challenge of separating what was most valuable in their faith tradition from alien cultural trappings while continuing to promote scientific progress. At the same time, along with other Christians across the world, they confronted the aftermath of horrific human rights abuses and the task of building a world where such atrocities were less likely to happen.

Thwarted progress, church divisions
Regrettably some of the widely-held hopes of that time, of people treating one another more justly and peacefully across social barriers and mutual cultural enrichment, were not fully realised. This was largely because those wielding greatest power interna-

tionally were unwilling to loosen their grip, for instance sponsoring coups against progressive southern leaders. But members of local elites who joined forces with them also played a part. Rivalry between western powers and the Soviet Union and its allies was also significant, as each tried to increase its influence in Africa, Asia and Latin America.

Religion, along with other forms of culture, became a site of intense (if not always visible) struggle. Systems of belief and types of worship which bolstered existing patterns of wealth and privilege or distracted people from their often wretched living conditions were favoured, and attempts made to win support away from more radical Christian organisations and networks.

Inculturation (or indigenisation) – the inclusion of aspects of local cultures (if not at odds with core Christian values) in the way that Christianity is taught and understood – has been central to the spread of faith from the earliest times. As churches sought to become more authentically rooted in colonial and post-colonial societies, this took various forms.

This approach could bring worship to life and enable the church to engage with the hopes and fears of parishioners. However, it could also reinforce rigid gender divisions and other forms of hierarchy when reactionary forms of Christianity coincided with existing social divisions. There was also a risk of oversimplifying 'tradition' and ignoring the varying forms it took and its dynamic nature, and of glossing over the issues of power and justice, so central to the Bible.

For example to Kenyan theologian John Mbiti, in his 1973 work Love and Marriage in Africa, "having sexual intercourse or intimacy with a person of the same sex is immoral, abnormal, unnatural, and a danger to society" since "two people of the same sex cannot establish the kind of relationship which can only come from a husband and wife relationship". He claimed that, from an African cultural and religious perspective, "It is on [in?] the creative dimension of marriage that you in fact become co-creator with God. In procreation you are fostering God's creative work in the world."

Procreation was, and remains, heavily emphasised in certain

African and Asian cultures and childless women are stigmatised. Nor is this unique to the south: for instance, older Germans may remember a time when motherhood was emphasised as a social obligation. But if Jesus was bold enough to question such attitudes, which can be deeply oppressive of women and sexual minorities, even in first-century Asia (e.g. Luke 11.27–28, Matthew 19.10–12), his followers today might reasonably be expected to follow suit.

At the same time, amidst growing urbanisation, LGBT visibility was increasing. It was all too easy (and sometimes convenient for global powers and their local partners) for people in countries wracked by blighted hopes to take out their frustrations on their neighbours and scapegoat ethnic or sexual minorities or others 'different' in some way. This in turn met with resistance.

Meanwhile, right-wingers in the west strove to undermine liberation theologies and those Christians opposed to their favoured regimes (including apartheid South Africa). For example, the Institute on Religion and Democracy (IRD), a right-wing think-tank, persuaded the makers of US television documentary series '60 Minutes' to smear the World Council of Churches and the National Council of Churches for supposedly diverting funds from American churchgoers to finance revolutionary violence (a decision the producer later regretted). Images included a collection plate being passed round at a United Methodist service, Cuban leader Fidel Castro and a murdered missionary in Zimbabwe.

This and other propaganda efforts helped to undermine mainstream denominations, while IRD and other bodies backed by far-right millionaires proved themselves skilled at tapping into disaffection among those churchgoers across the world who were worried about theological 'liberalism'.

Such organisations were also adept at exploiting resentment among certain churches in the south at their dependence on western Christians for funding, as well as at the condescending attitudes which some occasionally encountered. The notion that churches in Africa, Asia and Latin America, though materially poor, were spiritually richer than those in wealthier societies became popular. Some in the west who felt guilty about imperialism bought into this, stereotypical though it was.

Cry for life: following the Jesus of faith

A spectrum of views on sexuality, along with other issues, had developed among Christians in the south. In 1992 an assembly of the Ecumenical Association of Third World Theologians, meeting in Nairobi, Kenya, issued a powerful statement: 'A cry for life: the spirituality of the Third World':

> The Third World cry for life is one multi-tonal cry. It reflects the various ways oppression assaults Third World life. It carries the cries of countries protesting economic indenture to IMF and the World Bank... It carries the cries of refugees, children, displaced people and those afflicted with AIDS, the cries against the discrimination of homosexuals, of those who suffer from economic oppression ... It carries the cries of Blacks against apartheid. It carries the cries or the dalits against the apartheid or caste oppression. It carries the cries of women against patriarchal dominance and sexual violence...

> Our analysis of the global context is incomplete if we do not address ourselves to the growing divisions among our own people in the Third World and the violence committed on one another... Our elites perpetuate their dominance over the majority, increasing the misery of the poor. Among our religious institutions there are churches in most places which tend to be elitist, racist and sexist. By and large these churches have lost the moral credibility to respond to the cry of the world for life...

> To follow the Jesus of faith, first, is to follow one who is unrelentingly critical of the power relations in the structures of society that engender injustice and oppression. Second, it is to follow someone who believes that it is necessary to embody in community our vision of the new, more just society, as well as the discipline to work to realize our vi-

sion in this world. Third, following the Jesus of faith means following one who was dedicated to feeding the hungry, clothing the naked and fighting for the liberation of oppressed people...

God is present to us in him...

He comes so that we may have life and have it in abundance; he comes that we may be one; he comes not to be served but to serve and to lay down his life as a ransom for many (John 1:10; Mark 10:45)...

Commitment might lead to harassment, marginalization, ecclesiastical sanctions, arrest, torture or even death. To be committed means there is no cost too great when one joins God's mission to make the world a place where life is valued for all of God's creation...

The fullest democratic participation of all persons at all levels is a means of treating all persons and groups with dignity, of providing space for ethnic and cultural identity and spiritual development, of promoting relationships of mutuality irrespective of gender and sexual orientation, as well as of (at least) reducing exploitation, competition and waste...

It is the call of Jesus Christ to all disciples to take up our cross and go forward towards a more hopeful future for all.

The struggle of lesbians and gays against discrimination was here seen as an integral part of a wider movement towards a world freed from injustice of every kind, where destructive forces are confronted so that all have the chance to enjoy life in its abundance. That churches could be part of the problem as well as of the solution was also recognised.

'A cry for life' suggested that:

For many centuries the Bible has been interpreted from the point of view of a western patriarchal and dominant culture...

The people are now freeing the Bible from these wrong interpretations...

In the Bible itself one can see the struggle of people against the manipulation of scribes and the teachers of the law. The Bible teaches us to get over those texts which are oppressive in the new context. The Bible is self-critical and has the capacity to expose the oppressive elements in the lives, traditions and cultures of our people.

A new millennium

Some church leaders were more open to questioning the status quo than others. Famously in 2005, in response to South African archbishops questioning why Anglicans were so focused on homosexuality when Africa faced pressing issues such as war, AIDS and poverty, their Nigerian counterpart Peter Akinola told the media, "I didn't create poverty. This church didn't create poverty. Poverty is not an issue, human suffering is not an issue at all, they were there before the creation of mankind."

This is not to say that such churches were not engaged in charitable activity. But (with some exceptions) seriously challenging the imbalances of power at home and abroad that led to so much wretchedness was a different matter, t despite the Bible having far more to say about social and economic justice than about sexuality. The siphoning off of mineral wealth, manipulation of markets and exploitation of cheap labour profoundly affected all but the wealthiest in the south. However, certain Christian leaders tried to make out that inclusive sister-churches were the real imperialists (though those attacked were not all in the west).

Some moderates bought into this, blocking progress in their own countries to placate these leaders while not expecting the same standards from them which might be required of westerners. For instance, anti-inclusive senior clergy from the south were not expected to engage in rigorous theological debate, just express their displeasure and quote a few Bible verses, or even to consult those local LGBT people who lives were profoundly affected by their pronouncements. Adopting such double standards, however well-intended, is itself a form of racism. But not everyone bought into this approach and in North America and elsewhere, several churches moved towards greater acceptance, triggering intensified opposition.

"US conservatives mobilized African clergy in their domestic culture wars at a time when the demographic center of Christianity is shifting from the global North to the global South," wrote Kapya Kaoma in 'Globalizing the Culture Wars', Political Research Associates, 2009. "Traditionally, evangelical African churches have been biblically and doctrinally orthodox but progressive on such social issues as national liberation and poverty, making them natural partners of the politically liberal western churches."

But in some instances, "Right-wing groups have enticed African religious leaders to reject funding from mainline denominations – which require documentation of how the money is spent – and instead to accept funds from conservatives... Christian Right activists use rhetoric about 'family values' to foment homophobia in Africa with disastrous consequences."

Meanwhile some Anglican, Catholic and other churches in Uganda, Nigeria and beyond were benefiting from funding from the US government which, under George W Bush, was pursuing global dominance with renewed vigour. Through the President's Emergency Plan for AIDS Relief (PEPFAR) and USAID, money was lavished on faith-based organisations (FBOs) in the USA and Africa to combat AIDS and its impact.

These churches often cared conscientiously for the sick and orphaned, but also benefited from the gratitude and dependence of those people forced to rely on them for help. And all too frequently, ideology took precedence over saving lives, for instance promoting abstinence and fidelity but withholding the option of condoms, and accurate information for men having sex with men.

To quote a 2011 paper by Comfort David and other researchers: 'Comparing religious and secular NGOs in Nigeria: are faith-based organizations distinctive?' published by the University of Birmingham, FBOs "believe that they have a responsibility" to spread their religion "and often see their humanitarian activities as a means to that end... FBOs display symbols of their religion in the dress of their staff, in their facilities and on their vehicles."

Indeed, a USAID 2013 memorandum on "whether the Inter-Religious Council of Uganda used the President's Emergency Plan for AIDS Relief (PEPFAR) funds to support Uganda's Anti-Homosexuality Bill" was inconclusive, finding that "USAID is paying for IRCU activities that are outside the scope of its agreement", though it was unclear what this included.

Though the centre-left government of Barack Obama (who is of part-Kenyan descent) placed more emphasis on human rights, to the anger of some church leaders, FBOs have continued to receive extensive funding. The bolstering of the status and resources of associated churches is a form of western 'interference' to which they do not seem to object.

Hope of a different world
In much of the world, those strongly against inclusion may at present seem to have the upper hand. Yet bold people still organise for change, often seeing this as part of a wider movement for a more just and loving world.

In August 2014, over thirty African leaders from ten countries, meeting in South Africa with World Council of Churches support, issued the KwaZulu Natal Declaration, calling on all religious institutions – especially churches – to "care for the least amongst us as Christ has done" and "create safe spaces for encounter with the sexual diversity within the body of Christ".

A WCC gathering later in the year in India, with delegates from across the world, focused mainly on economic justice and the environment. However, the focus was on achieving an Economy of Life, "measured by the quality of life of those dwelling in the margins (Matthew 10:42)" and in which "all people – regardless of class, gender, race, caste, sexual orientation, indigenous identity and religion – have a voice and participate in decision-making at all levels."

Ultimately, if the Holy Spirit is at work in even the bleakest situations, the fruits of the earth will be more justly shared and truth and compassion will win out over scapegoating and prejudice.

[An earlier version of this article was first published in December 2014]

Part 3: Looking afresh at the Bible and tradition

Some people believe either that the Bible and Christian tradition contain nothing relevant to people in today's world or that these are strongly negative about any pattern of family life other than heterosexual marriage based on rigid gender roles. Many people, myself included, would disagree.

A range of reflections in this part of the book, covering chapters 26–32 explore various topics related to love, sexuality, gender and family life. While some of the biblical passages often referred to during debates on same-sex partnerships are examined, this is not an attempt to offer a systematic approach. However, it is hoped that some of the thoughts set out here will prompt others to consider such issues afresh, even if they come up with different conclusions.

Chapter Twenty-Six

Fruitful love: beyond the civil and legal in partnerships

The day of Friday 22 July 2011 was a terrible one for the people of Norway. Extreme-right winger Anders Behring Breivik bombed government buildings in Oslo, an action which resulted in eight deaths, and started shooting at a youth camp, killing 69 more. Many others were injured or traumatised. Yet amidst the horror, there were incidents of heroism.

This included the rescue of forty or so children by a married couple, who had been having a picnic when they heard the commotion and saw youngsters fleeing. They headed into the lake in a boat and pulled young people out of the water, taking them to safety on the shore. The side of the boat was riddled with bullets. Nevertheless they went back and forth four times, repeatedly risking their lives to save more of the children who had leapt into the lake.

Both partners, Hege Dalen and Toril Hansen, were women. In Norway, marriage is open to same-sex as well as opposite-sex couples.

One of the theological arguments sometimes used against same-sex partnership is that it is not 'fruitful', unlike heterosexual marriage. The parents of those children whose lives they saved might disagree.

The value of partnership
This raises the issue of what can be regarded as 'fruitfulness', and indeed why partnership should be valued, from a Christian perspective. One long-recognised purpose is companionship and mutual support

for better, for worse,
for richer, for poorer,
in sickness and in health,

to love and to cherish,
till death us do part

to quote the Church of England marriage service.

"It is not good that the man should be alone; I will make him a helper as his partner," declares God in a creation myth in the biblical book of Genesis 2. In marriage "a man leaves his father and his mother and clings to his wife, and they become one flesh", a passage Jesus later quotes in the Gospels.

The author of Ecclesiastes advises : "Two are better than one, because they have a good reward for their toil. For if they fall, one will lift up the other; but woe to one who is alone and falls and does not have another to help. Again, if two lie together, they keep warm; but how can one keep warm alone?" (Ecclesiastes 4.9–11).

Moreover, in marriage, desire can be directed towards enjoyment without injustice. The sexual impulse, and erotic love, can be powerful. As one of the lovers in the Song of Songs proclaims (Song of Solomon 8.6–7):

love is strong as death,
passion fierce as the grave.
Its flashes are flashes of fire,
a raging flame.
Many waters cannot quench love,
neither can floods drown it.
If one offered for love
all the wealth of one's house,
it would be utterly scorned

In one of the Epistles, Paul advises: "because of the temptation to sexual immorality, each man should have his own wife and each woman her own husband" (1 Corinthians 7.2). In modern times, there has been increasing recognition that justice requires not only respecting others' marriages but also equality between partners.

Love, of various kinds, is perceived in Scripture and Christian tradition as enabling spiritual growth. For instance, Jesus is portrayed in the Gospels as caring for many but also enjoying intimate friendships; and 1 John 4 urges: "Beloved, let us love one another, because love is from God; everyone who loves is born of God and knows God. Whoever does not love does not know God, for God is love. God's love was revealed among us in this way: God sent his only Son into the world so that we might live through him. In this is love, not that we loved God but that he loved us and sent his Son to be the atoning sacrifice for our sins. Beloved, since God loved us so much, we also ought to love one another. No one has ever seen God; if we love one another, God lives in us, and his love is perfected in us."

It is now widely (though not universally) acknowledged that same-sex, as well as opposite-sex, partnerships can offer space for loving, self-giving and lifelong companionship, and enable partners to grow in likeness to Christ. "Persons living in faithful heterosexual and homosexual partnerships, can through sharing sexual love be 'the grace of God to each other'. The fruit of the Spirit can grow in that soil," said the Anglican theologian and former Bishop of Salisbury John Austin Baker in a lecture in 1997. "I have seen the face of Christ in the sacrificial support of gay men for their lovers right to the end."

However, lesbian and gay relationships are sometimes condemned as invalid (or at least inferior to heterosexual relationships) on the grounds that they are not 'fruitful'. Though many in such partnerships have children as a result of previous relationships with the opposite sex, artificial insemination or adoption, same-gender intimacy cannot result in conceiving a child, unless one partner is trans or intersex.

Yet, even in Scripture and tradition, what it means to be 'fruitful' is more diverse than some Christians realise.

Fruitfulness in Christian thought

"Be fruitful and multiply, and fill the earth" God tells the humans, male and female, in the creation myth in Genesis 1. This has indeed happened.

It is estimated that the global population at the time of Jesus was just 300 million and it took more than 1600 years to double. Survival was precarious in ancient and mediaeval times: for instance in fourteenth century Europe, waves of epidemics wiped out much of the population. Not surprisingly, it seemed to some that procreation was an important social duty for adults of childbearing age. In addition there was an expectation that skills, tools and in some families, land, were to be handed down to future generations.

But in modern times the world's population grew rapidly, rising from 1.7 billion at the beginning of the twentieth century to 6 billion at its end. By late 2011, it had reached 7 billion. While much poverty, overcrowding and pressure on natural resources arise from the way that society is organised, excessive population growth challenges sustainability.

Many have come to believe that if humankind is to carry out its divinely-mandated responsibility of stewardship of the earth and the many species it sustains, family planning should be encouraged. Hence babies are to be treasured but as persons, not as means to an end.

And having baby after baby may be seen as less desirable than trying to make sure that children who are born (to oneself or others) are properly fed, clothed, sheltered, educated, provided with healthcare and protected from the devastating effects of modern warfare and environmental catastrophe. There are still some faith communities where leaders teach that the use of contraception is selfish but, even in these, laypeople often take a different view.

Meanwhile life expectancy has risen. There have always been some couples in which one or both partners was infertile (sometimes resulting in stigma as well as personal frustration), but now there are many marriages in which the wife or husband is too old to conceive, including partners who married in later life and never had children together.

In addition, there are sizeable numbers of sick and disabled adults, many of them elderly, who need support if they are to enjoy a reasonable quality of life. While some people care for both children and adult relatives or friends, others share caring responsibilities (e.g. for nieces or nephews, grandparents or neighbours) without being biological parents.

It is perhaps easier now than in earlier times to re-examine biblical and traditional concepts of 'fruitfulness' without reading these through the distorting lens of anxiety about having too few children.

In the Old Testament (Hebrew Scripture), fertility is indeed celebrated, but this is not the only way in which the image of plants bearing (or failing to bear) fruit is used. For instance, in Psalm 1 a righteous person is likened to a tree that "yields its fruit in its season", and in Proverbs 8 ,Wisdom tells her listeners that "My fruit is better than gold". In Jeremiah 11, the prophet conveys what he believes is a divine warning: because of the wrongdoing of nations which were once "'a green olive tree, beautiful with good fruit", disaster will come upon them.

In the New Testament, there is a radical shift of emphasis around family life. Jesus himself has no wife or children, and declares that "whoever does the will of God, he is my brother and sister and mother" (Mark 3.21, 31–35). Those who follow the way of love are invited to be part of a new family, united not by heredity but shared commitment to generosity and justice, heralds of a divine commonwealth (Mark 10.28–31).

The concept of fruitfulness is often used. For example, John the Baptist tells those flocking to him, "Bear fruits in keeping with repentance", urging them, "Whoever has two tunics is to share with him who has none, and whoever has food is to do likewise" (Luke 3.7–14). In the Sermon on the Mount (Matthew 5–7), Jesus sets out a vision of a new way of living characterised by love and peace-making, and warns that "A healthy tree cannot bear bad fruit, nor can a diseased tree bear good fruit. Every tree that does not bear good fruit is cut down and thrown into the fire. Thus you will recognise them by their fruits". This is a concept he returns to in Matthew 12 when he is accused of doing his works of mercy and healing by the power of Satan: "Either make the tree good and its fruit good, or make the tree bad and its fruit bad, for the tree is known by its fruit."

In John's Gospel, Jesus tells his followers, "Truly, truly, I say to you, unless a grain of wheat falls into the earth and dies, it remains alone; but if it dies, it bears much fruit" (John 12.24). In John 15, he describes himself as "the true vine, and my Father is the vinedresser. Every branch in me that does not bear fruit he takes away, and every branch that does bear fruit he prunes, that it may bear more fruit. Already you are clean because of the word that I have spoken to you. Abide in me, and I in you. As the branch cannot bear fruit by itself, unless it abides in the vine, neither can you, unless you abide in me." They are to be united in love: "I chose you and appointed you that you should go and bear fruit and that your fruit should abide, so that whatever you ask the Father in my name, he may give it to you. These things I command you, so that you will love one another."

Paul states in Galatians 5 that "the fruit of the Spirit is love, joy, peace, patience, kindness, goodness, faithfulness, gentleness, self-control". According to James, "where jealousy and selfish ambition exist, there will be disorder and every vile practice. But the wisdom from above is first pure, then peaceable, gentle, open to reason, full of mercy and good fruits, impartial and sincere" (James 3.16–17).

Various Christian thinkers through the ages have reflected on such texts. For instance John Chrysostom (347-407), in one of his homilies on the Gospel of Matthew, reflected that "what He had said before, this He establishes now also; that a good tree cannot bring forth evil fruit, nor again can the converse be." In a Treatise on the Love of God, Francis de Sales (1567–1622) suggests that "charity is truly the only fruit of the Holy Ghost, but because this one fruit has an infinity of excellent properties, the Apostle, who wishes to mention some of them by way of example, speaks of this one fruit as of many, because of the multitude of properties which it contains in its unity".

Fruitfulness and partnership

From this perspective, parenthood can indeed be fruitful, not because it adds to the world's population or the size of a particular family, tribe, ethnic group or nation but rather because it can enable people to become more kind, patient, generous and so forth. For example, parents may sit up through the night to care for a sick child, setting aside their own exhaustion. And this love will hopefully overspill to others outside the immediate family circle, for instance, in offering hospitality to one's child's playmate whose own caregivers are absent or neglectful.

However, a loving but childless union which enables partners to grow more compassionate and forgiving, and support one another in acts of peacemaking and mercy, might be more fruitful than that of rich parents who take little interest in their children as persons but rather want heirs to continue to amass wealth in the family business.

An emotionally and sexually intimate partnership is, for many people, a school of love. This is not as romantic as it might sound: fearfulness, selfishness, rivalry and other negative traits may surface, and hard work may be needed to overcome these. Yet this can be a path to spiritual growth, which may manifest itself in small ways or through acts of heroic altruism. Such relationships, whether between opposite-sex or same-sex partners, can help to bring forth good fruit.

Chapter Twenty-Seven

Wedding blessings: friendship across boundaries

Anecdotes can be illuminating as well as entertaining or moving. Sometimes an incident becomes the stuff of family or community legend, and is embroidered in the telling. Even so, it can shed light on the people involved. And, by engaging listeners' imagination and connecting with their experience, it can sometimes encourage them to look afresh at what is around them.

An unusual wedding party

Asian weddings can be big occasions, especially in cultures which emphasise the value of marriage and fertility. Many years ago, a young couple, their families and friends gathered for a wedding feast, where there was much merriment.

"Eat, O friends, and drink; drink your fill, O lovers," ran a popular love-song of the time. In the event, the wine flowed rather too freely, and ran out when the party was still in full swing – a social disaster.

Though the status of women was not high in that society, it was to a widow, wise and sometimes outspoken, that those in charge of the feast turned. She in turn called her son, who with his friends was also among the guests. Unusually for that time, he was unmarried.

He was at first reluctant to act. But he gave way to his mother's insistence, and told those serving to fill some water-jars. When the master of ceremonies tasted what was inside, he told the bridegroom, "Everyone serves the good wine first, and when people have drunk freely, then the poor wine. But you have kept the good wine until now."

Some readers will recognise this as the story of the wedding at Cana, in John 2 (and the love-song as the Song of Solomon). This Gospel is often regarded as largely a theological reflection on Jesus' life and work, which is true, but to me it is also rich in fascinating incidents and characters. Sometimes these involved food or drink, such as his encounter with a Samaritan woman at a well (John 4), in which refreshment was offered and barriers overcome.

John's Gospel (like the others) goes on to tell of many occasions when he brought freedom and healing to those in need, heralding a time of abundance though he himself apparently remained poor and celibate. He also encountered different kinds of families; John 12 describes how he dined in an unusual household made up of two sisters and a brother, whom he loved and whose lives he had transformed when tragedy struck. But he antagonised the powerful and self-righteous, who set out to destroy him.

The following chapter narrates how, shortly before he was arrested and sentenced to death, he had supper with his disciples. There he washed and dried their feet, taking on the role of a servant or wife, showing up the hollowness of the status-seeking and competitiveness that so often affects human relationships.

He urged them too to wash one another's feet, and told them, "Just as I have loved you, you also should love one another. By this everyone will know that you are my disciples, if you have love for one another."

As he hung dying on the cross, and his mother and the disciple whom he loved in a special way stood by, according to John 19, he told her that they would now be mother and son to each other, and this disciple took her into his home. The next chapter recounts how he was the first of Jesus' friends to see the empty tomb.

A partnership through the years
Centuries later, in a different part of Asia, another young couple got married. They were from different ethnic groups and there were some misgivings among their relatives, but they were idealistic and in love, and the wedding went ahead. The couple and their friends and families celebrated, and this time the refreshments did not (as far as I know) run out.

O Thou Who gavest power to love
That we might fix our hearts on Thee,
Preparing us for joys above
By that which here on earth we see

sang those at the wedding, and:

Grant them the joy which brightens earthly sorrow;
Grant them the peace which calms all earthly strife,
And to life's day the glorious unknown morrow
That dawns upon eternal love and life.

They went on to have children, grandchildren and great-grand-children – though one of their daughters was noticeably different from an early age, and ended up partnered with another young woman. They too pledged their commitment to each other, sur-rounded by family and friends.

This Asian couple's marriage was fruitful in other ways too: the husband and wife supported one another in being inspiring teachers, generous neighbours and passionate campaigners for justice. At times they faced hardship, danger and loss, but got through this together.

Many years later, the fresh-faced bride was wrinkled, frail, unsteady, and increasingly forgetful and confused. The dash-ing groom was now grey-haired and weary, though still devoted to his wife. They moved in with their lesbian daughter and her partner, of whom they were deeply fond and who in turn loved them as parents; and this made it possible to cope with domestic tasks and meet care needs.

Another daughter sometimes travelled long distances to help, other family members visited when they could, and care assis-tants too gave and received kindnesses from the couple. Though they struggled with health problems, in that home there was also music and laughter, the sharing of food, drink and tenderness.

No special guest dropped by to turn water into wine. But per-haps, in the love those in that household had for one another, de-spite their human weaknesses and failings, they sometimes en-countered the Love at the heart of the universe. If one or another occasionally felt so heavily laden that they could barely carry on, from somewhere they found refreshment and renewal.

At last the husband became seriously ill and died, to the deep sorrow of his wife. Though by this time her condition was poor and she needed a great deal of support, she remained in her home, where she regularly received communion.

Finally, surrounded by her children, she died peacefully in the room the couple had shared. A thanksgiving service for their lives was held in a place of worship with a beautiful picture of the wedding at Cana.

Beyond rivalry: love and family life

Through the centuries, at certain times and in some churches, celibacy has been exalted and marriage treated as second best, while at other times the reverse has been the case. Even now, in some circles, this rivalry continues.

However many people have come to recognise that different people have different callings, and that married people and celibates both make an important contribution to the wider 'family' of the church, and indeed humankind.

Perhaps Christians have a tendency to get trapped in sibling rivalry, convinced that, unless God disapproves of those with a different identity or way of life from their own, they themselves cannot feel secure in God's acceptance. The latest version of this is the claim by certain church leaders that too welcoming a stance towards same-sex partnerships involving the minority of the population that are lesbian, gay, bisexual or trans (LGBT) somehow devalue or threaten heterosexual marriage.

Yet the God portrayed in John's and other Gospels, who shared the joys and sorrows of human life and continues to offer refreshment and healing, is not like those parents who stir up rivalry among their children. God's love and goodness are abundant: nobody need fear that it will run out unless certain social groups are shouldered aside.

The psalmist wrote:

How precious is your steadfast love, O God!
The children of humankind take refuge in the shadow of your wings.

They feast on the abundance of your house,
and you give them drink from the river of your delights.
For with you is the fountain of life (Psalm 36.7–8)

Indeed:

You make springs gush forth in the valleys;
they flow between the hills;
they give drink to every beast of the field;
the wild donkeys quench their thirst (Psalm 104.10–11)

The Jesus whom Christians worship extends an invitation to all: "If anyone thirsts, let him come to me and drink" (John 7.37). No-one need fear that, if others drink deeply, they themselves will be left thirsty.

Men and women can become part of that abundance, organically connected with God and neighbour: "I am the vine, you are the branches. Those who abide in me and I in them bear much fruit, because apart from me you can do nothing... If you keep my commandments, you will abide in my love, just as I have kept my Father's commandments and abide in his love. I have said these things to you so that my joy may be in you, and that your joy may be complete. This is my commandment, that you love one another as I have loved you" (John 15.5, 10–12).

This is far removed from the patterns of envy and competitiveness that all too often affect human relationships, but which (with God's help) can be overcome.

Families and communities may be made up of single people, couples and smaller sub-groups or networks, differing in sexual orientation, gender identity and many other ways. All may make a unique contribution, and grow in unique ways while drawing closer to the One whose love sustains the universe, brings abundant blessings and satisfies the deepest thirst.

Chapter Twenty-Eight

Did God make snails? Diversity in creation

The beginning of the Hebrew Bible is often quoted in debates about gender and sexuality, particularly with regard to the role of lesbian, gay, bisexual, trans and intersex (LGBTI) people in church and society. Some Christians believe it clearly rules out same-sex relationships and emphasises distinct roles based on sex at birth. But it can be interpreted in different ways. Indeed the first chapters of Genesis, in the light of the Bible as a whole as well as through observation and reason, could be read as recognising and rejoicing in the diversity of living beings.

In the beginning

The opening chapters of Genesis, the first book in the Bible, have fascinated readers for thousands of years.

Today they are often read by Christians as being largely symbolic: while the world did indeed arise from God's loving creativity, the precise sequence of scientific and historical events is not the focus. For instance in the creation account from Genesis 1.1, plants are created before humans, while in the second story in Genesis 2 humans before plants.

However, what readers might understand these narratives to symbolise, especially with regard to sexuality and gender identity, is hotly disputed.

This is in part because they were written in ancient Hebrew thousands of years ago, in a civilisation remote from our own, and probably drew on even older oral traditions. These chapters are also read in the framework of different belief systems: Jewish and Christian approaches for instance may differ.

In addition, the cosmic scope and poetic quality which gives these narratives such power – and variety of ways in which people perceive and relate to God, who is at the heart of it – increase the ambiguity. Perhaps, most of all, readers approach these and other biblical stories in the light of social and personal expectations and experiences.

It may be useful to take another look at contrasting interpretations in the light of other biblical passages and modern knowledge, and examine how Christians today might draw on these ancient stories in understanding gender and sexuality.

Abundant life and the image of God

The first creation story can be read as emphasising reproduction and sexual difference. God creates "plants yielding seed, and fruit trees of every kind on earth that bear fruit with the seed in it." When sea creatures and birds are created, God blesses them, saying "Be fruitful and multiply", after which land animals are formed. The author repeatedly affirms, "God saw that it was good."

Then humans are created: God said, 'Let us make humankind in our image, according to our likeness...'

So God created humankind in his image, in the image of God he created them; male and female he created them.

God blesses the humans and tells them, "Be fruitful and multiply, and fill the earth and subdue it; and have dominion over the fish of the sea and over the birds of the air and over every living thing that moves upon the earth." God attends to the need of all these creatures for food, giving them plants to eat. Then "God saw everything that he had made, and indeed, it was very good", and rests.

Yet, even as the narrative celebrates the diversity and abundance of life on earth, perhaps even more remarkably it highlights what humans have in common. All are made in the image of God and are interconnected with other creatures, who also benefit from the generosity of the Creator.

This was in stark contrast to the creation myths of the surrounding nations, which included Babylon. There, a murderous power-struggle among gods was the backdrop to creation, while in Genesis the 'us' who creates humankind (later sometimes regarded by Christians as pointing towards the Trinity) is peaceful and promotes harmony. Admittedly , the passage has sometimes been used to justify ruthless misuse of the earth and other creatures by humans, yet this has resulted from failure to follow the lead of a Creator whose dominion involves taking responsibility for others' wellbeing. Responsible stewardship is called for, not a smash-and-grab attitude.

In Babylonian mythology, the subordinate gods were set to work but rebelled, so humans were created to carry out manual labour, serving as well as worshipping the gods. This and other empires were deeply hierarchical, with the king – sometimes portrayed as being in the image of a god – at the top and peasants and slaves at the bottom.

By contrast, in the Genesis account, all humans are made in God's image and not simply to be exploited. Even today, if taken seriously, this is a startlingly radical notion. Christian belief takes this even further, with God working as a carpenter in an outpost of another empire, then facing the death of a criminal before rising again and ushering in a new way of being.

Even more is known today about the complexity and wonder of nature and the capabilities of our own species, when it is allowed to develop and flourish.

It is now known that many types of creatures cannot be neatly divided into two sexes. For instance most snails – which play an important role in various ecosystems (even if they can occasionally be a nuisance to gardeners) – are hermaphrodites, with both male and female reproductive organs. Many species of coral are hermaphroditic too. Coral reefs enable numerous other species to breed and eat, protect coastal areas from storm damage and in other ways contribute to wellbeing: it is estimated that half a billion people are reliant on them.

Some might wish to claim that this must be a consequence of the Fall, that depiction in Genesis 3 of the fact that the universe is not entirely as it should be. Certainly, nature at its cruellest is far removed from the idyllic scenes at the beginning of the book, where there is no violence. But I think the onus is on anyone wedded to the notion that animals should always be straightforwardly male or female to make the case that such useful and (at least in the case of coral) beautiful creatures are not part of God's good creation.

It has also become apparent that, in numerous species of land animals and birds, same-sex sexual behaviour is not uncommon, nor is engagement in behaviour characteristic of the opposite sex. This may at first seem puzzling from an evolutionary perspective but there seem to be various benefits which go beyond the individual. Examples include a male penguin couple in a Kent zoo caring for a chick abandoned by its biological parents, and female bonobos having sex to promote bonding and to reduce the risk of aggression during intergroup encounters.

Of course, ethical guidance for people cannot be derived directly from the behaviour of other kinds of animals. However it is important to note that from earliest times surviving and thriving has involved far more than having as many babies as possible. A childless person with the skills to identify which plants were safe to eat, heal the sick or negotiate with another clan and thus avoid war might contribute more to collective welfare than even the most fecund man or woman, while romantic or erotic relationships might serve a range of purposes. It is possible that communities in which a minority of people was different from others in sexual orientation, biological sex or gender identity possessed certain advantages.

Today, thanks largely to modern medicine and disease prevention measures, humankind has indeed multiplied and filled the earth, to the point that responsible stewardship may not be properly exercised and the survival of some species is imperilled. While it is vital that some people continue to bear children, there is no compelling reason for everyone to do so, especially if this frees up more time for such tasks as the care of sick and frail older people, fostering and adoption, tackling mass poverty and the risk of war which would involve weapons of mass destruction.

The New Testament adds a further dimension, inviting readers to be part of a new kind of 'family' not based on blood ties but setting an example of compassion, justice and generosity. Almost everyone was expected to marry in the culture described in the Hebrew Bible and eunuchs were outsiders, as made clear in Leviticus 21.20 and Deuteronomy 23.1. To quote the latter, "No one whose testicles are crushed or whose penis is cut off shall be admitted to the assembly of the Lord." Yet Jesus remains unmarried and affirms eunuchs, however these are understood.

There is no reason to suppose that people who are intersex, transgender or disinclined or unable to conceive are any less made in God's image or part of God's good creation than anyone else.

Loving companionship

In the second account, in Genesis 2, God creates the first human from dust, breathing into his nostrils the breath of life, and sets him to till and care for the earth in the garden of Eden, full of beauty and fruit good to eat. God recognises that it is "not good that the human should be alone; I will make him a helper fit for him."

Jesus later refers to this passage in his teaching on marriage (e.g. Matthew 19.3–5). Some believe that, taken together with Genesis 1, it emphasises male-female complementarity, the notion that men and women are essentially different and that this is at the heart of marriage and society.

Yet others read the account as emphasising divine respect for human autonomy, as well as deep concern for its wellbeing. The beasts and birds are brought, one by one, and the human names them, but finds none of them suitable to be his partner.

Then God creates a second human from the rib (or side) of the first, so that the androgynous being becomes male and female. The reaction is one of delight at the meeting of a profound need: the companion is "bone of my bones and flesh of my flesh".

However, this is not as prescriptive as it may seem. If God had decided that it was not good for humans to be alone, and there were only one way to fix the problem – marrying a member of the opposite sex – celibacy would be ruled out. This is clearly not the case in the New Testament and Christian tradition, in which many have entered into religious communities offering a different kind of family life.

This does not necessarily mean that same-sex partnerships are also an acceptable way of being not alone, but the notion of a divinely-ordained one-size-fits-all pattern is not supported by the passage when read in a wider context.

For a small but significant minority, meeting a person of the same sex can bring the same sense of delighted recognition which heterosexual marriage, at best, brings, as well as involving the same challenge to overcome selfishness and grow spiritually through faithful self-giving love. Unlike most of the Babylonian gods, to whom ordinary people are merely a means to an end, God is not indifferent to human need and suffering and is acutely aware of each person, different but equally treasured.

Diversity and sexuality

In the rest of the Bible, even when humans betray God's trust, are expelled from the garden of delight and find themselves at odds with one another and other living beings, God does not abandon them. Life on earth falls short of its full potential, but through prophets and sages people are recalled to a better way; and in Christ there is hope of renewal and transformation for creation as a whole.

In a world not yet fully redeemed, human relationships – including the most intimate – are all too often tainted by power imbalances, egotism, greed and cruelty. This applies whether people are male, female or a combination of both, and attracted to the same or opposite sex, both sexes or neither.

Yet Genesis 1–2 perhaps offers a vision of diversity in which God delights and at the same time, a radical challenge to all societies which refuse to acknowledge that all people, whatever their ancestry or identity, are made in God's image. The invitation to join in protecting the environment, justly sharing the earth's abundance and filling the world with compassion and peace is not only for a select few.

Chapter Twenty-Nine

Using and misusing St Paul: wisdom, gender and sexuality

Some Christians look to St Paul as the guardian of a narrow doctrinal and moral purity, and cite his writings to 'prove', for example, the sinfulness of homosexual relationships. Others criticise him for the parallel reasons, seeing him as oppressive of women, gays and others. Indeed, he is sometimes regarded as radically altering the faith Jesus founded, replacing freedom in Christ with rule-based religion. Neither view, I will argue, is fair to Paul, to the radical transformation he underwent, or to the contradictions with which he wrestled – personally, theologically and as a leader of a growing movement.

This chapter focuses primarily on the use and misuses of St Paul in fractious contemporary church debates about sexuality and gender. It can also be read in parallel with the growing body of work on re-understanding one of the key figures in the history of Christianity – including, for example, the conversations opened up by Neil Elliot's book Liberating Paul, and the work of Ulrich Duchrow and others, suggesting that Paul's project was to create a new community and dynamic which was capable of re-energising the suppressed radicalism of Torah religion in a dangerously imperialistic setting.

Who was Paul?
A complex figure, Paul first appears in the Acts of the Apostles as Saul of Tarsus, a young religious fanatic who tries to stamp out Christianity by violence. After a dramatic conversion experience in which he encounters Christ, he becomes a Christian himself and, while Jewish himself, focuses on bringing the good news to other peoples.

His influence on the church has been profound. His letters (epistles) are part of the New Testament and are often quoted, though scholars now believe that several 'Pauline' epistles were actually written by other people.

According to John Dominic Crossan, Romans, 1–2 Corinthians, Galatians, Philippians, 1 Thessalonians and Philemon were by the historical Paul, but Ephesians, Colossians, 2 Thessalonians were probably not his work, and 1–2 Timothy and Titus were certainly not by him. (Jouette M Basler suggests that, while 2 Thessalonians and Colossians could possibly have been by Paul, there is overwhelming evidence that Ephesians, 1–2 Timothy and Titus were not.)

Difference in authorship explains some of the contradictions which have puzzled many readers, though other differences arise from the range of specific problems he was addressing, and the nature of the Wisdom tradition which helped to shape his approach.

Wisdom's call and Paul's response

The Wisdom tradition runs through much of the Hebrew Bible and is particularly marked in what are known as the Wisdom books – Job, Psalms, Proverbs, Ecclesiastes and Song of Songs. The later Jewish books of Wisdom (of Solomon) and Sirach (the Wisdom of Jesus the son of Sirach, sometimes known as Ecclesiasticus) are included in some Bibles and regarded as Deuterocanonical (though not Scriptural) works of value in certain other Christian traditions, and were influential in Paul's day.

The name of Solomon – the scholar-king with wide knowledge of natural history (1 Kings 4.29–34) and deep understanding of the human heart (1 Kings 3.16–28), whom people travelled from afar to hear – is often associated with Wisdom. Some now associate the figure of Wisdom (Sophia in Greek) with the Holy Spirit. Through observation, experience, learning and reflection, this tradition sought a deeper understanding of the universe, how God is at work in it and how people ought to live.

In the words of Proverbs:

Does not wisdom call?
Does not understanding raise her voice?...
"To you, O my people, I call,
And my cry is to all that live....

I love those who love me,
and those who seek me diligently find me"...
The mind of the wise makes their speech judicious
and adds persuasiveness to their lips.
(Proverbs 8.1, 17, 16.23)

Some passages in the Wisdom books are subjective (for instance the lament in Psalm 55 at betrayal by a friend and the sense of futility in Ecclesiastes 2), or are based on outmoded knowledge. For example, unlike the time when Psalm 19 was composed, it is known today that the sun's journey does not cover the whole of the heavens: the universe is far larger. However an illustration based on flawed science does not necessarily invalidate an argument.

Indeed, people in the twenty-first century have much to learn from those in earlier eras who, without modern scientific equipment, found out so much about the workings of the universe and without computers or printing, sought knowledge so diligently and made efforts to communicate it widely. And it is useful to remember that to many, even in the ancient world, religion was not seen as solely a matter of revelation detached from reason.

In Acts 17, Paul is portrayed sharing the good news in radically different contexts – with a mainly Jewish audience in Thessalonica, then in Beroea, and later with Gentiles in Athens. In Thessalonica, he went to the synagogue and "argued with them from the Scriptures, explaining and proving that it was necessary for the Messiah to suffer and to rise from the dead". So Paul drew creatively on the Hebrew Bible, reinterpreting it in the light of new experience.

In Athens "he was deeply distressed to see that the city was full of idols". But he did not launch into a fierce denunciation of Gentiles' wicked ways. Instead he entered into debate with philosophers and accepted an invitation to the Areopagus (named after the god Ares).

There, he engaged with them on their own intellectual as well as physical terrain, saying, "Athenians, I see how extremely religious you are in every way. For as I went through the city and looked carefully at the objects of your worship, I found among them an altar with the inscription, 'To an unknown god.' What therefore you worship as unknown, this I proclaim to you. The God who made the world and everything in it, he who is Lord of heaven and earth, does not live in shrines made by human hands".

Paul went on to explain that God made all nations from one ancestor, intending that "they would search for God and perhaps grope for him and find him – though indeed he is not far from each one of us. For 'In him we live and move and have our being'; as even some of your own poets have said, 'For we too are his offspring.'"

So he was able to affirm and build on what was positive in their culture, while challenging aspects which he believed alienated them from the living God.

He also acknowledged the importance of Wisdom, for instance in Romans 11, where he drew on Hebrew Scripture, including Job:

O the depth of the riches and wisdom and knowledge of God! How unsearchable are his judgements and how inscrutable his ways!

"For who has known the mind of the Lord?
Or who has been his counsellor?"

In 1 Corinthians 1–2 Paul contrasted worldly with true wisdom:

since, in the wisdom of God, the world did not know God through wisdom, God decided, through the foolishness of our proclamation, to save those who believe... Yet among the mature we do speak wisdom, though it is not a wisdom of this age or of the rulers of this age, who are doomed to perish. But we speak God's wisdom, secret and hidden, which God decreed before the ages.

He went on to write that "we have received not the spirit of the world, but the Spirit that is from God, so that we may understand the gifts bestowed on us by God." This resembles Wisdom

9: "Who has learned your counsel, unless you have given wisdom and sent your holy spirit from on high?"

1 Corinthians 8 declares that "for us there is one God, the Father, from whom are all things and for whom we exist, and one Lord, Jesus Christ, through whom are all things and through whom we exist." The author of Colossians (possibly Paul) extols Christ as "the image of the invisible God, the firstborn of all creation; for in him all things in heaven and on earth were created, things visible and invisible, whether thrones or dominions or rulers or powers – all things have been created through him and for him. He himself is before all things, and in him all things hold together." There are echoes perhaps of Wisdom 7–8, in which Wisdom:

> is a reflection of eternal light,
> a spotless mirror of the working of God,
> and an image of his goodness.
> Although she is but one, she can do all things,
> and while remaining in herself, she renews all things...
> She reaches mightily from one end of the earth to the other,
> and she orders all things well.

According to Sirach 1:

> Wisdom was created before all other things,
> and prudent understanding from eternity.

Thus the Christ to whom Christians are joined may be seen as an embodiment of divine Wisdom.

When considering what Paul said and wrote on particular topics, it is instructive to take account of his wider approach of seeking to discern, with the aid of the Holy Spirit, how God was and is at work, including in the lives of believers. Indeed, in 2 Corinthians 3, he informed his readers that "you show that you are a letter of Christ, prepared by us, written not with ink but with the Spirit of the living God, not on tablets of stone but on tablets of human hearts".

Paul and women

As has often been pointed out, Paul's attitudes to women were seemingly contradictory. This is explained to some extent, although not entirely, by the different authorship of some 'Pauline' epistles.

Paul wrote appreciatively about female fellow-evangelists and church leaders, including the deacon Phoebe, and Junia, "prominent among the apostles" (Romans 16). He also stated in Galatians 3 that "There is no longer Jew or Greek, there is no longer slave or free, there is no longer male and female; for all of you are one in Christ Jesus." Some regard this statement as being solely about spiritual equality, without implications for social relationships, but this distinction is questionable: for instance Paul was critical of Jewish believers who shied away from eating with Gentiles.

In 1 Corinthians 7, Paul wrote on marriage in terms of mutuality. Yet in 1 Corinthians 11 he declared:

> I want you to understand that Christ is the head of every man, and the husband is the head of his wife, and God is the head of Christ. Any man who prays or prophesies with something on his head disgraces his head, but any woman who prays or prophesies with her head unveiled disgraces her head... a man ought not to have his head veiled, since he is the image and reflection of God; but woman is the reflection of man.

(We should note that this is contrary to Genesis 1, cited by Jesus in Matthew 19 and Mark 10, in which both man and women are created in God's image. Peter Williams and others have suggested an alternative reading of this 'headship' language, pointing out that in Hebrew anthropology, the source of decision-making authority is the gut, not the head, and that 'head' was understood as denoting source or origin. In which case Paul is here citing the Genesis account of woman being created out of the rib of a man – itself meant as an alternative to violent Mesopotamian myths that required the destruction of the feminine as the condition for creation – and stretching it into an argument about propriety and church order. There may be something in this, but it is hard to avoid the conclusion that Paul ends up with a depiction which is inherently subordinationist, even if this is not the intention.)

There are strong cultural factors at work here. In Paul's day, women's hair was believed to inflame men's passions and going about with free-flowing hair was frowned upon, rather like going topless in some societies today. He was concerned not to stoke the prejudice which Christians were already likely to face from those around them, as well as being swayed by the prejudices of the Jewish and Hellenistic cultures of his day in which gender distinctions and male dominance were heavily emphasised.

In chapter 14 he went on to urge, in the context of avoiding disorderly worship:

> As in all the churches of the saints, women should be silent in the churches. For they are not permitted to speak, but should be subordinate, as the law also says. If there is anything they desire to know, let them ask their husbands at home. For it is shameful for a woman to speak in church.

Confusingly, he then advises the Christians in Corinth (presumably of both sexes) to "be eager to prophesy". It has been suggested that the practical concern he was addressing arose when women and men were sitting apart (as was customary in worship) and wives called out to their husbands, disrupting the service.

In addition the authors of Ephesians, Colossians, 1 Timothy and Titus urged female submission.

It would seem likely that Paul experienced a tension between, on one hand, the freedom of a new community where barriers were broken down in Christ and roles determined charismatically and, on the other hand, the pressure of social and cultural expectations, as well as practical challenges.

However, especially when taken out of context, these passages appeared to endorse women's inferiority. They could also be read as criticising anyone who sought to change gender, since this could be perceived as either abandoning one's God-given dignity if born male, or improperly aspiring to a higher status if born female. Later teachers and leaders, including the authors of other 'Pauline' epistles, tended to shy away even further from the radical implications of being "one in Christ".

Far more evidence is now available on the suffering and waste resulting from sexual inequality and rigid gender roles, and of the benefits to church and society as well as individual women of recognising their gifts. The fruits of scholars' knowledge and many people's experience should be taken into account: as Sirach 6 puts it:

> If you love to listen you will gain knowledge,
> and if you pay attention you will become wise...
> If you see an intelligent person, rise early to visit him;
> let your foot wear out his doorstep.

(Or, in the era of modern communication, search out the relevant journal articles or websites as well as listening to others in person before reaching firm conclusions.)

Paul and homosexuality

Paul's stance on sexuality has also been the subject of much debate. This is complicated by the fact that the modern concept of homosexual orientation was probably unknown in the ancient world, though of course some people engaged in sexual relationships with those of the same biological sex (and might today have been regarded as LGBT – lesbian, gay, bisexual or trans).

Ancient Jewish law forbade sex between men, a practice largely seen as associated with other, idolatrous nations, though not sex between women. The Greeks and Romans tended to approve of sex between males only if one was clearly socially inferior to the other (e.g. a youth or slave penetrated by an adult freeman), while a man who chose to 'play the woman' would face mockery or worse.

1 Corinthians 6.9–11 and the pseudo-Pauline 1 Timothy 1.8–11 are often quoted as forbidding gay sex, yet there are widely varying views on how the relevant terms should be translated,

let alone what weight they should be given today. 1 Corinthians 6 includes a list of those who will not inherit the kingdom of heaven, including *malakoi* and *arsenokoitai*, while the latter term is part of a list in 1 Timothy 1 of those to whom the law applies. The term *malakoi* (soft/weak/unmanly) may or may not have sexual connotations, while the obscure *arsenokoitai* may refer to male prostitutes, pimps or men having sex with men in general.

In the Authorised (King James) version, 1 Corinthians 6.9–11 reads, "Know ye not that the unrighteous shall not inherit the kingdom of God? Be not deceived: neither fornicators, nor idolaters, nor adulterers, nor effeminate, nor abusers of themselves with mankind, Nor thieves, nor covetous, nor drunkards, nor revilers, nor extortioners, shall inherit the kingdom of God. And such were some of you: but ye are washed, but ye are sanctified, but ye are justified in the name of the Lord Jesus, and by the Spirit of our God."

This might indicate that Paul set the bar higher than Jesus, who was himself labelled as a glutton and drunkard by the religious leaders of his day (Matthew 11.19), and who warned them that "the tax collectors and the prostitutes go into the kingdom of God before you" (Matthew 21.31). Indeed Paul's warning would appear to be at odds with other Pauline teachings such as Romans 10.9 ("if you confess with your lips that Jesus is Lord and believe in your heart that God raised him from the dead, you will be saved").

However, it is understandable that Paul would want to affirm the positive changes made by people joining the church and like other Wisdom writers, encourage virtuous living. It is unclear what bearing 1 Corinthians has on equal relationships between adult men.

Romans 1 possibly comes the closest to addressing what might be regarded today as homosexuality. To quote the New Revised Standard Version (NRSV):

the wrath of God is revealed from heaven against all ungodliness and wickedness of those who by their wickedness suppress the truth... Claiming to be wise, they became fools; and they exchanged the glory of the immortal God for images resembling a mortal human being or birds or four-footed animals or reptiles...

For this reason God gave them up to degrading passions. Their women exchanged natural intercourse for unnatural, and in the same way also the men, giving up natural intercourse with women, were consumed with passion for one another. Men committed shameless acts with men and received in their own persons the due penalty for their error...

They were filled with every kind of wickedness, evil, covetousness, malice. Full of envy, murder, strife, deceit, craftiness, they are gossips, slanderers, God-haters, insolent, haughty, boastful, inventors of evil, rebellious towards parents, foolish, faithless, heartless, ruthless.

The main thrust of the argument is that those who condemn them are also sinners: "you have no excuse, whoever you are, when you judge others; for in passing judgement on another you condemn yourself" (Romans 2.1), in the context of an argument against legalism. He chose behaviour which pious Jews would abhor in order to drive home the notion that both Jews and Gentiles were reliant on God's grace, and could be saved by faith. So using the passage legalistically misses the point.

Nevertheless, the theory Paul seems to be espousing deserves attention: of idolatry leading to 'perverse' heterosexual behaviour, probably anal sex, giving men a taste for 'unnatural' sex which they then indulged with one another. (It is also possible, though unlikely, that the passage alludes to lesbian sex.) After all, it is not impossible for the direction of desire to be influenced by social ideals, e.g. of feminine or masculine attractiveness.

He seems to refer to the theory in Wisdom 13–14 about the origins of immorality:

all people who were ignorant of God were foolish by nature;

and they were unable from the good things that are seen to

know the one who exists...

the idea of making idols was the beginning of fornication,

and the invention of them was the corruption of life...

they no longer keep either their lives or their marriages pure,

but they either treacherously kill one another, or grieve one another by adultery,

and all is a raging riot of blood and murder, theft and deceit, corruption, faithlessness, tumult, perjury,

confusion over what is good, forgetfulness of favours,

defiling of souls, sexual perversion,

disorder in marriages, adultery, and debauchery.

The behaviour of some members of the Roman ruling class in the first century, including Emperor Nero and his family, would have given further credence to this belief. However, in Romans, Paul questioned whether even those who worshipped one God were as righteous as they supposed.

As has been pointed out in recent decades, Romans 1 does not appear to fit LGBT people, partnered or otherwise, whose orientation has not arisen from idol-worship and who are no more prone to vices such as envy and malice than their heterosexual neighbours.

In addition, far more is known now about sexuality than two thousand years ago, for instance that same-sex acts or pair-bonding occur in many species. Also, across cultures and throughout history, a minority of people have been mainly homosexual in orientation, and physical intimacy and/or marriage have often taken place between partners of the same biological sex. However, how same-sex desire is perceived and expressed has varied considerably. As Paul sought out and learnt from the most plausible theories of his day, we would do well to do the same today.

More positively for LGBT people, at a time when there was heavy emphasis on procreation, and the single and childless risked being marginalised, Paul upheld the acceptability of being unmarried (as Jesus had done), creating space for sexual minorities. He also encouraged a sense of 'family' that went beyond biological bonds, urging Christians to "Love one another with brotherly affection. Outdo one another in showing honour" (Romans 12.10).

Though almost certainly celibate himself, Paul was also realistic about the fact that most people were not cut out for lifelong abstinence. His suggestion that "because of the temptation to sexual immorality, each man should have his own wife and each woman her own husband... To the unmarried and the widows I say that it is good for them to remain single as I am. But if they cannot exercise self-control, they should marry. For it is better to marry than to burn" was not the most enthusiastic endorsement of marriage! However it is still an important practical point that partnership allows people to channel desire constructively.

He thus prudently steered a path between the extremes of taking all sexual feelings at face value and suggesting that people could easily refrain from ever expressing their sexuality physically.

There is now extensive evidence that heterosexual marriages entered into by lesbian and gay people, though occasionally successful, are often tokenistic, short-lived or damaging to both partners; and that permanent celibacy works well for only for a minority of people, LGBT or heterosexual. In contrast, same-sex partnerships can be stable, joyful and a source of love which overspills to others in the community. It could be argued that "it is better to marry than to burn" could apply to same-sex as well as opposite-sex marriage.

Wider principles and ethical trajectories

Other writings by Paul are indirectly relevant when wrestling with ethical issues linked with gender and sexuality.

He made it clear that, in his view, moral conduct was not a

matter of following arbitrary commands supposedly issued by God. In Romans 13, he wrote:

> Owe no one anything, except to love one another; for the one who loves another has fulfilled the law. The commandments, 'You shall not commit adultery; You shall not murder; You shall not steal; You shall not covet'; and any other commandment, are summed up in this word, 'Love your neighbour as yourself.' Love does no wrong to a neighbour; therefore, love is the fulfilling of the law.

In Galatians, likewise, Paul strongly criticised legalism: "For freedom Christ has set us free. Stand firm, therefore, and do not submit again to a yoke of slavery... You who want to be justified by the law have cut yourselves off from Christ... the whole law is summed up in a single commandment, 'You shall love your neighbour as yourself.'"

Love is not a sentimental notion: Paul writes at some length about what this might involve in practice (e.g. 1 Corinthians 13), and elsewhere suggests criteria for determining whether the Holy Spirit is at work in particular relationships and situations (Galatians 5.22–23).

There is an overlap with Jesus' 'Golden Rule' in Matthew 7.12: "whatever you wish that others would do to you, do also to them, for this is the Law and the Prophets."

In addition, he advocated – and strove to build – a community not fundamentally based on hierarchy or competitiveness, an approach that remains radical even today. For instance he portrayed the church as a body with Christ as the head:

> just as the body is one and has many members, and all the members of the body, though many, are one body, so it is with Christ. For in the one Spirit we were all baptised into one body – Jews or Greeks, slaves or free – and we were all made to drink of one Spirit... God has so arranged the body, giving the greater honour to the inferior member, that there may be no dissension within the body, but the members may have the same care for one another. If one

member suffers, all suffer together with it; if one member is honoured, all rejoice together with it. (1 Corinthians 12)

Thus exclusion of any comes at a cost to all. And, within this ethos, there is no reason to suppose that improving the status of women or LGBT people will necessarily result in reduced status for men and masculinity, or heterosexuals and heterosexual marriage.

He also went to considerable lengths to challenge the marginalisation of converts and insistence that they adopt Jewish law to be fully included in Christian worship, to the point of challenging the main church leaders (Galatians 2.11–14, Acts 15). Attitudes and measures that discourage some groups of people from joining, or fully participating in, the church should not be lightly adopted.

Learning from Paul

Paul's writings are sometimes cited by both supporters and opponents of women's equality. Likewise, in debates on sexuality, he is often quoted by those who regard same-sex partnerships as wrong, while others believe such passages are not relevant to committed and equal relationships today.

However, perhaps even more important than Paul's perspective on specific issues, is how he reached his conclusions. Using particular passages as a new 'law' that means that other Christian views can be rubbished and the fruits of experience, learning and reflection ignored, misses the point of much of what he taught, and how he himself worked.

Steeped in the Wisdom tradition, he set an example of grappling with difficult issues. Christians today would be well advised to learn from him to study Scripture diligently yet to approach it creatively, engage critically with surrounding cultures and advances in knowledge, and seek to determine whether particular acts or omissions involve harming one's neighbour. The building of a community in which all are valued and brought to fullness of life, through the grace of Christ who died and rose again, is also of crucial importance, even if this involves challenging the seemingly important and self-righteous.

If indeed the refusal of full equality is demonstrably causing damage at both a personal and community level, we might be well advised to follow the advice in Sirach 4.26:

Do not be ashamed to confess your sins,
and do not try to stop the current of a river.

Chapter Thirty

Belief in 'clarity of Scripture' complicates debate

Some Christians are convinced that biblical teaching on sexual ethics is clear and consistent, despite extensive evidence to the contrary. Often this belief is linked with the doctrine of the clarity – sometimes known as perspicuity – of Scripture.

Even insistence on taking the whole Bible literally does not result in a straightforward moral code covering such matters as marriage and same-sex relationships. Simplistic and dogmatic approaches are harmful to people and do not do justice to the richness and complexity of the Bible.

Yet overcoming these is a challenge, when the craving for order and certainty can lead people to ignore anything which does not fit an expected pattern.

The 'perspicuity' of Scripture

"The clarity of Scripture means that the Bible is written in such a way that its teachings are able to be understood by all who will read it seeking God's help and being willing to follow it," wrote Wayne Grudem in Systematic Theology in 1994. A professor and theologian, he later edited the English Standard Version Study Bible.

Belief in the perspicuity (clarity) of Scripture was championed by leading figures during the Reformation, though there were differences in how this was understood among Protestants. "Let miserable men," urged Martin Luther, "stop imputing with blasphemous perversity the darkness and obscurity of their own hearts to the wholly clear Scriptures of God."

"All things in Scripture are not alike plain in themselves, nor alike clear unto all: yet those things which are necessary to be known, believed, and observed for salvation are so clearly propounded, and opened in some place of Scripture or other, that not only the learned, but the unlearned... may attain unto a sufficient understanding of them," declared the Westminster Confession of Faith.

This might imply that if, despite striving to think and do what is right, people are mistaken on certain ethical or doctrinal issues on which biblical teaching seems unclear, they will not be damned. But if an individual or faction becomes convinced that particular views or acts are crucial to salvation, it is all too easy then to assume that the Bible must be clear on this matter.

In many ways, the notion that ordinary Christians could grasp the Bible's meaning, and did not have to rely on a pope or bishop to tell them what to think, was liberating. In the modern age, some (though not all) approaches to biblical scholarship might again appear to marginalise all but a learned few.

Some aspects might be described as clear, for instance the emphasis on a God who is greater than any local deity or object of worship, impossible to bully or bribe and who invites humans into a relationship of faithfulness and trust. There are also other consistent themes, such as the importance of sharing the fruits of the earth so generously given by the Creator.

But, taken to an extreme, the doctrine has sometimes resulted in a new bondage, as interpreters read their era's (or their own) preconceptions into the Bible and refuse even to consider alternative approaches. In addition, fellow-Christians whose selection of passages, translation or interpretation results in a different opinion may be condemned as perverse or wicked.

Since the Reformation, devout believers have argued contradictory positions on several topics, including whether the earth goes round the sun, slavery and racial segregation. This has led some people to conclude that the Bible may offer valuable insights but not always clear instruction on everything of importance, taking into account the constraints on understanding which affect readers in a particular generation. However others cling to the doctrine and insist on applying it to the issue of sexuality.

A more cautious approach does not necessarily mean devaluing the Bible as a source of learning and inspiration. If one teacher presents his students with straightforward facts and principles which they must then regurgitate, while another makes them think hard and work together to discover the truth, the latter is not necessarily worse at teaching.

A quick look at some biblical instructions, advice and stories touching on sexuality and gender follow. These illustrate how belief in the clarity of Scripture on sexual ethics can be problematic. Quotes are from the New Revised Standard Version unless otherwise stated.

Remarriage of widows

The issue of remarriage after the death of one's spouse has not been especially contentious in recent decades. Most Christians perhaps assume (in accordance with Romans 7.2–3) that a woman is free to remarry if her husband dies. In the laws in the Hebrew Bible, a husband is anyway free to marry additional wives; but it seems logical, if monogamy is favoured for both sexes, to assume that widowers likewise may – but need not – remarry.

However things are not that simple.

According to Deuteronomy 25.5–10, under certain circumstances a widow who bears her husband no sons is required to marry his brother unless he refuses (referred to in Matthew 22.23–33), their firstborn son being regarded as the dead man's child. Scripture treats failure to follow this obligation as a serious matter (Genesis 38.8–10). Otherwise widows may remarry outside the extended family but if they do not, they and their children should be offered support by the community to fend off destitution (see e.g. Deuteronomy 24.17–22, 26.12–15).

In the Acts of the Apostles and various epistles, Paul indicates that, in his view, Christians need not be bound by Jewish law. But various eminent Christians, including Thomas Aquinas, have suggested that this could be subdivided into moral, ceremonial and judicial laws. It has also been argued that, in the words of the 1689 Baptist Confession, "The moral law doth for ever bind all, as well justified persons as others, to the obedience thereof" – which might suggest that a Christian widow and her brother-in-law might be obliged under certain circumstances to marry (at least if he were not already married).

Yet Christians who hold the much-contested belief that the Hebrew Bible can be subdivided in this way, and 'moral law' still applies, do not generally insist on marriage in such circumstances. Perhaps this is because they believe that some rules related to sexuality in the Hebrew Bible are not part of the moral law while others are, but the rationale is unclear.

Rules and teachings may reflect broader ethical principles, for instance justice and mercy (Micah 6.8) but be applied in ways specific to an era and culture. This law would appear to address men's anxieties in the ancient world about dying without a son to inherit from them and keep their name alive, to maintain property within the extended family and also to provide financial support for widows.

Even devoutly Orthodox Jewish people today might conduct a ceremony to mark the renunciation of this right but would not expect bereaved in-laws to marry. If churches were to argue that modern Christians should obey this law – ostensibly about sexual ethics, in that it forbids certain people from acting on their own desires and inclinations – this would be unjust and unmerciful.

Various New Testament writers have their own take on the matter of widowhood. The Epistle of James suggests that "Religion that is pure and undefiled before God, the Father, is this: to care for orphans and widows in their distress, and to keep oneself unstained by the world" (James 1.27).

In 1 Corinthians, Paul states that widows may remarry but it is fine, indeed admirable, for them to remain single: "To the unmarried and the widows I say that it is well for them to remain unmarried as I am. But if they are not practising self-control, they should marry. For it is better to marry than to be aflame with passion... A wife is bound as long as her husband lives. But if the husband dies, she is free to marry anyone she wishes, only in the Lord. But in my judgement she is more blessed if she remains as she is. And I think that I too have the Spirit of God" (1 Corinthians 7.8–9, 39–40).

However, the author of 1 Timothy appears more contemptuous than sympathetic to widows under sixty, stating that "their sensual desires alienate them from Christ... and they are not merely idle, but also gossips and busybodies" and "some have already turned away to follow Satan." He forbids assistance to them and demands that they remarry (1 Timothy 5.11–15).

A young or middle-aged widow who decides not to remarry should be commended, according to 1 Corinthians, but condemned, according to 1 Timothy.

That all widows under sixty not under a husband's control, then and now, are idle gossips alienated from Christ may also seem improbable. Some church leaders are scornful of anyone who admits that experience affects their interpretation of the Bible. Yet even these might be hesitant to denounce the wickedness of such women, since Christians who have (or are) mothers or grandmothers who stayed single after suffering untimely bereavement might be sceptical and maybe indignant.

Moreover the Gospel narratives give an honoured place to widows, from the prophet Anna (Luke 2.36–38) – widowed at an early age and remaining single – to the widow of Nain (Luke 7.11–15), on whom Jesus has compassion when her son dies. In fact, by the time Jesus is an adult, his own mother appears to be a widow who has not remarried.

Rather as someone designing a newsletter on a computer may barely have to think before he clicks commands such as 'bring to front', 'send to back' or 'delete', readers of the Bible may prioritise certain texts and play down or even disregard others without being aware. They may then be convinced that the Bible is absolutely clear on a particular topic – but someone else may be equally confident while reaching a different conclusion. The human brain is wonderful but sometimes deceptive; and optical illusions are a reminder that, even at the most basic level, perceptions can be different from reality.

Translation, culture and acceptability

Another example of how parts of the 'moral law' can be bypassed by Christians who claim to uphold it in its entirety, is the reluctance – for good reason – to insist on Deuteronomy 22.28–29. This also illustrates how difficult translation and interpretation can be and the importance of cultural context.

According to the New International Version, this decrees that "If a man happens to meet a virgin who is not pledged to be married and rapes her and they are discovered, he shall pay her father fifty shekels of silver. He must marry the young woman, for he has violated her. He can never divorce her as long as he lives."

Biblica, which produced this translation, believes "In the divine inspiration of all 66 books of the Old and New Testaments as originally given, guaranteeing their infallibility, entire trustworthiness, and supreme authority in all matters of faith and conduct." If indeed the passage clearly sets out an infallible moral law, applicable now as in the past, this would suggest that a rapist whose female victim is unmarried should not be jailed but instead the woman should be punished by forcing her to relive her trauma every day as his wife.

Yet other translations are ambiguous and might cover both rape and consensual sex without parental consent, for instance: "If a man find a damsel that is a virgin, which is not betrothed, and lay hold on her, and lie with her, and they be found; then the man that lay with her shall give unto the damsel's father fifty shekels of silver, and she shall be his wife; because he hath humbled her, he may not put her away all his days" (Authorised Version).

Meanwhile Exodus 22.16–17 decrees that "If a man seduces a virgin who is not pledged to be married and sleeps with her, he must pay the bride-price, and she shall be his wife. If her father absolutely refuses to give her to him, he must still pay the bride-price for virgins" (NIV). The AV version is broadly similar.

Apparently, then, if an unmarried woman had consensual sex with a man, the father might or might not be legally obliged to let them marry; and in the case of rape (at least if the father agreed to marriage in these circumstances), the victim might be forced to be the lifelong wife of her attacker.

This law arose in a deeply patriarchal society in which stigma might leave a rape victim shamed and destitute, or her family at a financial loss if she could not then marry. Lawmakers might wish to ensure that she had some means of support or that the head of the household was compensated for his loss, which makes this passage rather more explicable. Israa Tawalbeh, the first female coroner in Jordan, one of the few countries of have laws of this kind in modern times, suggested that it was mainly used when under-18s had consensual sex with their boyfriends (deemed statutory rape) and that such marriages are "better than leaving girls to be killed by their parents or relatives."

However, others have argued out that such laws are unfair and cruel, given what is now known about the impact of sexual assault. Certainly if church leaders were to argue that Christians today should faithfully observe Deuteronomy 22.28–29, this would give rise to justifiable anger and disgust.

The meaning of Scripture in this case would appear unclear and, whatever translation is used, at odds with both the moral reasoning applied elsewhere in the Bible (for instance the repeated calls for justice and mercy) and what is morally acceptable today. In any event, even church leaders who claim to believe that the 'moral law' came directly from God and must still be obeyed, do not generally seek to champion it in this instance.

Filtering out, adding in

While those who think they believe in the clarity of the Bible sometimes filter out what does not fit their preconceptions, they may also add in what is not there. One example is the treatment of the story of Sodom through the ages.

The biblical account is the second part of a longer narrative, Genesis 18.1–19.29 and is set in an often harsh landscape where travellers could die of thirst or exposure to the elements if they were not offered hospitality. Jewish law insisted on the care of foreigners; "You shall not oppress a resident alien; you know the heart of an alien, for you were aliens in the land of Egypt," states Exodus 23.9.

Tradition also taught that messengers from God might appear in the guise of outsiders (see e.g. Judges 13.2–24, Joshua 5.13–15); as Hebrews 13.2 later put it, "Do not neglect to show hospitality to strangers, for by doing that some have entertained angels without knowing it."

At the start, the narrator describes how Abraham, sitting at the entrance of his tent, sees three men nearby. He runs out to meet them, bows, invites them in, arranges for a meal to be prepared and serves them, and as a result encounters God.

He and his wife have long wanted a son but they have grown old. To his astonishment, God promises that their wish will be fulfilled, and readers learn that Abraham will become the ancestor of "a great and mighty nation, and all the nations of the earth shall be blessed in him."

In case the reader has any doubt about Abraham's compassion for people of other nations and cultures, God tells him of the outcry against the wickedness of nearby Sodom and Gomorrah and how they are about to be destroyed, but Abraham is willing to argue even with God to try to save them. He manages to strike a deal that, if at least ten just men can be found, it will be spared.

Two angels then go on to Sodom, where Abraham's nephew Lot comes to meet them, bows, and invites them to his home where a meal is prepared for them. But the men of Sodom surround the house and demand that the visitors be brought out "so that we may know them." The intention appears to be gang-rape or maybe some other form of brutality which would assert their power over the newcomers (the Hebrew term 'yadha' is ambiguous). Lot refuses and even offers his daughters (this was indeed a patriarchal society), pleading "do nothing to these men, for they have come under my roof."

However the attackers have no regard for the ancient code of hospitality. In case the reader has any doubt about their hostility to people of other nations and cultures, they threaten Lot, saying, "This fellow came here as an alien, and he would play the judge."

The angels lead Lot's family to safety and Sodom and Gomorrah are destroyed. The narrative ends by highlighting the contrast between the fate of the hospitable Abraham and the violently inhospitable attackers: "when God destroyed the cities of the Plain, God remembered Abraham, and sent Lot out of the midst of the overthrow, when he overthrew the cities in which Lot had settled."

There is another parallel story to the fall of Sodom in Judges 19.1–20.48. In this instance, a concubine who has left her partner, a Levite, is persuaded to return home with him. On the journey he stops in the territory of the tribe of Benjamin, thinking he will be safe, and waits in Gibeah town square; but no-one offers them shelter until an old man coming home from work in the fields, himself from another area, does so.

The Benjaminites threateningly surround the house, demanding that the stranger be brought out so that they can assault him; instead, to save himself, he shoves his partner outside. They can thus humiliate the outsider from another tribe by gang-raping a woman reserved for his use, so to speak; though a man was permitted have multiple wives and concubines and also sleep with single women, a woman in effect belonged to just one man. In the morning he finds her dead.

Instead of burying her, the Levite cuts up her body and sends parts to the other tribes, rallying them for a ferocious attack on the Benjaminites. This can hardly be said to offer a flattering portrayal of heterosexuality but sadly, in today's world too, tribes and nations battle for supremacy and there are plenty of men who betray or brutalise women and sometimes other men.

Jesus refers to Sodom in the context of inhospitality (e.g. Matthew 10.5–15), while other biblical writers broaden this to other forms of injustice (e.g. Ezekiel 16.49 states that Sodom "had pride, excess of food, and prosperous ease, but did not aid the poor and needy").

Yet amazingly, for many centuries, Christians regarded the sin of Sodom as being sex between men, even if consensual, and not as violent inhospitality. Some appeared to find it hard to believe that mistreating outsiders could really bother God that much unless 'deviant' sex was involved, though Matthew 25 indicates that treating strangers unlovingly means rejecting Christ. Many today recognise the flaws in this view, whether or not they approve of same-sex partnerships. Yet some still believe that this is the 'clear meaning', seeing what they expect rather than what is there. This is an example of how society's prejudices may distort biblical interpretation.

Clarity and contradiction

Traditionally, the Hebrew Bible was read not as a sort of do-it-yourself manual with clear instructions for every eventuality, but rather in the context of reflection and debate. The community of faith was, and is, invited to engage in the interpretive process, rather than being spoon-fed.

For example, Leviticus 20.12 decrees that "If a man lies with his daughter-in-law, both of them shall be put to death; they have committed perversion; their blood is upon them"; but after Tamar contrives to sleep with her father-in-law, he declares that "She hath been more righteous than I" (Genesis 38, Authorised Version; one of the twins they conceive is named as an ancestor of Jesus in Matthew 1.3).

According to Deuteronomy 22.5, "A woman shall not wear a man's apparel, nor shall a man put on a woman's garment; for whoever does such things is abhorrent to the Lord your God"; but Joseph is dressed in a garment of many colours (Genesis 37:3), the type of robe worn by a king's virgin daughter (.2 Samuel 13:18–19), yet goes on to become one of the great patriarchs.

"No Ammonite or Moabite shall be admitted to the assembly of the Lord. Even to the tenth generation, none of their descendants shall be admitted to the assembly of the Lord," Deuteronomy 23.3 states; but the Moabite Ruth (Ruth 1.1–18) sets an example of faithful love and becomes the great-grandmother of king David (and another ancestor of Jesus).

This is not because the Bible is a collection of outdated and sometimes contradictory texts. On the contrary, its power and relevance lies, in part, in its continual resistance to simplistic reading. Key themes, such as God's transforming love at work and the call to embody and communicate this, can assist Christians in interpreting the Bible in ways that are life-giving rather than deadly (2 Corinthians 2.6).

So can guiding principles set out in the New Testament, such as the advice: "In everything do to others as you would have them do to you; for this is the law and the prophets" (Matthew 7.12), as well as Paul's precept that "Love does no wrong to a neighbour; therefore, love is the fulfilling of the law" (Romans 13.8–10).

Defending or discrediting the Bible

The passion evoked by debates on sexuality, especially same-sex partnership, are probably partly because some defenders of the doctrine of the clarity of Scripture see this as a last-ditch stand.

Reputable scholars and devout Christians disagree about the interpretation and sometimes the translation of key passages on sexuality. Many believe that committed faithful relationships should be accepted, or at least that theological diversity is legitimate. Yet some insist that if any church respects conscientious difference on this topic, it is abandoning its claim to be authentically Christian.

In certain instances, this may be a result of prejudice, inability to see others' point of view or a lack of awareness that loving partnerships are very different from the predatory and power-seeking behaviour portrayed in certain biblical passages. I think others genuinely fear that if teaching on the issue is open to question, doubt is cast on the perspicuity of the Bible, thus leaving no reliable guide on matters of faith.

However, such insistence can lead other people to reject the Bible altogether if they disagree on ethical or factual grounds with its 'clear teaching' on a particular matter. And it takes no account of the many times eminent Christians with wide support have historically quoted biblical passages in support of a position which later turned out to be wrong.

In a different sense, the Bible is clear. It vividly depicts humankind's encounter with a God beyond imagination, yet made known in Christ, and invites readers to be transformed and play a part in the transformation of the universe. Love and willingness to venture into the unknown – like Jesus' first disciples who heard the call to "Follow me" – are emphasised, rather than confidence that one currently possesses all truth. Seeking to understand the Bible correctly is important, but the possibility of error cannot always be ruled out; though Christians may trust that ultimately the Spirit will guide them into all the truth (John 16.13).

Chapter Thirty-One

The washing of feet: a call to love and a challenge to gender and privilege

The Gospel account of Jesus washing the feet of his disciples is widely known among Christians. Some churches re-enact it on Maundy Thursday. Yet it is not always recognised quite how subversive this was.

Hierarchy based on gender, class and other factors has been a feature of numerous human societies since ancient times. Rigid roles, though oppressive (especially for those at the lower levels), offer a certain security, and people can react with anger and even violence if others fail to comply. The alternative way offered by Jesus as depicted in the gospels is challenging even today.

"Do you know what I have done to you?"

The foot-washing scene occurs only in John's gospel, though Matthew, Mark and Luke also depict the 'last supper'. By this point, Jesus has gathered a large following, especially among the marginalised and dispossessed, but has become a focus for the hostility of much of the religious and political elite.

Though, highly unusually for a Jewish man of that era, there is no indication that Jesus ever married, some of his followers form an alternative type of family. John 11–12 describes his love for the members of a household in Bethany, Mary and Martha and their brother Lazarus, for whom he weeps and then raises from the dead.

In Luke 10, Mary has annoyed her sister by sitting at Jesus' feet listening, as male disciples of rabbis often did, rather than joining in the housework. John 12 describes how they give a dinner for him at which Mary anoints Jesus' feet, wiping them with her hair, to the annoyance of Judas Iscariot, the apostle who will betray him. The atmosphere is sombre as Jesus, defending Mary, refers to his own impending death.

John 13 tells how, during Jesus' final supper with his followers before his betrayal, arrest and crucifixion:

Jesus, knowing that the Father had given all things into his hands, and that he had come from God and was going to God, got up from the table, took off his outer robe, and tied a towel around himself. Then he poured water into a basin and began to wash the disciples' feet and to wipe them with the towel that was tied around him.

He came to Simon Peter, who said to him, 'Lord, are you going to wash my feet?' Jesus answered, 'You do not know now what I am doing, but later you will understand.' Peter said to him, 'You will never wash my feet.' Jesus answered, 'Unless I wash you, you have no share with me.' Simon Peter said to him, 'Lord, not my feet only but also my hands and my head!' Jesus said to him, 'One who has bathed does not need to wash, except for the feet, but is entirely clean. And you are clean, though not all of you.' For he knew who was to betray him; for this reason he said, 'Not all of you are clean.'

After he had washed their feet, had put on his robe, and had returned to the table, he said to them, 'Do you know what I have done to you? You call me Teacher and Lord – and you are right, for that is what I am. So if I, your Lord and Teacher, have washed your feet, you also ought to wash one another's feet. For I have set you an example, that you also should do as I have done to you. Very truly, I tell you, servants are not greater than their master, nor are messengers greater than the one who sent them. If you know these things, you are blessed if you do them.'

Later he tells them, "I give you a new commandment, that you love one another. Just as I have loved you, you also should love one another. By this everyone will know that you are my disciples, if you have love for one another."

John 15 elaborates on this: "This is my commandment, that you love one another as I have loved you. No one has greater love than this, to lay down one's life for one's friends. You are my friends if you do what I command you. I do not call you servants any longer, because the servant does not know what the master is doing; but I have called you friends, because I have made known to you everything that I have heard from my Father."

The duties of a wife

It is often pointed out that foot -washing was the duty of a servant (or slave) and so it was an act of great humility on the part of Jesus which others, especially leaders, should emulate. This is true. Peter's reaction – first to refuse, then to go to the other extreme and ask that his hands and head be washed too – is sometimes attributed to his flawed understanding and impulsive nature, which is not entirely fair.

Obviously not every Jewish man, especially one from a poorer background, had domestic servants, but almost all were part of a patriarchal family system which gave them certain privileges over their wives and children. Indeed, in the book of Genesis, the first form of human inequality which arises from humankind's fall from grace is women's subservience to men.

As the 1906 Jewish Encyclopaedia (now online) explains, in rabbinical literature washing feet "was a service which the wife was expected to render her husband (Yer). Ket. v. 30a); according to Rab Huna, it was one of the personal attentions to which her husband was entitled, no matter how many maids she may have had; likewise, according to the Babylonian Talmud (Ket. 61a), besides preparing his drink and bed, the wife had to wash her husband's face and feet (comp. Maimonides, 'Yad,' Ishut, xxi. 3; Shulan 'Aruk, Eben ha-'Ezer, 80, 4)."

Foot -washing was therefore connected not only with status but also intimacy.

The story of Joseph and Aseneth is an imaginative rendering of the marriage of Joseph (who has become an important figure in Egypt) to the daughter of a pagan priest in Genesis 41. It is thought to have been written between the first century BCE and second century CE. In this, the upper-class Aseneth is at first appalled at the notion of being married off to a former shepherd and slave of another race.

Then she sees Joseph and falls heavily in love with him. After the barriers to their marriage are overcome and they have embraced, she brings water to wash his feet. At first he urges that one of her maids do this instead, but she insists, "No, my lord, for my hands are your hands, and your feet my feet, and no one else shall wash your feet" (HFD Sparks version).

Unsurprisingly for Peter (who may be used to having his feet washed by his wife, if at all), it is profoundly disconcerting when he finds Jesus kneeling at his feet. And when he volunteers, "Lord, not my feet only but also my hands and my head!" this indicates that he has grasped what his teacher and redeemer is trying to convey.

The foot -washing helps to bind together a new type of family brought together not by ancestry but through the Holy Spirit, a community intimately linked not only with one another but also with Christ and the heavenly Father with whom he is one. They are still fallible humans, but part of the nucleus of a transformed humanity.

Beyond the 'destiny' of gender and social status

Even in movements for change with egalitarian ideals, it is easy to reproduce old ways of relating, in which God or Truth is at the top, mediated through a ruling class or central leadership via a set of intermediaries down to those at the bottom. There may be limited opportunities for advancement for members of the 'lower orders' who may be especially talented or ambitious, as long as the system remains intact.

Even a home where there is love may instill gender and other norms in a way that allows no scope for deviation, acting as a training ground for a world in which people know their place. Yet this ethos is called into question in the gospels, particularly at the foot washing.

In the first few verses of John's gospel, God is depicted as beyond human-made categories such as gender. The universal Christ is identified with the Word who was with God, and was God, from the beginning. God is spirit, and those who worship him must worship in spirit and truth. Those who accept that life which is the light of all people, which shines in the darkness, are given power to become children of God.

At the last supper, Christ's followers are urged to remain as branches of this true vine.

This newness of life is more than a metaphysical concept which allows oppressive relationships to continue while people take comfort in the fact that at some level, they are more free than they appear to be. Throughout all the gospels, Jesus constantly overturns expectations of how society is supposed to function and indeed, of what God is like.

In John's gospel, the day after Jesus washed his disciples' feet, he is condemned by the secular and religious authorities and crucified. His mother and the disciple Jesus loves in a special way, who lay against his breast during supper, are standing by. He tells them, "Woman, here is your son", and "Here is your mother", after which the disciple takes her into his own home, joined in a family linked through love and faith, not birth. And, though society does not greatly value women's testimony, on the third day it is another woman, Mary of Magdala, who is chosen to be the first witness of the resurrection.

The way of love, where food and drink are shared with the physically hungry and God's own self is offered as spiritual nourishment, is profoundly challenging. Following this path may involve straying far outside one's comfort zone, even risking one's life. Yet it leads to hope, and – Christians believe – triumph over death itself.

Chapter Thirty-Two

Same-sex love, self-denial and the cross

Partly as a result of developments in biblical scholarship, many Christians now believe that it can be acceptable to enter a same-sex partnership. Those who disagree sometimes cite Christ's call in the gospels, "If any want to become my followers, let them deny themselves and take up their cross and follow me." (Matthew 16.24, Mark 8.34, Luke 9.23). They argue that people attracted to members of the same sex should abstain, if necessary, staying celibate for life.

Undoubtedly following Christ can be challenging. But the language of the cross has sometimes been used in ways that contradict Jesus' teaching and example. It is worth carefully examining at what this call does, and does not, mean.

The need for caution in using the language of the cross
Certainly everyone who follows Christ will be called on to give up some things they previously held on to, which may be painful. However, it is risky to be too quick to insist that to be faithful to Christ, a set of people with less power or prestige in church or society should give up hope of enjoying what a dominant group takes for granted.

Theologians have sometimes used the language of the cross in questionable ways. For instance they have sought to imply that slaves seeking an end to slavery and wives resisting domestic violence are being un-Christian.

Many slave-owners in the eighteenth and nineteenth centuries argued that abolitionism was against God's will. Modern Bible study notes on 1 Peter from St Helen's Bishopgate argue that "a slave must submit even to a perverse master... Christians are called to follow in the footsteps of the Christ who persevered in godliness in the face of much provocation and suffering. His death on the cross not only saves His people... but also establishes the blueprint for our life and especially for the way that we are to respond to unjust suffering."

They state, "That astonishing obedience is the template for Christians to follow in life, especially at the time that it will be most difficult to do so – when we are being violated and receiving unjust treatment from others... God has providentially ordered society... Only if I trust in his ultimate vindication of His people (as Christ did) will I be able to sit loose to my 'rights' in this world and recognise that any unjust suffering I endure is, ultimately, His will."

In the case of domestic violence too, victims have often been told that any questioning of their lot is a rebellion against God. John Calvin's position on wife-beating has been adopted by many church leaders through the centuries.

He wrote, "We have a special sympathy for poor women who are evilly and roughly treated by their husbands, because of the roughness and cruelty of the tyranny and captivity which is their lot. We do not find ourselves permitted by the Word of God, however, to advise a woman to leave her husband, except by force of necessity; and we do not understand this force to be operative when a husband behaves roughly and uses threats to his wife, nor even when he beats her, but when there is imminent peril to her life... [We] exhort her to bear with patience the cross which God has seen fit to place upon her; and meanwhile not to deviate from the duty which she has before God to please her husband, but to be faithful whatever happens."

There are serious problems with using the language of the cross to sanctify passivity in the face of stark inequality. To begin with, such an approach may stifle alternative interpretations of what God wants, including different readings of the Bible. If Jesus indeed came to proclaim freedom to those in captivity and let the oppressed go free (Luke 4.18–19), using his name to sanction enslavement and cruelty is wrong. Yet using God's name to sanction imbalances of power and privilege in society is an effective way of silencing dissent.

As a 2006 Church of England document, Responding to domestic abuse: Guidelines for those with pastoral responsibilities, points out:

> It has been forgotten that Jesus' teaching and ministry not only humbled the exalted but exalted the humble.

> ....the theology of self-denial and redemptive suffering which flows from the crucifixion of Jesus and the symbol of the cross has often undermined people's recognition of the evils being done to them and implanted masochistic attitudes of acceptance, or even celebration, of their afflictions...

> Part of the Spirit's function is to help the Christian community to interpret the Bible and tradition in the light of 'what belongs to Jesus' (John 16.15), so that we may sift the healthy from the unhealthy elements of our inheritance and be 'guided into all the truth' (John 16.13).

The concepts of self-denial and the way of the cross can be wrongly applied, with damaging consequences. This does not, in itself, demonstrate that it is wrong to urge lesbian, gay, bisexual and transgender (LGBT) people to abstain from same-sex partnerships. However it suggests that caution is advisable.

It may be useful to look again at what Jesus said, in context, and then review how it might be applied to LGBT people's situation.

The way of love: losing and gaining life
In the Gospels, the exalted are indeed brought low and the lowly exalted. When Jesus is conceived, his mother, Mary, rejoices that God has:

> brought down the powerful from their thrones,
> and lifted up the lowly;
> he has filled the hungry with good things,
> and sent the rich away empty (Luke 1.52–53).

Lives are transformed as, in word and deed, Jesus proclaims God's realm of peace and love, announcing that he has come to bring good news to the poor and freedom to the oppressed.

(Luke 4.18). Many are attracted to him but many of the most pious are outraged when his commitment to the marginalised and attentiveness to human need leads him to act in ways which they believe are contrary to Scripture.

For instance he defends his disciples when they are accused of breaking a commandment by plucking corn on the day of rest because they are hungry, declaring that "The Sabbath was made for humankind, and not humankind for the Sabbath." (Mark 2.27). "If you had known what this means, 'I desire mercy and not sacrifice', you would not have condemned the guiltless", he tells their accusers. (Matthew 12.7, Hosea 6.6).

When he heals a man with a withered arm in a place of worship on the Sabbath, Jesus' enemies begin plotting to destroy him. (Mark 3.6). To them, it seems improper that the desire to relieve hardship, especially when it afflicts someone so unimportant in the world's terms, should come above sacred duty, but Jesus' view of what God requires is radically different.

"In everything do to others as you would have them do to you; for this is the law and the prophets," he advises. Even if people are told that something is willed by God, they must look critically at the claim, being attentive to the consequences: "A good tree cannot bear bad fruit, nor can a bad tree bear good fruit. Every tree that does not bear good fruit is cut down and thrown into the fire. Thus you will know them by their fruits." (Matthew 7.12, 18–20).

"Whoever loves father or mother more than me is not worthy of me; and whoever loves son or daughter more than me is not worthy of me; and whoever does not take up the cross and follow me is not worthy of me. Those who find their life will lose it, and those who lose their life for my sake will find it", he says (Matthew 10.37–39). God's realm is like a pearl of great value, for which his followers should be willing to give up all they have. (Matthew 13.45–46).

On the other hand, he offers to ease the load of those weighed down by legalistic religiosity and an oppressive social order: "Come to me, all you that are weary and are carrying heavy burdens, and I will give you rest. Take my yoke upon you, and learn from me; for I am gentle and humble in heart, and you will find rest for your souls. For my yoke is easy, and my burden is light". (Matthew 11.28–30).

He is also accused of being a glutton and drunkard, a friend of tax collectors and sinners (Luke 7.34), indicating that he is willing to be condemned as self-indulgent and morally lax if needs be. Food, drink, shelter, fellowship and life itself (provided these are not acquired through harming or depriving others) are good things to be enjoyed, gifts of a generous Father: though Jesus' concern that none should be denied such benefits means that he is willing to forego these himself if needs be.

Aware that his opponents are out to have him killed, though his disciples are in denial about the suffering that lies ahead, Jesus warns them that "If any want to become my followers, let them deny themselves and take up their cross and follow me."

'Deny' is sometimes translated as 'disown' or 'forsake'. According to Strong's concordance, the Greek word *aparnéomai* may suggest 'strongly reject': the instinct for self-preservation must be set aside.

Love is costly, especially in a world so often dominated by greed, cruelty, prejudice and callous indifference and in which scapegoating is rife. "This is my commandment, that you love one another as I have loved you. No one has greater love than this, to lay down one's life for one's friends", Jesus tells his followers in John's gospel, shortly before his betrayal and arrest.

He is abandoned, convicted of blasphemy and subversion, beaten, mocked and crucified, a painful form of execution used against slaves and rebels in the Roman empire. Yet according to Christian belief, he is raised from the dead, signalling the ultimate triumph of life, love and truth and offering hope to humankind.

God has been willing to experience suffering and death so that humans may be freed from their grasp, the divine image no longer tarnished but able to shine brightly, the old self replaced with what is imperishable, this tradition claims. The Epistles reflect on this new life.

For instance, Galatians calls for an approach to righteousness based not on legalism but on right relationship with God and neighbour: "through the law I died to the law, so that I might live to God. I have been crucified with Christ; and it is no longer I who live, but it is Christ who lives in me. And the life I now live in the flesh I live by faith in the Son of God, who loved me and gave himself for me," Paul writes. (Galatians 2.19–20).

He warns that if followers of Christ cling to the notion that they must be circumcised (an act mandated by Scripture for men), "the offence of the cross has been removed... you were called to freedom, brothers and sisters; only do not use your freedom as an opportunity for self-indulgence, but through love become slaves to one another. For the whole law is summed up in a single commandment, 'You shall love your neighbour as yourself'". (Galatians 5.11, 13–14).

Through the cross, barriers are broken down, between humankind and God and among different sets of people. Though those who were Jewish and Gentile were once divided, Christ has "broken down the dividing wall, that is, the hostility between us" so that "he might create in himself one new humanity in place of the two, thus making peace, and might reconcile both groups to God in one body through the cross, thus putting to death that hostility through it". (Ephesians 2.14–16).

In the light of New Testament teaching, it is worth re-examining the relevance of such concepts to the sexuality debate.

Taking up the cross, living the resurrection life

Some Christians argue that the biblical view is straightforward. The way of the cross means, for the majority, urging one's LGBT neighbours to renounce any hope of a same-sex partnership, even if this means staying single and celibate for life; and, for the minority, embracing this renunciation oneself.

"The truth of the matter is that while we are a very sexualised culture and we see sexuality as a right; the reality is that sexual relationships is (sic) not what makes us happy," stated Dale Kuehne, a professor at St Anselm College in the USA.

He claimed, "We may have been profoundly impacted by this world but whether we have gay inclinations, bi inclinations, whether we're inclined toward any variety of things the fact of the matter is that all of us are called to the same sacrifice. None of us get to do what pleases us. None of us get to do what we want. We may have different challenges. Some of us may have different sexual challenges. For me, my biggest challenge is money. But the reality is, is that all of us have to stand at the cross, deny ourselves and follow Christ."

However, many couples (heterosexual or otherwise) do find happiness in marriage, though this also involves discipline, vulnerability and self-sacrifice. Indeed, at best, loving and committed partnerships involve dying to self in order to live a life of love that overspills beyond the household, supporting one another in caring for those in need and helping to usher in God's realm on earth. The impact of depriving people of even the hope of such intimacy and companionship should not be trivialised, especially if they do not feel called to celibacy.

To quote Michael Bussee from the USA, who used to be one of the leaders of an 'ex-gay' ministry but later changed his views:

> I need to say that some had a positive, life-changing experience attending our Bible studies and support groups... There were some real "changes"—but not one of the hundreds of people we counseled became straight.

> Instead, many of our clients began to fall apart – sinking deeper into patterns of guilt, anxiety and self-loathing. Why weren't they "changing"? The answers from church leaders made the pain even worse: "You might not be a real Christian." "You don't have enough faith." "You aren't praying and reading the Bible enough." "Maybe you have a demon." The message always seemed to be: "You're not enough. You're not trying hard enough. You don't have enough faith."

> Some simply dropped out and were never heard from again. I think they were the lucky ones. Others became very self-destructive. One young man got drunk and deliberately drove his car into a tree... One of my most dedicated

clients, Mark, took a razor blade to his genitals, slashed himself repeatedly, and then poured drain-cleaner on the wounds—because after months of celibacy he had a "fall."

As another former 'ex-gay' leader who changed his stance, John Smid, explained:

Some people believe that homosexuality is merely a sexual desire. They believe it is simply a sexual appetite that can be controlled by repentance and self -discipline, and that it should be. This mindset often comes from people who have never been gay...

For my entire life I have had deep needs for an intimate connection with another man. The kind of connection that finds peace and fulfillment in merely holding one close, or laughing freely in such a way that can lead to an intimate hug without fear...

To be told for over two decades that this kind of connection is against God's nature, sinful, and that one can never have this kind of fulfillment has been disheartening. It has led me to depression, sadness, and has caused many years of feeling separated from my very soul...

I worked diligently to help gay men lay aside addictive practices with sex and pornography. Some found abatement for a season, but many never found the freedom they desired... The ongoing shame often led to a complete separation of their souls from God or anything spiritual.

This is until they finally release themselves from the cultural message that would refuse to acknowledge the deep need within them. Once they went on to find the true intimate connection with another person that matched their nature it seemed somehow that their road of life began anew.

He admitted that it was hard when those he had known for years broke off their connection with him and unsettling to deconstruct facades which he had used to hold up a false reality, but regarded it as worthwhile as he experienced the grace of God in a more authentic way.

Hence there are contrasting views of what it might mean to live the resurrection life.

Taking a stance for full acceptance of LGBT people, or even their human rights, can be costly, bringing the risk of condemnation, job loss or worse. Some Christians have been murdered for seeking greater equality.

For instance, San Francisco mayor George Moscone, who was heterosexual himself but worked to promote inclusion for minorities, women and the poor, was shot dead in 1978; while Cameroonian journalist and LGBT rights activist Eric Lembembe was brutally murdered in 2013 in what is widely believed to have been a homophobic killing. Perhaps they witness in an especially direct way to what it might mean to bear the cross.

Faithfulness and suffering

While following Christ will inevitably involve suffering, not all sacrifice is God-ordained. Indeed Jesus' example and teaching should make Christians more, rather than less, willing to examine whether the burdens laid on certain sets of people are truly justified.

Not following one's vocation can also be a source of sadness, for instance, like the rich young ruler in the gospels (Matthew 19.16–30, Mark 10.17–31, Luke 18.18–30), who goes away grieving because he has chosen a life of devout, law-abiding respectability and prosperity over the loss and uncertainty of joining Jesus' band of followers.

Those who insist that LGBT people who love God should abandon any hope of a entering a loving and committed same-sex partnership should at least consider the possibility that they might be wrong. The fact that some people who are mainly attracted to the same sex successfully lead celibate lives is not enough to insist that it is not only possible, but also right, for all others. The ethic proposed, though working well for some, has driven others to depression, despair and even suicide, so love and justice require that it be carefully examined.

If the chief executive of a firm insisted, because one or two of his employees had run a marathon, that all should do so, contemptuously sacking those who collapsed with heat-stroke or heart attacks, there would be an outcry. Portraying God in such a way can damage Christian witness.

I would suggest that, in following Christ and dying to the old way of life, both LGBT people and heterosexuals should be encouraged to look more deeply at society and the church as well, examining whether the patterns of relationships are truly conducive to abundance of life.

This may involve, for heterosexual people, scrutinising the privileges which they may take for granted, for instance being able to remark on the attractiveness of a member of the opposite sex, or mention a current or former romantic partner, without being afraid of being verbally or physically attacked or threatened with hellfire. For those who are LGBT, it may involve reawakening parts of oneself that had been kept buried, a sometimes painful process; and confronting one's own self-hatred and others' misconceptions, even if this involves conflict, so as to move towards a more authentic and lasting peace.

Further prayer, study and dialogue may be helpful to churches seeking to discern where the Holy Spirit is leading. Meanwhile, all should be united in combating mistreatment and violence and affirming God's generous love for all, whatever their ethnicity, socio-economic status, gender or sexual orientation.

Part 4: Living with disagreement

Chapter 13 discussed how debates on sexuality could be conducted in ways that are just and mutually respectful. The final part of the book, made up of chapters 33–34, examines this further.

This includes the suggestion that churches which have been open to discussing sexuality in a thoughtful manner are moving towards a middle ground where those with different views can coexist until there is broader agreement. It is based on an essay first published, and widely shared, at the end of 2013 but has been slightly modified in the light of comments received.

If Christians can get better at living with disagreement on this subject without pretending that the truth does not matter, there are lessons to be learnt, in the church and beyond. Among other people of goodwill too, who seek to act ethically and make the world better, conflict often arises and is all the more painful because it may divide those who thought they shared the same ideals and values.

Consensus will probably be reached sooner or later but this may take decades or even centuries. Meanwhile, controversy will continue but it need not lead to bitterness and rejection.

Chapter Thirty-Three

Church views on sexuality: recovering the middle ground

It is clear that Christians hold a spectrum of views on sexuality and marriage.

However, the popular idea that there are two warring blocks which may straightforwardly be labelled 'traditionalists' and 'revisionists', is simplistic and can be misleading as well as unhelpful. Current tensions could be reduced and reframed significantly if more church leaders acknowledged the extent of common ground in the middle of this continuum, allowed limited flexibility of practice, and enabled their communities to develop practices of discernment oriented towards the "grace and truth" (John 1.13–15) that lies at the heart of the Christian message.

Identifying the spectrum of views among Christians

There have been heated debates over sexuality in many churches. Some people fear that divisions on this issue, in particular as to how same-sex partnerships should be viewed, are too deep to overcome.

Yet there has been increasing convergence on a relatively narrow range within the broad spectrum of views held by Christians about sexuality. Those with supposedly opposing views often have more in common than they may at first think.

Practically, it should be possible for churches to accept that congregations and their members may, for the time being, occupy different spaces within this middle ground – not simply reducing conflict but also, through conversation and engagement, reframing and recasting it.

Moreover, the theological conviction of this paper is that, in time, if Christians continue to think, pray, talk and listen to one another, the Spirit can be trusted to lead us into what different church traditions call "the fullness of truth" on this matter.

The spectrum of widely held views set out below is broadly

indicative rather than narrowly prescriptive. People may shift their position somewhat or it may be hard to categorise, rather as an object may appear green in one light and blue in another.

Yet this may be a useful starting-point for identifying what areas of agreement and disagreement exist. A similar continuum can be drawn up on gender identity.

There is, not surprisingly, a similar range of views among people of other faiths and none. However, the reasons which Christians may have for accepting or rejecting particular positions are likely to be influenced by their faith.

The seven main positions could broadly be described as:

1. Me first, anything goes
2. Treat others decently, whether relationships are sexual or not
3. Support marriage between partners of the same or opposite sex
4. Support marriage for opposite-sex couples and lifelong faithful partnership for same-sex couples
5. Support marriage for opposite-sex couples based on equality, welcome lesbians and gays but abstinence is best for them
6. Support marriage for opposite-sex couples based on male headship, encourage lesbians and gays to abstain or try to change
7. The husband is boss, lesbians and gays are not acceptable

It is worth noting in passing that historically, there have also been varying views among Christians (ranging from Evangelicals and Pentecostals to Catholics and Orthodox) on whether marriage is (or can be) regarded as a sacrament – a ceremony regarded as imparting spiritual grace – and, if so, what this implies.

This matter is not the focus of my attention here.

Instead, I will examine the positions (set out in outline above) in more depth, looking at which might be considered as 'mainstream' by churches today. I will then examine possible ways forward for Christians who disagree on sexual ethics but would like to remain in fellowship.

It should also be noted that, as in other areas of conduct, Christians may sometimes fall short of acting upon their ethical beliefs (or occasionally behave better than might be predicted). Also, there is a difference between an ethical and legal code, and between setting ideals for oneself and judging others.

Unacceptable extremes

Positions 1 and 7 on the spectrum set out above might seem to reflect opposite extremes of unrestrained individualism and rigid sexism, yet they share certain characteristics. While relatively few Christians would argue publicly for these, they may underpin the attitudes and actions of some.

Position 1 says that it is acceptable to pursue any sexual relationship that brings one pleasure or profit, whatever the impact on others. The most extreme form would permit sexual violence, abuse of under-age children and bestiality, though not all would go so far. However deception and manipulation would not be ruled out.

Lesbian, gay, bisexual and trans (LGBT) people would be equal to heterosexual people in this set-up but other forms of inequality would be rife, as people used their power – based on status, wealth, beauty or other factors – to get what they wanted.

Individuals might appear to have complete freedom but, in practice, some would be less free than others, for instance those forced into the sex industry by extreme poverty, or the naive and emotionally needy who are seduced by those who claim to love them.

People who hold position 1 would not usually be particularly interested in the reasons why someone very poor, or whose upbringing was deeply damaging, ended up as a prostitute, provided she or he could offer them gratification. Likewise, if they broke up with a lover who had fallen in love with them but of whom they had tired, they would regard that as his or her tough luck.

Position 7 is that, in sexual partnerships, men's interests

should come first and they should be in charge, while women should serve them. Same-sex relationships should be frowned upon and LGBT people may be treated with hostility or contempt.

The most extreme form of this position would permit infidelity by husbands though not wives (the sexual double standard) or polygamy, and even violent coercion against women and gays, though not all would go so far.

Empathy with those who are attracted to, or fall in love with, members of the same sex, or indeed women who do not easily fit into subordinate roles, would not be encouraged. Macho behaviour and patriarchal patterns of family life would be regarded as natural. This position would promote selfishness among the more powerful in marriages and wider society, while others would be at risk of being exploited and oppressed.

Indeed, some people may see-saw between these positions, for instance acting the patriarch at home while secretly having sex with those in vulnerable positions.

Likewise, during wars and gang or communal conflicts, rigid and unequal family patterns may sometimes coexist alongside the no-holds-barred abuse of women and weaker men from other communities.

In addition, same-sex sexual activity takes place even in the most patriarchal societies, whether or not the feelings involved are publicly acknowledged. So position 7 tends to result in dysfunctional social patterns.

It is to be hoped that the majority of churches would strongly reject both these positions as harmful to humans made in God's image and as not being in keeping with the command to love one's neighbour as oneself. This does not mean that those who live by these codes should be rejected as people by the church, but certainly such patterns of behaviour would be hard to justify theologically, though some may try.

Christians as well as non-Christians may hold these positions for various reasons, for instance because of their upbringing or because they fit in with particular views of how society should be run. For example, people who have embraced consumerism may favour 1, while supporters of authoritarianism may be drawn to 7.

But they may nevertheless learn to behave differently through the influence of love, which the church can nurture and encourage by offering a community in which justice and compassion are not regarded as weak or 'letting the side down'.

Positions sincerely endorsed by some Christians, but which are less than satisfactory

Positions 2 and 6 are less extreme and theological arguments can be made for both of them, though I would suggest that they are outweighed by reasons against.

Position 2 is that there the same ethical code should be used for sexual and non-sexual relationships. Other people should be treated unselfishly and honestly, but exclusivity / faithfulness and permanence are not necessary between lovers unless this is explicitly promised or, perhaps, if a couple have children or other dependants who might be harmed if they split up or took other partners.

Equality and justice would be emphasised, whether people are LGBT or heterosexual. Indeed, some might think such distinctions questionable. Likewise friendship would be highly valued and kindness and openness encouraged.

Position 6 believes that sex should only happen between married opposite-sex couples in faithful lifelong relationships, though people who fall short of the ideal may be treated compassionately. Both partners should put each other first and the husband should consult his wife but take responsibility for key decisions as head of the household. Those attracted to the same sex should be encouraged to abstain from sexual relationships unless they marry a member of the opposite sex.

Some who hold this position, while regarding marital breakdown with great regret, would accept the possibility of remarriage after annulment or divorce.

The case for position 2 could include the difficulty of identifying a consistent sexual ethic in the Bible (for instance there are varying attitudes to eunuchs and to polygamy), and of the gap which exists between the ancient world it was set in and today's world.

Jesus' and Paul's rejection of legalism, emphasising instead love of God and neighbour and treating others as one would wish to be treated (Matthew 7.12, 22.36–40, Romans 13.8–10, Galatians 5.13–14), might seem a more reliable guide for all human relationships.

However position 2 fails to take enough account of the emotional vulnerability which many feel in sexual contexts and of the potential for joy, spiritual growth and mutual support in doing good which many find in committed faithful partnerships. There may be different perspectives on the biblical concept of partners becoming 'one flesh' (Genesis 2.18–24, Matthew 19.4–6), but it does reflect a very common experience. Underestimating the power of sexuality can lead to hurt, even if this is unintentional, and to a loss of opportunity.

Position 6 does acknowledge the potential for both good and ill in sexual relationships, in line with warnings in the New Testament epistles about sexual immorality. Potential benefits include conceiving children and bringing them up in a stable and caring setting. The concept of male headship can be argued from Ephesians 5.21–33 and is consistent with certain other passages in the epistles.

The emphasis on gender hierarchy is not however, in keeping with the insight in Galatians 3.28 that "There is no longer Jew or Greek, there is no longer slave or free, there is no longer male and female; for all of you are one in Christ Jesus." In the new creation, barriers are broken down and those on whom the Holy Spirit is poured are no longer trapped by the roles which society might allocate, but rather freed to use their gifts as part of a new body in which all members are equally honoured (Acts 2.1–21, 1 Corinthians 12.4–26).

It is insensitive to the damaging impact of sexism and prejudice on grounds of sexual orientation. In its treatment of women and gays, position 6 fails to do justice – a central theme in the Bible. And its promotion of hierarchical relationships among humans can displace the reverence due only to God.

Supporters of positions 2 or 6 are often sincere Christians, may have some useful insights and should be treated courteously and listened to attentively. Their views are still influential, as are combinations which include these. For instance some believe in a hybrid of positions 2 and 3 which embraces lifelong partnerships but not monogamy, or vice versa. Likewise, others hold to a hybrid of positions 6 and 5 which is positive about women's position but negative about people who are LGBT.

However in the longer term it would appear that these are losing ground and those who champion position 2 or 6 are unlikely to convince the rest of us that theirs should be the church's stance.

The middle ground
A comparatively narrow range of views makes up the middle ground towards which many churches have in practice been converging. A process of discernment is under way, though many church leaders do not explicitly recognise this, and some members may be unaware that a sizeable proportion of their fellow-worshippers think differently from themselves.

In some parts of the world, harsh state repression or prejudiced public attitudes to LGBT people may make it hard for Christians to find out about and seriously consider alternative perspectives. But where there have been opportunities for broad discussion which takes account of the Bible, tradition, reason and experience, many have settled on position 3, 4 or 5.

These share the perspective that love of God and neighbour are inextricably linked. Treating others justly and compassionately and, through closeness to others, becoming more loving is important, for "everyone who loves is born of God and knows God. Whoever does not love does not know God, for God is love" (1 John 4.7–8).

While love, in Christian terms, may involve showing mercy and generosity to all (Matthew 5.42–48) and loyalty and care towards others of one's faith (John 13.34–35), emotionally close relationships also matter.

In the Hebrew Bible, the soul of Jonathan is bound to the soul of David, whom he loves as his own soul, and they make a covenant (1 Samuel 18.1–4), a bond of love which endures despite the most difficult circumstances (1 Samuel 20, 23.15–18, 2 Samuel 1.26). This exemplifies the trustworthiness of the divine covenant of love with God's people. In John's Gospel, Jesus loves all his followers while relating in a special way to "the disciple Jesus loved" (John 13.21–26, 19.25–27, 21.20–23).

Church tradition draws on this gospel in developing a doctrine of the Holy Trinity, joined in intimate love (e.g. John 3.34–35, 14.8–17), which outflows to humankind.

Sexual relationships should not be entered into lightly or in an exploitative manner. Faithful, self-giving, lifelong faithful marriage founded on equality can offer unmatched opportunities for emotional and spiritual growth, as well as the nurture of children (if any). LGBT people should be welcomed and respected, and committed same-sex as well as opposite-sex partnerships can be deeply loving.

The emphasis on constancy and justice in these positions would make them all counter-cultural in many settings. Yet there are also important differences.

In position 3, churches should support and celebrate the marriage of both opposite-sex and same-sex couples, and all forms of ministry should be open to LGBT as well as heterosexual people. While lifelong celibacy is to be respected as a vocation, relatively few people are called to it. Being married offers a constructive channel for the yearning for intimacy and enables partners to understand more deeply, and reflect more fully, the trustworthy and generous love of God. Fruitfulness matters but this is not always about having biological children: there are various ways in which couples' love could benefit others.

Position 4 would celebrate committed loving same-sex partnerships involving emotional and physical intimacy but regard them as different from marriage, reserving this term for opposite-sex couples. Those who hold this view might or might not agree that the civil authorities and people of other beliefs should be free to regard same-sex relationships as marriages.

While some advocates of this stance regard same-sex relationships as not being as good, or at least not as central to humankind as heterosexual marriage, others might think of them as equally valid but different in character and even, in a few cases, better because they do not carry the legacy of patriarchy attached to the notion of being married.

Supporters of position 5 would, while recognising that sexually intimate lesbian and gay partnerships can be exemplary in many ways, regard lifelong celibacy as more in keeping with biblical teaching and church tradition. While opposing human rights abuses, some (though not all) of those who hold this view would be reluctant to appoint ministers who were non-celibate and partnered with someone of the same sex.

In recent years, many theologians have argued the case for each of these three positions. At a leadership and grassroots level in various churches, many members have wrestled with the issue of sexuality and likewise have come to hold one of these positions, sometimes shifting their stance. Some are still trying to decide which position seems best.

The debate can become unhelpful and even destructive if positions 1–3 or 5–7 are treated as identical (sometimes lumping position 4 in with one set or the other). This also makes it harder to raise awareness of the damaging consequences of positions 1 and 7.

Indeed, fellow Christians who disagree on sexuality may be treated as if they have abandoned all respect for Scripture and tradition, or any attention to reason and experience. Yet there may be sincere disagreement on how these are interpreted by those who seek to follow Christ today in their own settings, while being part of a universal fellowship that crosses time and space.

In seeking to do justice, love kindness and walk humbly with God (Micah 6.7–9), avoid false witness (Exodus 20.16), love one another with mutual affection and outdo one another in showing honour (Romans 12.10), clarity matters.

This does not mean glossing over the tensions that can exist near the middle of the spectrum.

For instance, supporters of position 3 (myself included) might point to the unnecessary loneliness faced by many LGBT people who are persuaded to steer clear of committed partnerships by advocates of position 5, the loss of faith some experience and the damage to the church's mission when it is perceived as narrow-minded and unjust.

Similarly, supporters of position 5 might regard those who favour position 3 as encouraging a way of life which is ultimately unhelpful to the practice of Christian discipleship. It can be hard work to be part of a faith community where sizeable numbers of people disagree on such matters.

Yet churches hold together despite disagreement on a range of important issues, doctrinal and ethical. As in the days of the early church, unity need not be based on uniformity of opinion on all matters.

Moving forward amid uncertainty

There are various approaches to dealing with disagreement in faith communities. Suppression of dissent can lead either to unthinking conformity and/or splits, while refusal ever to challenge erroneous views may erode credibility and convey the impression of indifference to truth, justice and faithfulness to God's will.

Ultimately, the Spirit of truth can be trusted to lead seekers into all truth (John 16.13), Christians believe. But in the interim they may get things wrong. The New Testament offers examples of different ways of dealing with difference.

Paul starts as Saul, a religious fanatic who condones violence against those he thinks are wrong, until he realises that he is persecuting the very God whose honour he thinks he is defending. In contrast, the wise rabbi Gamaliel argues that "if this plan or this undertaking is of human origin, it will fail; but if it is of God, you will not be able to overthrow them – in that case you may even be found fighting against God!" (Acts 5.34–38).

Later, Paul has a showdown with the top church leaders of his day over the issue of demanding that converts to Christianity should obey Jewish law (Galatians 2), which would have hampered the spread of faith. Yet on the issue of eating food offered to idols, he takes the view that it is worth making concessions to others' conscientious scruples, even if these are wrong, if not doing so might undermine their faith (1 Corinthians 8). Being loving matters more than proving that one is right: "Knowledge puffs up, but love builds up."

On sexuality, senior leaders in some churches present position 5 (or even a mixture of this and position 6) as a clear biblical norm while, in practice, other clergy or elders and congregations adopt position 4, or possibly 3. This is less than satisfactory, since it may appear to promote duplicity, while LGBT people and their friends may still feel unwelcome. However, it is better than purging churches of minorities and dissidents and, possibly, fighting against God.

Yet if position 3 or 4 is believed by the majority of members to be most in accord with God's will, with a sizeable minority not yet convinced, obliging all congregations and ministers to celebrate same-sex partnerships could alienate those who are reluctant and may inflame divisions.

It would seem that the most constructive approach is for church leaders to be open about the differences that exist, while acknowledging the extent of common ground in the middle of the spectrum, and allowing some flexibility of practice. Some ministers and churches might conscientiously choose to celebrate partnerships between same-sex couples, while others might opt not to do so.

At the same time, in order to move the debate forward, churches should challenge those with strong views on sexuality to spell out clearly the practical and theological reasoning behind positions they may take for granted, even if this seems obvious to them, and to engage with others' arguments.

This may be difficult for people who feel vulnerable, because it seems to them that their identity and deepest relationships are in question, or that the world is changing in ways which leave them bewildered and disempowered. However, both advocates of change and church leaders should be encouraged to set a helpful tone in debating issues constructively and supporting human dignity for all.

Bishops and other senior clergy (or elders and ministers in other traditions) who coordinate diverse Christian communities would not be able to please everyone, but should be able to articulate their own views coherently while listening to and caring for those who disagree. They in turn, should try to be supportive of their bishop even if not entirely happy with his or her views and (if relevant) partnership.

This is not to say that positions 3, 4 and 5 will be regarded by their different proponents as equally valid. Indeed, bringing differences into the open and encouraging prayerful and reasoned debate may bring forward the day when there is broad consensus on sexual ethics.

If churches can deal constructively with disagreement on this matter, it will surely also contribute to the overall quality of theological understanding and discussion. As the family therapist and priest Sue Walrond-Skinner once asked: how will people discover, by the way we disagree as well as by our agreement, that we are committed to Christ and seeking the kingdom (or commonwealth) of God?

Meanwhile, Christians sharing the 'middle ground' of the spectrum should be able to coexist, jointly seeking to make God's love known and practised and allowing one another some measure of freedom, recognising their deeper unity in Christ.

Such a stance is not about weak compromise. In theological terms it is truly radical – that is, both deeply rooted in Scripture and tradition and open to the change and transformation that a living community requires in order not to be left behind by the God who, in biblical terms, is always ahead of us, inviting us to discover more of the ways of love, truth and justice.

Chapter Thirty-Four

Coping with difference and moving forward

Many churches are now formally discussing whether same-sex partnerships should be accepted. Among Christians in general, conversations on the issues are taking place, though sometimes on a low-key basis. Such debates are likely to continue for some years to come.

Some people still regard church unity as a matter of minimising public disagreement. All too often, this favours those with most power and downplays the importance of justice and truth. However, there is now greater awareness that conflict, if handled in a constructive way, may lead to growth, even if this is painful. In addition, it is more widely known that LGBT people often pay a heavy cost when their reality is ignored, and their families and friends may be affected too.

This ties in with a wider challenge facing churches: to undertake what an Anglican conference in 1930 described as "the duty of thinking and learning as essential elements in the Christian life." Indeed, for all people of goodwill, in a world where there is so much suffering and the very future of humankind is threatened, personal spirituality and immediate care for those in need – while important – are not enough.

All too often, churches have failed to challenge attitudes and systems which impoverish millions and push disabled and ethnic minority people, women and other groups to the margins, sometimes seeking to sanctify injustice. It is vital not to take for granted the claims of people in authority and instead look more deeply at important issues. Inevitably, this will involve conflict. At the same time, it is important to probe new ideas and calls for change, while seeking to understand whether these truly offer liberation or are themselves oppressive.

There may be both positive and negative lessons to be learnt from the manner in which church debates over sexuality have been handled. Trying to understand others' views, reflecting them fairly, communicating one's own beliefs and experiences with clarity while seeking common ground without glossing over differences may be hard work. But with practice this can become easier.

Human rights abuses however, make matters far harder. Those churches which encourage the jailing, dismissal or eviction of LGBT people and their friends undermine their own ability to share the Gospel with any credibility. Their overseas allies should also examine their own role in intensifying the suffering of those already marginalised and in making hatred seem respectable.

At the same time, attempts to persuade less homophobic and transphobic governments to force the adoption of full equality by churches – which are made by a few people who support greater acceptance – are unhelpful. Not only are these highly unlikely to succeed, since religious freedom is deeply entrenched, but they fail to recognise the risks of giving the state too much power. It is right that publicly-funded projects, even if run by religious organisations, should not discriminate against LGBT users and employees, partnered or single. But people of faith themselves must draw on their own values and traditions in taking responsibility for changing the way that worshipping communities treat women and LGBT people.

Some churches have made more progress than others in coming up with models for living with difference in situations where conscience leads sizeable numbers of church members in different directions. This may involve respecting the choices of ministers and congregations. For example, in the United Reformed Church, ministers may decide whether or not to celebrate civil partnerships and a similar arrangement is being considered for marriages involving same-sex couples.

Consensus will probably be reached at some point, but this is likely to take decades or even centuries. For the time being, even when Christians disagree about sexual ethics, they may be able to unite on other matters, which in turn, may shed new light on areas of disagreement.

It may be useful to look more deeply at how intimate relationships fit in with Christ's call to seek first God's realm, that commonwealth of justice, peace and love where the hungry are fed and the marginalised welcomed. Meanwhile, however people define their beliefs and sexuality, all are faced with the joys and challenges of living with diversity.

Autobiographical notes

Author **Savitri Hensman** was born in Sri Lanka in 1962 and moved to England as a small child. As well as being a writer, she worked for many years in the voluntary sector, largely around involvement in equalities, health and social care. She has also worked as a consultant.

Savi writes:

I first became interested in the sexuality debate when I was about twelve years old. I was a devout young Anglican when it gradually dawned on me that I was more attracted to the same than the opposite sex. It was only a few decades since churches had begun to accept even the use of contraceptives between married couples, and sex between men had only been legal for a few years (in Scotland, Northern Ireland and numerous countries outside the UK, it was still a crime).

I had grown up believing that same-sex relationships were always wrong. In addition, stereotyping was widespread and it was widely believed that such relationships were superficial or would end in misery (something I later discovered was completely false). It took me years of study and reflection, including revisiting what the Bible actually said, before I changed my mind.

Since then I have continued to follow, and take part in, discussions among Christians on this and various other matters, as well as seeking greater inclusion in church and society. I have been fortunate to belong to congregations whose members have remained in fellowship with one another while grappling with controversial issues. I was also privileged to spend twenty-four years with my life-partner until she died of cancer, and through this experience, to deepen my understanding of the joys and challenges of loving partnerships.

In other churches too, and among people of other faiths and none, conversations have been taking place about sexuality. Those taking part include heterosexual people who are no longer content with rigid gender roles in marriage. It has been a time of learning and sometimes painful growth and I have tried to give a flavour of this in the book.

Rachel Mann, who wrote the Foreword to this book, is an English Anglican priest, poet and feminist theologian. Since 2008 she has been Priest-in-Charge at the Church of St Nicholas, Burnage. She is also Resident Poet at Manchester Cathedral.

Notes and resources

Some chapters have endnotes (reproduced below), others do not – or have sources cited in or at the end of the chapter. We have followed the referencing style that was adopted with the original article where it has been reproduced here, and the author's preference for original material. All major sources are noted. Citations from the Internet were current as of 15 November 2015. Full URLs have been cited. Readers may find it more convenient and quicker to search for articles by title and author online rather than to type in URLs.

Chapter Three

[1]   See e.g. Reddie R, The Church: Enslaver or Liberator?, BBC, http://www.bbc.co.uk/history/british/abolition/church_and_slavery_article_01.shtml; Noll MA, 'Battle for the Bible', Christian Century, 2 May 2006, http://www.religion-online.org/showarticle.asp?title=3403

[2]   Those who would like more information might wish to visit the section on sexuality on the Fulcrum website for an Anglican perspective from a less extreme position than that taken by some opponents of same-sex unions, http://www.fulcrum-anglican.org.uk/tag/sexuality/, and for a Roman Catholic perspective, visit the Pontifical Council for the Family webpage, http://www.vatican.va/roman_curia/pontifical_councils/family/index.htm

[3]   For example Anselm, who was to become Archbishop of Canterbury, wrote to his friend Gilbert Crispin in the eleventh century, "Sweet are the gifts, sweet friend, which your sweet love sends ; but they are utterly powerless to console my heart, which is desolated by your absence. No, not if you sent me all the most fragrant spices, the most glittering metals, the most precious stones, the most delicate embroidery, could my soul consent to be comforted, for it is quite beyond its power, unless its other half which has been torn away be given back to it again. My heart's pain bears me witness as I think of this; so do the tears which cloud my eyes and wet my fingers as I write... To you our very separation has given the presence of another, whom you love not less, yea more, than me ; but I have lost you, I say; and none has been given me in your place" (Robinson JA, Notes and documents relating to Westminster Abbey: Abbot Gilbert Crispin, Cambridge University Press 1911, http://www.archive.org/stream/gilbertcrispinab00robiuoft/gilbertcrispinab00robiuoft_djvu.txt).

[4]   Seventeenth century English mystic Thomas Traherne was unusually

explicit in his poem 'Love' (http://www.bartleby.com/236/49.html), which compares the ecstasy of being loved by God with the joys of Danae and Ganymede, female and male lovers of Jove in classical mythology.

[5] See e.g. 'Contraception', BBC, http://www.bbc.co.uk/religion/religions/christianity/christianethics/contraception_1.shtml

[6] Florensky P (translated Jakim B), Letters 4 and 11 in The Pillar and Ground of the Truth, Princeton University Press, 1997.

[7] Hilliard D, 'UnEnglish and unmanly: Anglo-Catholicism and homosexuality', Victorian Studies, Vol. 25, No. 2, Winter, 1982, pp.181–210. http://anglicanhistory.org/academic/hilliard_unenglish.pdf

[8] Ingram AK, Sex-Morality Tomorrow, George Allen and Unwin, 1940.

[9] Ingram AK, Christianity and sexual morality – a modernist view, Union of Modern Free Churchmen, 1944

[10] Carey JS, 'DS Bailey and the "name forbidden among Christians"', Anglican Theological Review, 1988, vol. 70, no2, pp. 152–173, http://www.williamapercy.com/wiki/images/DS_bailey_and_the_name_forbidden_among_christians_studies_of_homosexuality_volume_12.pdf

[11] Derrick Sherwin Bailey, Homosexuality and the Western Christian tradition (London, New York and Toronto: Longmans, 1955); see especially pp.153–174.

[12] Towards a Quaker View of Sex, Friends Home Services Committee, 1964; see extracts on http://www.worldpolicy.org/sites/default/files/uploaded/image/Quakers-1964-Towards%20a%20Quaker%20View%20of%20Sex.pdf

[13] Childs J, 'Helmut Thielicke: A Formative Voice of Evangelical Ethics', Journal of Lutheran Ethics (JLE) Volume 9, Issue 9, September 2009, http://downloads.elca.org/html/jle/www.elca.org/what-we-believe/social-issues/a-formative-voice-of-evangelical-ee8ffdf7c.htm

[14] Rhymes D, No new morality: Christian personal values and sexual morality, Constable, 1964

[15] Nolan RT, 'Dr. W. Norman Pittenger', LGBT Religious Archives Network, http://www.lgbtran.org/Profile.aspx?ID=158

[16] See obituary in the Guardian by Michael de-la-Noy, http://www.guardian.co.uk/news/2005/may/14/guardianobituaries.religion

[17] 'Harry Williams' (obituary), Guardian, 20 February 2006, http://www.guardian.co.uk/news/2006/feb/20/guardianobituaries.obituaries

[18] See e.g. 'Michel Foucault', Stanford Encyclopedia of Philosophy, http://plato.stanford.edu/entries/foucault/

[19] Quoted on http://churchdraft.wordpress.com/2010/04/29/rd6p-k1rkp/

[20] See e.g. Wylie-Kellerman B, 'Not vice versa. Reading the powers biblically: Stringfellow, hermeneutics, and the principalities', Anglican Theological Review, Fall 1999, http://prodigal.typepad.com/prodigal_kiwi/files/william_stringfellow_not_vice_versa.%20

Reading%20the%20Powers%20Biblically%20-%20Stringfellow,%20
Hermeneutics,and%20the%20Principalities%20by%20Bill%20Wylie-
Kellermann.pdf

[21] Stringfellow W, 'The Incarnation and Social Responsibility', http://www.
justice.net.nz/writings-to-share/the-incarnation-and-social-respon-
sability/

[22] http://www.malcolmboyd.com/home.htm

Chapter Four

[1] See e.g. http://mccchurch.org/overview/history-of-mcc/

[2] Henry P, 'Homosexuals: Identity and Dignity', Theology Today, April
1976

[3] McNeill JJ, "Homosexuality: Challenging the Church to Grow", Christian
Century, 11 March 1987, http://www.religion-online.org/showarticle.
asp?title=122

[4] http://www.religion-online.org/showarticle.asp?title=430

[5] http://www.amazon.com/Homosexual-Neighbor-Revised-Updated-
Christian/dp/0060670789#reader_0060670789

[6] See e.g. Harvard Educational Review, Summer 1996, http://www.hepg.
org/her/booknote/255

[7] http://www.welcomingresources.org/campolo

[8] Moss B and Moss R, Humanity and Sexuality, Church Information Office,
1978

[9] See e.g. profile in LGBT Religious Archive Network, http://www.lgbtran.
org/Profile.aspx?ID=100

[10] http://www.religion-online.org/showarticle.asp?title=429

[11] http://www.religion-online.org/showarticle.asp?title=1265

[12] See e.g. Ellison MM and Legge MJ, 'Justice in the Making' foreword,
https://tspace.library.utoronto.ca/bitstream/1807/24209/2/Legge-
justice.pdf

[13] http://www.outhistory.org/exhibits/show/religion_homosex/presby-
terian

[14] See obituary of John Yates by Richard Eyre in the Guardian, http://www.
guardian.co.uk/world/2008/mar/14/religion.gayrights

[15] See e.g. John Boswell page on 'People with a History: an online guide
to LGBT history', http://www.fordham.edu/halsall/pwh/index-bos.
html#reviews

[16] Davidson J, 'Mr and Mr and Mrs and Mrs': review of The Friend by Alan
Bray, London Review of Books, 2 June 2005, http://www.lrb.co.uk/v27/
n11/james-davidson/mr-and-mr-and-mrs-and-mrs

[17] http://people.brandeis.edu/~brooten/

[18] http://rowanwilliams.archbishopofcanterbury.org/pages/about-row-
an-williams.html

[19] See e.g. transcript of 'Homosexuality and the Churches' in the Religion

Report, Radio National, 5 March 2003, http://www.abc.net.au/radio-national/programs/religionreport/full-transcript-homosexuality-and-the-churches-pt-2/3531400

[20] Countryman LW, Dirt, Greed, and Sex: sexual ethics in the New Testament and their implications for today, Fortress Press, 1988

[21] See e.g. biographical note by Chris Hughes on Spring Hill College website, http://www.shc.edu/theolibrary/resources/baum.htm

[22] Baum G, 'Homosexuality and the Natural Law', The Ecumenist, Vol. 1, No. 2, 1994; quoted on http://thewildreed.blogspot.com/2009/01/perspectives-on-natural-law.html

[23] See 2010 profile by Stephen Bates in The Guardian, http://www.guardian.co.uk/world/2010/jul/08/jeffrey-john-gay-bishop-bid, also Davies L, 'Anglican stance on same-sex marriage "morally contemptible", says gay cleric', Guardian, 14 August 2012, http://www.guardian.co.uk/world/2012/aug/14/anglicans-gay-marriage-jeffrey-john

[24] Lamb ML, 'Liberation Theology and Social Justice', from Process Studies, pp. 102–122, Vol. 14, Number 2, Summer, 1985; available on Religion Online, http://www.religion-online.org/showarticle.asp?title=2570

[25] Abraham KC, Spirituality Of The Third World: A Cry For Life: Papers And Reflections From The Third General Assembly Of The Ecumenical Association Of Third World Theologians, Wipf & Stock Publishers, 2005

[26] 'Cornel West on Heterosexism and Transformation: An Interview', Harvard Educational Review, Summer 1996 issue, http://www.hepg.org/her/abstract/281

[27] Hopkins DN, 'Toward a Positive Black Male Heterosexuality', Anglican Theological Review, Summer 2008, http://www.anglicantheologicalreview.org/static/pdf/articles/hopkins.pdf

[28] http://www.richardcleaver.net/home/about

[29] Shepard B, 'Dancing in the Streets: Contested Public Spaces and the History of Queer Life', Dissent, 23 June 2011, https://www.dissentmagazine.org/online_articles/dancing-in-the-streets-contested-public-spaces-and-the-history-of-queer-life

[30] See e.g. pages on queer theory on website theory.org.uk, http://www.theory.org.uk/ctr-que1.htm

[31] See e.g. review on Wordtrade.com of Queer Theology: Rethinking the Western Body, edited by Gerard Loughlin, http://www.wordtrade.com/religion/christianity/queertheologyR.htm

[32] http://www.lgbtran.org/Profile.aspx?ID=56

[33] Goss RE, 'Proleptic Sexual Love: God's Promiscuity Reflected in Christian Polyamory', Theology and Sexuality, Vol. 11, No. 1, 52–63 (2004), http://tse.sagepub.com/cgi/content/abstract/11/1/52

[34] http://www.lgbtran.org/Profile.aspx?ID=88

[35] http://www.chrisglaser.com/

[36] See e.g. Bloomsbury Publishing's profile of Ken Stone, http://www.

bloomsbury.com/author/kenneth-stone

[37] See e.g. Wilson N, 'Queer Theology as Change Agent', 2009, http://www.moderatorscorner.mccchurch.org/?p=234

[38] http://www.lgbtran.org/Profile.aspx?ID=24

[39] Stuart E, Gay and Lesbian Theologies: Repetitions with Critical Difference, Ashgate, 2002.

[40] https://www.dur.ac.uk/theology.religion/staff/profile/?id=2394

[41] http://www.chch.ox.ac.uk/college/profile/academics/graham-ward

[42] Comstock GD and Henking SE, Que(e)Rying Religion: A Critical Anthology, Continuum, 1997

[43] Comstock GD, Gay Theology Without Apology, Pilgrim Press, 1993

[44] In Literature and Theology (2001) 15 (3), http://litthe.oxfordjournals.org/content/15/3/276.abstract

[45] See review by Mary E Hunt for The Witness, http://thewitness.org/archive/julyaug2001/mollenkott.html

[46] See e.g. entry on 'Remembering Marcella Althaus-Reid, "Indecent Theologian"' on Queer Saints and Martyrs (and Others) blog, http://queering-the-church.blogspot.co.uk/2012/02/remembering-marcella-althaus-reid.html

[47] Quoted in Project Gutenberg entry on Marcella Althaus-Reid, http://self.gutenberg.org/article/whebn0002538129/queer%20theology

[48] http://news.harvard.edu/gazette/story/2015/07/peter-j-gomes/

[49] Boynton RS, 'God and Harvard: A profile of Rev. Peter Gomes', New Yorker, 11 November 1996, http://www.robertboynton.com/articleDisplay.php?article_id=35

[50] http://www.harpercollins.com/9780061744426/good-book

[51] http://melwhite.org/

[52] See review by Ralph Blair on http://ecinc.org/review-fall-1996-vol-21-no-4/

[53] See e.g. http://www.courage.org.uk/articles/articles.asp?CID=4

[54] See e.g. Faith, Hope & Homosexuality, Evangelical Alliance, 1998, http://www.evangeliskalliance.dk/media/12397/faith,%20hope%20and%20homosexuality.pdf

[55] http://www.forthebibletellsmeso.org/indexa.htm

[56] http://www.queens.ac.uk/about/staff/dr-nicola-slee /

[57] See BFI Screenonline entry, http://www.screenonline.org.uk/film/id/444107/index.html, and entry in Jim's Film Reviews, http://jclark-media.com/film/filmreviewvictim.html

[58] See e.g. Moore MR, 'Black Church, Black Patriarchy, and the '"Brilliant Queer"': Competing Masculinities in Langston Hughes's "Blessed Assurance"', African American Review, Fall-Winter 2008, http://www.jstor.org/discover/10.2307/40301249?uid=2129&uid=2&uid=70&uid=4&sid=21101005669963

[59] http://news.bbc.co.uk/onthisday/hi/dates/stories/july/11/news-

id_2499000/2499721.stm

[60] See e.g. biography on Wildcat International website, http://www.wild-catintl.com/pnw.cfm?view=bio

[61] See Hensman S, 'A heavy grace: fiction, theology and same-sex love', Ekklesia, 2008, http://www.ekklesia.co.uk/node/8026

[62] See e.g. entry in New Georgia Encyclopedia, http://www.georgiaency-clopedia.org/nge/Article.jsp?id=h-1243

[63] See Bomb magazine interview by Susan Shacter with director, http://bombsite.com/issues/51/articles/1854

[64] http://www.prayersforbobby.com/

[65] http://www.michaelarditti.com/

[66] Sneed RA, Representations of Homosexuality: Black Liberation Theology and Cultural Criticism, Palgrave Macmillan, 2010

Chapter Five

[1] http://divinity.vanderbilt.edu/people/bio/leong-seow

[2] Baker JA, Homosexuality and Christian ethics – a new way forward together, St Martin-in-the-Fields, 1997; see also 'Retired Bishop Speaks out on Homosexuality', Anglican Communion News Service, 25 April 1997, http://www.anglicannews.org/news/1997/04/retired-bishop-speaks-out-on-homosexuality.aspx

[3] See e.g. Clare Garner's report in the Independent, http://www.independent.co.uk/news/how-i-felt-the-wrath-of-a-bishop-fury-as-the-church-votes-for-gay-ban-1169824.html

[4] See e.g. the author's research piece 'Re-writing History: the Episcopal Church struggle', Ekklesia, 2007, http://www.ekklesia.co.uk/research/rewriting_history

[5] See e.g. http://news.bbc.co.uk/2/hi/7100295.stm

[6] See e.g. New York Times reports on the Righter heresy trial on http://www.nytimes.com/1995/08/28/us/bishop-now-faces-the-heretic-s-brand.html?ref=waltercrighter&pagewanted=1 and http://www.nytimes.com/1996/05/16/us/episcopal-bishop-absolved-in-gay-ordination.html?ref=waltercrighter

[7] Kaoma K, 'The U.S. Christian Right and the Attack on Gays in Africa', Public Eye, Winter 09/Spring 10, http://www.publiceye.org/magazine/v24n4/us-christian-right-attack-on-gays-in-africa.html

[8] Macaulay RJ, 'Africa and Homosexuality', Witness, http://www.thewitness.org/agw/macauley121604.html

[9] Pui-lan K, Introducing Asian Feminist Theology, Sheffield Academic Press, 2000

[10] Varghese W, 'Christian Outcasts: Dalit Theology', The Witness, 19 May 2004, http://www.thewitness.org/agw/varghese051904.html

[11] See e.g. Ambridge C, '"Emerging Common Ground": a Toronto experiment', http://toronto.integritycanada.org/docs/witart.html

[12] http://www.vatican.va/roman_curia/congregations/cfaith/docu-ments/rc_con_cfaith_doc_19861001_homosexual-persons_en.html

[13] Matzko McCarthy D, 'Homosexuality and the Practices of Marriage', Modern Theology,13 July 1997, http://web.archive.org/web/20041223095640/jesusradicals.com/library/matzko/homosexu-ality.html

[14] See e.g. 'Gay Catholics Dismayed and Angry at Vatican Authorities', Dignity USA, 13 July 1999, http://www.dignityusa.org/press/gay-cath-olics-dismayed-and-angry-vatican-authorities

[15] http://web.archive.org/web/20070205105806/www.americamaga-zine.org/articles/SilencingNugentGramick.cfm

[16] http://www.bc.edu/schools/cas/theology/faculty/lcahill.html

[17] 9.5 Theses on Homosexuality in Modern Catholicism, http://www.press.uchicago.edu/Misc/Chicago/410412.html

[18] Keenan JF, 'The open debate: moral theology and the lives of gay and lesbian persons', Theological Studies, March 2003, http://cdn.theologi-calstudies.net/64/64.1/64.1.7.pdf

[19] See e.g. review in the Tablet, http://archive.thetablet.co.uk/article/2nd-august-2003/13/a-question-of-truth-christianity-and-homosexuality

[20] More information about the life of this important scholar is giv-en in an obituary on http://www.findagrave.com/cgi-bin/fg.cgi?page=gr&GRid=23691955

[21] http://www.jamesalison.co.uk/ ; see also Ruddy C, 'In defense of desire: the theology of James Alison', Commonweal, 30 January 2009, http://commonwealmagazine.org/defense-desire-0 Alison's work has been very highly valued by former Archbishop of Canterbury and scholar Rowan Williams, and by many Ekklesia associates and partners. He con-tributed a chapter to Barrow S, and Bartley J, Consuming Passion: Why the killing of Jesus really matters, Darton, Longman and Todd, 2005.

[22] From 'Blindsided by God: Reconciliation from the underside', http://www.jamesalison.co.uk/texts/eng26.html

[23] http://www.othersheepexecsite.com/Tom_Hanks_in_Buenos_Aires.html

[24] Brueggemann W, Placher WC, Blount BK, Struggling with Scripture, Westminster John Knox Press, 2002; see also review by Candace Chellew in Whosoever, http://www.whosoever.org/v7i1/scripture.html

[25] For more on Walter Brueggemann, see http://www.walterbruegge-mann.com/; William C Placher's obituary on the Wabash College web-site is on http://wabash.edu/news/displaystory.cfm?news_ID=6499; Brian K Blount is described on http://www.upsem.edu/academics/fac-ulty_staff/brian_k_blount1/

[26] See e.g. entry in Logos Almanac of the Christian World, https://almanac.logos.com/Theodore_W._Jennings,_Jr.$

[27] See entry in Christian Alternative, http://www.christian-alternative.

com/authors/keith-sharpe

[28] Ind J, Memories of Bliss: God, Sex and Us, SCM Press, 2003

[29] Rogers EF, 'An argument for gay marriage', The Christian Century, 15 June 2004, http://www.religion-online.org/showarticle.asp?title=3069

[30] Rogers EF, 'Same-sex complementarity', The Christian Century, 11 May 2011, http://www.christiancentury.org/article/2011-04/same-sex-complementarity

[31] Allen CW, 'We Will Not Let You Go, Unless You Bless Us: The Gospel's Preferential Option for Eccentric Relationality,' Encounter 63 (2002):3–12, http://www.therevdrcharleswallen.com/WeWillNotLetYouGoUnlessYouBlessUs.pdf

[32] See To Set Our Hope on Christ, http://www.philosophy-religion.org/beliefs/pdfs/ToSetOurHopeOnChrist.pdf, and St Michael Report, http://www.anglican.ca/primate/tfc/ptc/smr/

[33] Musskopf AS, 'Open letter to the World Forum on Theology and Liberation: How far are we willing to go?', 2005, http://wftlofficial.org/pdf/musskopf.pdf

[34] Countryman LW, Love Human and Divine: Reflections on Love, Sexuality and Friendship, Morehouse Publishing, 2005

[35] See review by Barry Morgan on http://www.thinkinganglicans.org.uk/archives/001341.html

[36] More information on Andrew Linzey can be found on http://www.oxfordanimalethics.com/who-we-are/director/; on Richard Kirker in a New Statesman article by Simon Edge on http://www.newstatesman.com/life-and-society/2008/01/gay-kirker-church-bishop; on Keith Ward on http://www.keithward.org.uk/; Lisa Isherwood on http://www.winchester.ac.uk/aboutus/lifelonglearning/Theologicalpartnerships/peopleprofiles/Pages/LisaIsherwood.aspx; Vincent Strudwick on http://www.gtfeducation.org/faculty-staff/Strudwick.cfm; Marilyn McCord Adams on http://www.nationalcathedral.org/staff/PE-5H7BE-CN001N.shtml; Rowan Greer on http://episcopaldigitalnetwork.com/ens/2014/03/24/rip-yale-professor-emeritus-rowan-greer-dies-at-79/; George Pattison on http://www.gla.ac.uk/schools/critical/staff/georgepattison/; Thomas Breidenthal on http://www.episcopalchurch.org/staff/rt-rev-thomas-breidenthal; Elaine Graham on http://www.chester.ac.uk/departments/trs/staff/graham; Martyn Percy on http://www.chch.ox.ac.uk/college/profile/academics/martyn-percy; and Adrian Thatcher, who has written extensively on sexuality and marriage, on http://www.adrianthatcher.org/

[37] See Terry Brown's piece on the book on Rethinking Mission, http://www.rethinkingmission.org.uk/article_terry.html,

[38] For more information on Winston Halapua see http://anglicantaonga.org.nz/Features/Bible/winston-background; Aruna Gnanadason is a feminist theologian who has been active in the international ecumenical

movement, http://www.united-church.ca/communications/news/general/140910; anti-apartheid activist Bishop David Russell later became involved in Inclusive and Affirming Ministries, http://www.sahistory.org.za/people/david-patrick-russell; Charles Hefling on http://www.bc.edu/schools/cas/theology/faculty/chefling.html; articles by Mario Ribas can be found on The Witness site on http://www.thewitness.org/agw/ribas111203.html and http://www.thewitness.org/agw/ribas080703.html

[39] See e.g. Grossman CL, 'Presbyterian Church debates issue of gay elders', USA Today, 22 June 2006, http://www.usatoday.com/news/religion/2006-06-12-presbyerian-meeting_x.htm

[40] Formerly a Professor of New Testament at the General Theological Seminary, New York City, she blogs on http://notbeingasausage.blogspot.co.uk/

[41] See extract on http://www.ekklesia.co.uk/node/4844 and article for Ekklesia, http://www.ekklesia.co.uk/node/5162

[42] See review by Ian Gibson on GoodBookStall, http://www.thegoodbookstall.org.uk/review/9781853117411/steven-shakespeare-and-hugh-rayment-pickard/the-inclusive-god/

[43] Martin DB, Sex and the Single Savior: Gender and Sexuality in Biblical Interpretation, Westminster John Knox Press, 2006.

[44] See review by Alun Brookfield for Ministry Today on http://ministrytoday.org.uk/magazine/issues/40/reviews/121/

[45] More information on Duncan Dormor can be found on http://www.joh.cam.ac.uk/dean-chapel; Jeremy Morris on http://www.kings.cam.ac.uk/research/fellows/jeremy-morris.html; Maggi Dawn on http://divinity.yale.edu/dawn; Andrew Mein on http://www.westcott.cam.ac.uk/andrew-mein/; and Jessica Martin on http://www.ely.anglican.org/news_events/media/announcements/details.html?id=244

[46] http://www.ajol.info/index.php/hts/article/viewFile/41268/8648

[47] http://www.kcl.ac.uk/artshums/depts/trs/people/staff/academic/burridge/index.aspx

[48] Burridge R, Imitating Jesus: An Inclusive Approach to New Testament Ethics Today, Eerdmans, 2007.

[49] http://episcopaldigitalnetwork.com/ens/2012/01/18/cdsp-professor-louis-weil-receives-ecumenical-liturgy-award/

[50] http://www.associatedparishes.org/images/Open_Spring_2008_full_issue.pdf, pp. 5–9

[51] http://www.canterburypress.co.uk/books/9781853119163/Space-for-Grace

[52] See e.g. Arana G, 'My So-Called Ex-Gay Life', American Prospect, 11 April 2012, http://prospect.org/article/my-so-called-ex-gay-life?utm_source=Huge+News%3A+Dr.+Robert+Spitzer+Renounces+His+Infamous+2001+Ex-Gay++Study+&utm_campaign=Kony+Mass&utm_

medium=email

[53] http://www.courage.org.uk/intro/introducing.shtml

[54] Examples include Darlene Bogle and Michael Bussee, http://www.be-yondexgay.com/article/apology.html; Kim Brett, Wendy Lawson and Vonnie Pitts, http://www.beyondexgay.com/article/apology2.html; and John Smid, http://www.gracerivers.com/gays-repent/ and http://www.gracerivers.com/new-observation/

[55] Dreyer Y, 'Pastoral care and gays against the background of same-sex relationships in the Umwelt of the New Testament', Theological Studies, Vol 64, No 2 (2008), http://www.hts.org.za/index.php/HTS/article/view/42/39

[56] See relevant page on his blog, http://peacetheology.net/homosexuality/

[57] See excerpt from Reasoning Together: A Conversation on Homosexuality (Herald Press, 2008), on http://peacetheology.net/homosexuality/welcome/

[58] http://divinity.yale.edu/farley

[59] http://www.anglicantheologicalreview.org/static/pdf/articles/90.3_norris.pdf

[60] http://www.anglicantheologicalreview.org/static/pdf/articles/farley.pdf

[61] Nickoloff JB, '"Intrinsically Disordered": Gay People And The Holiness Of The Church', http://www.scu.edu/ic/publications/articles.cfm?c=17821

[62] Zachariah G, 'The Church: A Rainbow Community of the Beloved and Equals: Reflections on Christian Reponses to Homosexuality', Religion and Society, Vol 54 No 4, December 2009, http://orinam.net/content/wp-content/uploads/2011/12/Zachariah_Church_A_Rainbow_Community.pdf

[63] http://www.chicagoconsultation.org/?p=145

[64] More information on Ruth Meyers can be found on http://cdsp.edu/faculty/ruth-meyers/; Fredrica Harris Thompsett on https://almanac.logos.com/Fredrica_Harris_Thompsett; William H Petersen on http://theadventproject.org/Who-Are-We.htm; and Katherine Grieb on http://www.vts.edu/katherinegrieb

[65] See review by Charles Hefling in Anglican Theological Review, http://reasonableandholy.blogspot.co.uk/2010/02/review-from-anglican-theological-review.html

[66] http://jintoku.blogspot.com/

[67] Galilee Report, Primate's Theological Commission, Anglican Church of Canada, 2009, http://www.anglican.ca/primate/files/2010/11/galilee-report-full-with-papers.pdf

[68] http://www.collegeforbishops.org/assets/1145/ss_document_final.pdf

[69] Cheng PS, 'Rethinking Sin and Grace for LGBT People Today', in Sexuality and the Sacred. 2nd edition, ed Ellison MM and Brown Douglas K. Westminster John Knox Press 2010, http://www.patrickcheng.net/uploads/7/0/3/7/7037096/cheng_rethinking_sin_and_grace.pdf

[70] Punt J, 'Family in the New Testament. Social location, households and "traditional family values"', Joint International meeting of the Society of Biblical Literature and the European Association of Biblical Studies (EABS), Tartu, Estonia, July.2010, http://www.uva.nl/binaries/content/documents/personalpages/b/r/a.brenner/en/tab-three/tab-three/cpitem%5B21%5D/asset?1355373309110

[71] Gunda MR, The Bible and Homosexuality in Zimbabwe, University of Bamberg Press, 2010, http://www.academia.edu/2949283/The_Bible_and_Homosexuality_in_Zimbabwe

Chapter Six

[1] http://www.bloomsbury.com/uk/a-theology-of-love-9780567646927/

[2] McGarry P, 'Vatican ban on writing by Irish priest "unwise"', Irish Times, 15 November 2010, http://www.irishtimes.com/newspaper/ireland/2010/1115/1224283325842.html; extracts from original article can be found on http://queertheology.blogspot.com/2010_11_01_archive.html

[3] Scally D, 'Theologian says much of clergy is gay', Irish Times, 22 November 2010, http://www.irishtimes.com/newspaper/world/2010/1122/1224283832839.html

[4] Hockenos P, '144 theologians confront hierarchy', National Catholic Reporter, 14 February 2011, http://ncronline.org/news/accountability/144-theologians-confront-hierarchy?page=3

[5] 'German theologians' letter – bishops respond', Independent Catholic News, 9 February 2011, http://www.indcatholicnews.com/news.php?viewStory=17625

[6] http://www.memorandum-freiheit.de/unterzeichner/

[7] See entry on Ignatian Spirituality website, http://ignatianspirituality.com/ignatian-voices/21st-century-ignatian-voices/jon-sobrino-sj/

[8] Dom Sebastian Moore interviewed by Noel Debien, 13 February 2011, Australian Broadcasting Corporation, http://www.abc.net.au/sundaynights/stories/s3138282.htm

[9] Keneally K, 'Why I support gay marriage', The Drum, 26 September 2011, http://www.abc.net.au/unleashed/2942868.html

[10] Thatcher A, 'God, sex and gender', lecture, 4 November 2011, http://www.adrianthatcher.org/data/resources/god,%20sex%20and%20gender%20%5Bleuven%5D.pdf

[11] See e.g. Coakley S, 'Taming desire: Celibacy, sexuality and the Church', Australian Broadcasting Corporation, 20 May 2011, http://www.abc.net.au/religion/articles/2011/05/20/3222443.htm

[12] Cornwall, S, Controversies in queer theology, SCM Press, 2011.

[13] See for instance Rowan Williams' 2009 document 'Communion, Covenant and our Anglican Future', http://rowanwilliams.archbishop-ofcanterbury.org/articles.php/1505/communion-covenant-and-our-anglican-future

[14] See e.g. Andrew Marin's website, http://www.loveisanorientation.com/, and Andrew Goddard's review on Fulcrum of the book Love is an orientation, http://www.fulcrum-anglican.org.uk/articles/review-of-andrew-marins-love-is-an-orientation-elevating-the-conversation-with-the-gay-community/

[15] Special Commission on Same-Sex Relationships and the Ministry, Church of Scotland, May 2011, http://www.churchofscotland.org.uk/_data/assets/pdf_file/0006/5757/ga11_specssrm.pdf

16. 'ELCIC National Convention Delegates Approve Social Statement on Human Sexuality', news release, 16 July 2011, http://www.elcic.ca/news.cfm?article=276

[17] ELCIC Social Statement on Human Sexuality, http://elcic.ca/Human-Sexuality/documents/APPROVEDELCICSocialStatementonHumanSexuality.pdf

[18] See Interview with Rev Dr Arlo Duba, http://covnetpres.org/2011/01/interview-with-rev-dr-arlo-duba/

[19] Dudley J, 'Evangelicals and Gay Marriage: Why "Love the Sinner, Hate the Sin" Doesn't Work', Huffington Post, 22 October 2011, http://www.huffingtonpost.com/jonathan-dudley/evangelicals-gay-marriage-why-love-the-sinner-hate-_b_1017934.html

[20] http://publicreligion.org/research/2011/08/generations-at-odds/

[21] Snyder D, 'Young Evangelicals Are Shifting on Marriage Equality', Huffington Post, 15 September 2011, http://www.huffingtonpost.com/rev-dean-snyder/evangelical-marriage-equality_b_958686.html

[22] Scharen CB, 'Blessed and Broken: Gay Marriage in Church and Society', talk at Valparaiso Institute of Liturgical Studies, 2012, http://christian-scharen.com/uploads/pdf/Blessed%20and%20Broken-ILS%202012.pdf

[23] See Thinking Anglicans, 14 March 2012, http://www.thinkinganglicans.org.uk/archives/005412.html

[24] Robinson GJ, 'Sexual Relationships: Where Does Our Morality Come From?', http://gcvi.ie/docs/Christian%20Basis%20for%20Teaching%20on%20Sex.pdf; see also media reports, e.g. http://ncronline.org/news/spirituality/bishop-urges-change-church-teaching-concerning-all-sexual-relationships

[25] Goh JN, 'Mary and the Mak Nyahs: Queer Theological Imaginings of Malaysian Male-to-Female Transsexuals', Theology & Sexuality 18, no. 3 (2012)

[26] Lings KR, Love Lost in Translation: Homosexuality and the Bible,

Trafford Publishing, 2013.

[27] Methuen C, 'Marriage: one man and one woman?', Open Democracy, 12 April 2013, https://www.opendemocracy.net/ourkingdom/charlotte-methuen/marriage-one-man-and-one-woman

[28] Pilling Report, House of Bishops Working Group on Human Sexuality, 2013, https://www.churchofengland.org/media/1891063/pilling_re-port_gs_1929_web.pdf

[29] Wilson A, More Perfect Union: Understanding Same-Sex Christian Marriage, Darton, Longman and Todd, 2014

[30] Taylor SJ, 'An invitation to the feast: A positive Biblical approach to equal marriage', To Have and To Hold conference, 2014, http://www.inclu-sive-church.org/sites/default/files/files/Simon%20Taylor-%20%20 biblical%20perspective%2C%20An%20Invitation%20To%20the%20 Feast%20.pdf

[31] Dick JA, 'Belgian bishop advocates church recognition of gay relation-ships', National Catholic Reporter, 30 Dec 2014, http://ncronline.org/ news/faith-parish/belgian-bishop-advocates-church-recognition-gay-relationships

[32] Bonny J, 'Synod on the Family: Expectations of a Diocesan Bishop', Flanders Church website, September 2014, http://kerknet.be/admin/ files/assets/subsites/4/documenten/SYNOD_ON_FAMILY_ENG.pdf

[33] Lee J, Torn: Rescuing the Gospel from the Gays-vs.-Christians debate, Hachette UK, 2012.

[34] Vines M, God and the Gay Christian: The Biblical Case in Support of Same-Sex Relationships, Convergent Books, 2014.

[35] Chalke S, 'A Matter of Integrity: The Church, sexuality, inclusion and an open conversation', Christianity, January 2013, http://www.oasisuk. org/sites/default/files/A%20MATTER%20OF%20INTEGRITY%20 Expanded%20version.pdf

[36] Brownson JV, Bible, Gender, Sexuality: Reframing the Church's Debate on Same-Sex Relationships, Eerdmans, 2013.

[37] Gushee DP, Changing Our Mind, Read The Spirit Books, 2014.

[38] Song R, Covenant and Calling: Towards a Theology of Same-Sex Relationships, SCM Press, 2014.

[39] Conradie EM, 'What on Earth did God create? Overtures to an ecumenical theology of creation', Ecumenical Review, December 2014, Vol 66, Issue 4, http://repository.uwc.ac.za/xmlui/bitstream/handle/10566/1314/ ConradieWhatOnEarth2014.pdf?sequence=1

Chapter Eleven

[1] See Barrow S (ed), Fear or Freedom?: Why a Warring Church Must Change, Shoving Leopard/Ekklesia, 2008; Hassett MK, Anglican Communion in Crisis: How Episcopal Dissidents and Their African Allies Are Reshaping Anglicanism, Princeton University Press, 2007, http://

press.princeton.edu/titles/8413.html

[2] Acts 10.1–11.18

[3] Galatians 2.6–14

[4] See e.g. http://justus.anglican.org/resources/timeline/06reformation. html

[5] http://www.bbc.co.uk/religion/religions/christianity/christianethics/ contraception_4.shtml

[6] See e.g. http://www.catholic.com/tracts/birth-control

[7] Crowther, Samuel Ajayi, Elijah Olu Akinwumi, Dictionary of African Christian Biography, http://www.dacb.org/stories/nigeria/crowther4_ samajayi.html

[8] See e.g. Sanecki K, 'Protestant Christian missions, race and empire', pp. 97–99, http://etd.gsu.edu/theses/available/etd-07062006-114644/ unrestricted/sanecki_kim_200608_ma.pdf.

[9] http://www.episcopalchurch.org/library/article/reflecting-35th-anni- versary-ordination-women-priesthood

[10] https://viaintegra.wordpress.com/church-same-sex-blessings-across- europe/

[11] Romans 12.10, 16.

[12] The author's 2007 essay Rewriting history: scapegoating the Episcopal Church, on http://ekklesia.co.uk/research/rewriting_history, covers this in some detail.

[13] 'Learned Discourse on Justification', Richard Hooker, http://elvis.rowan. edu/~kilroy/CHRISTIA/old_library/hooker-learned.htm

[14] http://www.anglicancommunion.org/resources/document-library/ lambeth-conference/1930/resolution-6-the-christian-doctrine-of-god? author=Lambeth+Conference&year=1930

[15] http://www.anglicancommunion.org/resources/document-library/ lambeth-conference/1958/resolution-4-the-bible?author=Lambeth+C onference&year=1958

[16] http://www.anglicancommunion.org/resources/document-library/ lambeth-conference/1958/resolution-8-the-bible?author=Lambeth+C onference&year=1958

[17] See e.g. Lambeth 1878, Recommendation 1, http://www.anglicancom- munion.org/resources/document-library/lambeth-conference/1878/ recommendation-1-union-among-the-churches-of-the-anglican- communion-encyclical-letter-15?author=Lambeth+Conference&ye ar=1878; Lambeth 1930, Resolution 48, http://www.anglicancommu- nion.org/resources/document-library/lambeth-conference/1930/ resolution-48-the-anglican-communion?author=Lambeth+Conference &year=1930; Lambeth 1988, Resolution 72, http://www.anglicancom- munion.org/resources/document-library/lambeth-conference/1988/ resolution-72-epsicopal-responsibilities-and-diocesan-boundaries?aut hor=Lambeth+Conference&year=1988

[18] John 16.12–13

[19] http://www.anglicancommunion.org/resources/document-library/lambeth-conference/1978/resolution-10-human-relationships-and-sexuality?author=Lambeth+Conference&year=1978

[20] http://www.anglicancommunion.org/resources/document-library/lambeth-conference/1988/resolution-64-human-rights-for-those-of-homosexual-orientation?author=Lambeth+Conference&year=1988

[21] http://www.anglicancommunion.org/resources/document-library/lambeth-conference/1998/section-i-called-to-full-humanity/section-i10-human-sexuality?author=Lambeth+Conference&year=1998

[22] For background to this statement, see e.g. http://justus.anglican.org/newsarchive/lambeth98/sjn16.html

[23] http://www.anglicancommunion.org/media/100357/The-Listening-Process.pdf?author=The+Windsor+Process#page=6

[24] http://www.anglicancommunion.org/resources/document-library/lambeth-conference/1948/resolution-8-the-church-and-the-modern-world-human-rights?author=Lambeth+Conference&year=1948

[25] http://anglicanexaminer.com/ER.html

[26] http://www.anglicancommunion.org/communion/acc/meetings/acc2/resolutions.cfm#s12

[27] http://www.anglicancommunion.org/communion/acc/meetings/acc4/resolutions.cfm#s10

[28] http://www.anglicancommunion.org/resources/document-library/lambeth-conference/1998/section-i-called-to-full-humanity/section-i1-affirmation-and-adoption-of-the-united-nations-universal-declaration-of-human-rights?author=Lambeth+Conference&year=1998

[29] See e.g. the Yogyakarta Principles, 2007, http://www.yogyakartaprinciples.org/principles_en.htm; Love, hate and the law, Amnesty International, 2008, https://www.amnesty.org/en/documents/POL30/003/2008/en/; Together, Apart, Human Rights Watch, 2009, https://www.hrw.org/report/2009/06/11/together-apart/organizing-around-sexual-orientation-and-gender-identity-worldwide

[30] Ephesians 5.21.

Chapter Eighteen

[1] https://www.churchofengland.org/our-views/marriage,-family-and-sexuality-issues/human-sexuality/pilling-report.aspx

[2] http://www.thelancet.com/journals/lancet/issue/vol382no9907/PIIS0140-6736%2813%29X6059-3; see in particular Mercer CH et al, 'Changes in sexual attitudes and lifestyles in Britain through the life course and over time: findings from the National Surveys of Sexual Attitudes and Lifestyles' (Natsal), Lancet, 26 November 2013, http://dx.doi.org/10.1016/S0140-6736(13)62035-8

[3] See e.g. 'Hayes J et al, 'Prevalence of Same-Sex Behavior and Orientation

in England: Results from a National Survey', Archives of Sexual Behavior, June 2012, Volume 41, Issue 3, pp. 631–639, http://link.springer.com/article/10.1007/s10508-011-9856-8#page-1

[4] Moreton C, 'The man who believes he can turn gay people straight', Telegraph, 21 April 2012, http://www.telegraph.co.uk/news/religion/9218545/The-man-who-believes-he-can-help-gay-people-turnstraight.html

[5] Nolland LS, 'Gay marriage: hidden implications and impact', Anglican Mainstream, 12 October 2011, http://anglicanmainstream.org/gay-marriage-hidden-implications-and-impact-2/

[6] See e.g. Jivani A, It's not unusual: a history of lesbian and gay Britain in the twentieth century, Michael O'Mara Books, 1997.

[7] Report of the American Psychological Association Task Force on Appropriate Therapeutic Responses to Sexual Orientation, APA, 2009, http://www.apa.org/pi/lgbt/resources/therapeutic-response.pdf

[8] King M et al, 'Treatments of homosexuality in Britain since the 1950s—an oral history: the experience of professionals', British Medical Journal (BMJ), 29 January 2004, http://www.bmj.com/content/328/7437/429.pdf%2Bhtml; Smith G et al, 'Treatments of homosexuality in Britain since the 1950s—an oral history: the experience of patients', BMJ, 29 January 2004, http://www.bmj.com/content/328/7437/427.pdf%2Bhtml

[9] See e.g. Drescher J, 'Sexual conversion therapies', http://www.researchgate.net/publication/228772317_Sexual_Conversion_Therapies; 'Psychiatry giant sorry for backing gay "cure"', New York Times, 18 May 2012, http://www.nytimes.com/2012/05/19/health/dr-robert-l-spitzer-noted-psychiatrist-apologizes-for-study-on-gay-cure.html; Besen W, 'The Walls Are Closing In on the Ex-Gay Industry', Huffington Post, 29 Nov 2012, http://www.huffingtonpost.com/wayne-besen/the-walls-are-closing-in-on-the-ex-gayindustry_b_2203814.html

[10] Cianciotto J and Cahill S, Youth in the crosshairs: the third wave of ex-gay activism, National Gay and Lesbian Task Force Policy Institute, 2006, http://www.thetaskforce.org/downloads/reports/reports/YouthInTheCrosshairs.pdf

[11] Chakraborty A et al, 'Mental health of the non-heterosexual population of England', British Journal of Psychiatry (2011) 198: 143–148, http://bjp.rcpsych.org/content/198/2/143.full

[12] Haas AP, 'Suicide and suicide risk in lesbian, gay, bisexual, and transgender populations: review and recommendations', J Homosex, 2011 January; 58(1): 10–51, http://www.ncbi.nlm.nih.gov/pmc/articles/PMC3662085/

[13] For instance, those of us in the UK with darker-than-average skin may have higher-than-average rates of diabetes, both of these having a hereditary component. But this does not mean that skin-colour causes diabetes, and if I were to slather skin-lightening products on myself or

stay out of the sun I could damage my health without reducing my risk of becoming diabetic.

[14] Frisell T et al, 'Psychiatric morbidity associated with same-sex sexual behaviour: influence of minority stress and familial factors', Psychological Medicine (2010), 40, 315–324, http://www.researchgate.net/publication/24444347_Psychiatric_morbidity_associated_with_samesex_sexual_behaviour_influence_of_minority_stress_and_familial_factors/file/9fcfd50f9451d6d47c.pdf

[15] Mooallem J, 'Can animals be gay?', New York Times, 31 March 2010, http://www.nytimes.com/2010/04/04/magazine/04animals-t.html?pagewanted=all&_r=0

[16] Wight RG et al, 'Same-sex legal marriage and psychological well-being: findings from the California Health Interview Survey', American Journal of Public Health, February 2013, http://www.ncbi.nlm.nih.gov/pubmed/23237155

Thanks to financial supporters

The publication of this book has been made possible by financial contributions from a number of individuals. We are extremely grateful to the following for their generosity and support:

Dirg Aaab-Richards
Jonathan Adams
David Austin
Ken Ball
Peter Bennett
Bloomsbury Central Baptist
   Church
Kieran Bohan
Nick Burr
Ray Descombes
Edward Drake
Michael Egan
Susanna Ferrar
Zoe Franklin
Richard Fisher
Ruth Goldbourne
David &Vicky Harknett
David Hancock

Robin Hanford
Germaine Hanbury
Pam Hunt
S Holtom
J Humphreys
Kathleen Jowitt
David Lockett
David Maloney
Iain McDonald
Hannah Morgan
Carol Myers
Jayne Ozanne
Joc Sanders
Michael Scott
Laura Sykes
Teresa Sumption
Rosie Venner
Tony Weekes

About Ekklesia

Ekklesia is an independent, not-for-profit think tank which orients its work around the changing role of beliefs, values and faith or non-faith in public life.

We advocate transformative ideas and solutions to societal challenges based on a strong commitment to social justice, non-violence, environmental responsibility, nonconformist styles of Christianity, and a creative exchange among those of different convictions (religious and otherwise).

Ekklesia is committed to promoting – alongside others – new models of mutual economy, conflict transformation, social power, restorative justice, community engagement and political participation.

We are also working to encourage alternative perspectives on humanitarian challenges in a globalised world, not least a positive, affirming approach to migration.

Overall, we are concerned both with the policy, practice and theology of moving beyond a top-down 'church of power', and with challenging top-down, unjust models of economy and politics in society as a whole.

This means that, while we are a Christian political think-tank rooted in Anabaptist values, we are happy to work with people of many backgrounds, both 'religious' and 'non-religious', who share common values and approaches.

Ekklesia's reports, analysis and commentary can be accessed via our website here: www.ekklesia.co.uk

CPSIA information can be obtained at www.ICGtesting.com
Printed in the USA
BVOW06s1824020816

457706BV00012B/71/P